LAOS

ELECTORAL, POLITICAL PARTIES LAWS AND REGULATIONS HANDBOOK
STRATEGIC INFORMATION, REGULATIONS, PROCEDURES

International Business Publications, USA
Washington DC. USA - Laos

LAOS
ELECTORAL, POLITICAL PARTIES LAWS AND REGULATIONS HANDBOOK
STRATEGIC INFORMATION, REGULATIONS, PROCEDURES

UPDATED ANNUALLY

We express our sincere appreciation to all government agencies and international organizations which provided information and other materials for this handbook

Cover Design: International Business Publications, USA

International Business Publications, USA *has used its best efforts in collecting, analyzing and preparing data, information and materials for this unique handbook. Due to the dynamic nature and fast development of the economy and business environment, we cannot warrant that all information herein is complete and accurate. IBP does not assume and hereby disclaim any liability to any person for any loss or damage caused by possible errors or omissions in the handbook.*
This handbook is for noncommercial use only. Use this handbook for any other purpose, included but not limited to reproducing and storing in a retrieval system by any means, electronic, photocopying or using the addresses or other information contained in this handbook for any commercial purposes requires a special written permission from the publisher.

2017 Edition Updated Reprint International Business Publications, USA
ISBN 978-1-5145-1718-5

For additional analytical, business and investment opportunities information,
please contact Global Investment & Business Center, USA
at (703) 370-8082. Fax: (703) 370-8083. E-mail: ibpusa3@gmail.com
Global Business and Investment Info Databank - www.ibpus.com

Printed in the USA

LAOS

ELECTORAL, POLITICAL PARTIES LAWS AND REGULATIONS HANDBOOK
STRATEGIC INFORMATION, REGULATIONS, PROCEDURES

TABLE OF CONTENTS

LAOS STRATEGIC AND DEVELOPMENT PROFILES 7

- STRATEGIC PROFILE 7
  - Geography 9
  - People 11
  - Government 12
  - Economy 14
  - Energy 19
  - Communications 21
  - Transportation 22
  - Military 22
  - Transnational Issues 23
- IMPORTANT INFORMATION FOR UNDERSTANDING LAOS 24
  - PROFILE 24
  - GEOGRAPHY, TOPOGRAPHY AND CLIMATE 25
  - WATER RESOURCES 25
  - FOREST RESOURCES 25
  - MINERAL RESOURCES 26
  - ADMINISTRATIVE STRUCTURE OF LAOS 26
  - PEOPLE 31
  - HISTORY 32
  - GOVERNMENT AND POLITICAL CONDITIONS 33
  - ECONOMY 35
  - FOREIGN RELATIONS 37
  - U.S.-LAO RELATIONS 38
  - TRAVEL AND BUSINESS INFORMATION 39

LAOS JUDICIAL AND LEGAL SYSTEM 41

- LEGAL AND JUDICIAL SYSTEM 41
- LEGAL SYSTEM DEVELOPMENTS 41
  - Legal System in Transition 41
  - Investment Procedures 42

For additional analytical, business and investment opportunities information,
please contact Global Investment & Business Center, USA
at (703) 370-8082. Fax: (703) 370-8083. E-mail: ibpusa3@gmail.com
Global Business and Investment Info Databank - www.ibpus.com

Investment License	*42*
Investment Guarantees	*43*
Investment Incentives	*43*
Investment Sectors	*44*
Investment Structures	*44*
Taxation	*44*
Dispute Resolution	*46*
CIVIL LIBERTIES AND HUMAN RIGHTS	48
Detention centers	*49*
DEMOCRACY AND HUIMAN RIGHTS	51
Section 1 Respect for the Integrity of the Person, Including Freedom From:	*52*
Section 2 Respect for Civil Liberties	*57*
Section 3 Respect for Political Rights: The Right of Citizens to Change Their Government	*63*
Section 4 Governmental Attitude Regarding International and Nongovernmental Investigation of Alleged Violations of Human Rights	*64*
Section 5 Discrimination Based on Race, Sex, Religion, Disability, Language, or Social Status	*65*
Section 6 Worker Rights	*67*

POLITICAL AND GOVERNMENT SYSTEM 70

STRUCTURE OF THE GOVERNMENT 70
Executive	*70*
Legislature	*70*
Judiciary	*71*
Political Opposition	*72*
Refugees	*73*
Insurgents	*73*
Bureaucratic Culture	*74*

ORGANIZATION OF THE GOVERNMENT STATE AND GOVERNMENT LEADERS .. 76
Embassy of the Lao People's Democratic Republic	*78*
THE LAO PEOPLE'S REVOLUTIONARY PARTY	*80*
Origins of the Party	*80*
Semisecrecy of the Lao People's Revolutionary Party	*83*
Ideology of the Lao People's Revolutionary Party	*84*

LEADERSHIP 85
Internal Stability and External Influences	*85*

THE CONSTITUTION 86
Development of the Constitution	*86*
Highlights of the Constitution	*88*

LAOS ELECTORAL SYSTEM - STRATEGIC INFORMATION AND DEVELOPMENTS 91

ELECTIONS IN LAOS - BASIC INFORMATION 91
ELECTORAL SYSTEM	*91*
Electoral Process: 0 / 12	*91*
Political Pluralism and Participation: 0 / 16	*92*

LATEST ELECTION 92
LAO PEOPLE'S REVOLUTIONARY PARTY 92

  Party structure *95*
  Ideology *96*
  Leaders *96*
IMPORTANT LAWS AND REGULATIONS AFFECTING ELECTORAL PROCESS ... 98
 CONSTITUTION OF THE LAO PEOPLE'S DEMOCRATIC REPUBLIC 98
  PREAMBLE *98*
  CHAPTER I THE POLITICAL REGIME *98*
  CHAPTER II THE SOCIO - ECONOMIC SYSTEM *100*
  CHAPTER III FUNDAMENTAL RIGHTS AND OBLIGATIONS OF THE CITIZEN *101*
  CHAPTER IV THE NATIONAL ASSEMBLY *103*
  CHAPTER V THE PRESIDENT OF STATE *105*
  CHAPTER VI THE GOVERNMENT *106*
  CHAPTER VII THE LOCAL ADMINISTRATION *107*
  CHAPTER VIII THE JUDICIARY ORGANISATIONS *108*
  CHAPTER IX LANGUAGE, SCRIPT, NATIONAL EMBLEM, NATIONAL FLAG,
  NATIONAL ANTHEM AND CAPITAL CITY *109*
  CHAPTER X THE LAST PROVISION *109*
 LAW ON THE ELECTION OF MEMBERS OF THE NATIONAL ASSEMBLY 110
  Chapter 2 Determination of the Number of National Assembly Members *113*
  Chapter 3 Determination of Constituencies for Election and Polling Units *115*
  Chapter 4 Registration of Voters *116*
  Chapter 5 Election Committees at Different Levels *117*
  Chapter 6 Time, Date and Rules for Voting 20 .... *120*
  Chapter 7 Counting of Votes and Announcement of Results *122*
  Chapter 8 Election of Replacement Members of the National Assembly *123*
  Chapter 9 Policies for Outstanding Performance *124*
  Chapter 10 Final Provisions *124*
 LAW ON LOCAL ADMINISTRATION OF THE LAO PDR 125
  Part I General Provisions *125*
  Part II Provincial and City Administrations *126*
  Part III District Administration *131*
  Part IV Municipal Administration *136*
  Part V Village Administration *142*
  Part VI Working Methods and Local Administration Finance *145*
  Part VII Final Provisions *146*
 LAW ON THE GOVERNMENT OF THE LAO PDR 147
  Chapter I General Provisions *147*
  Chapter II The structure, duties and responsibilities of the Government *147*
  Chapter III Government meetings *149*
  Chapter IV Role, rights and duties of the Prime Minister *150*
  Chapter V The Prime Minister's Office *152*
  Chapter VI Ministries and Ministry-equivalent Organizations *154*
  Chapter VII Working methods of the Government. *157*
  Chapter VIII Final Provisions *159*
 PUBLIC SERVICE REGULATIONS OF LAO PDR 160
TRAVELING TO LAOS **175**

**For additional analytical, business and investment opportunities information,
please contact Global Investment & Business Center, USA
at (703) 370-8082. Fax: (703) 370-8083. E-mail: ibpusa3@gmail.com
Global Business and Investment Info Databank - www.ibpus.com**

US STATE DEPARTMENT SUGGESTIONS	175
PRACTIVCAL INFORMATION FOR TRAVELERS	179
Cultural Festivals	*179*
Official Holidays	*181*
VIENTIANE	*181*
SPORT AND LEISURE ACTIVITIES	*183*
SHOPPER'S HEAVEN	*184*
TRAVELLING OUTSIDE VIENTIANE	*186*
Business Information	*186*
SUPPLEMENTS	**188**
IMPORTANT WEBSITES	188
Web sites of organizations in Laos	*189*
IMPORTANT CONTACTS	190
Ministries	*190*
Banks	*192*
Consultants	*192*
Multilateral Aid Agencies	*193*
CUSTOMS OFFICE CODES	194
COUNTRY AND CURRENCY CODES	195
THE DECLARATION FORM	204
STRATEGIC STATISTICS	212
Basic Data	*212*
LAOS GLOSSARY	213
SELECTED TOUR OPERATORS IN LAOS	218
LAO PDR EMBASSIES AND CONSULTATE-GENERAL	219
BASIC TITLE FOR LAOS	222

**For additional analytical, business and investment opportunities information,
please contact Global Investment & Business Center, USA
at (703) 370-8082. Fax: (703) 370-8083. E-mail: ibpusa3@gmail.com
Global Business and Investment Info Databank - www.ibpus.com**

LAOS STRATEGIC AND DEVELOPMENT PROFILES

STRATEGIC PROFILE

Capital and largest city	Vientiane 17°58′N 102°36′E
Official languages	Lao
Spoken languages	Lao Hmong Khmu
Ethnic groups	55% Lao 11% Khmu 8% Hmong 26% other[a]
Religion	Buddhism
Demonym	Laotian Lao
Government	Marxist–Leninistone-party socialist state
• **General Secretary and President**	Bounnhang Vorachith
• **Prime Minister**	Thongloun Sisoulith
• **Vice President**	Phankham Viphavanh
Legislature	National Assembly
Formation	
• **Kingdom of Lan Xang**	1354–1707
• **Luang Phrabang, Vientiane and Champasak**	1707–1778
• **Vassal of Thonburi and Siam**	1778–1893
• **War of Succession**	1826–8
• **French Indochina**	1893–1949
• **Independence from France**	19 July 1949
• **Declared Independence**	22 October 1953
• **Laotian civil war**	9 November 1953 – 2 December 1975
• **Lao Monarchy abolished**	2 December 1975
• **Current constitution**	14 August 1991
Area	
• **Total**	237,955 km^2 (84th)

	91,428.991 sq mi
• Water (%)	2
Population	
• 2014 (Jul) estimate	6,803,699(104th)
• 2015 census	6,492,228
• Density	26.7/km^2 (177th)
	69.2/sq mi
GDP (PPP)	2014 estimate
• Total	US$34.400 billion
• Per capita	US$4,986
GDP (nominal)	2014 estimate
• Total	US$11.676 billion
• Per capita	US$1,692
Gini (2008)	36.7
	medium
HDI (2014)	0.575
	medium · 141st
Currency	Kip (LAK)
Time zone	ICT
Date format	dd/mm/yyyy
Drives on the	right
Calling code	+856
ISO 3166 code	LA
Internet TLD	.la

Laos, officially the **Lao People's Democratic Republic**, is a landlocked socialist republic communist state in southeast Asia, bordered by Myanmar (Burma) and the People's Republic of China to the northwest, Vietnam to the east, Cambodia to the south, and Thailand to the west. Laos traces its history to the Kingdom of Lan Xang or *Land of a Million Elephants*, which existed from the 14th to the 18th century. After a period as a French colony, it gained independence in 1949. A long civil war ended when the communist Pathet Lao came to power in 1975.

Private enterprise has increased since the mid-1980s, but development has been hampered by poor communications in the heavily forested and mountainous landscape. 80% of those employed practice subsistence agriculture; this is coupled with widespread starvation due to the many failures of communism and the state's command economy.

The country's ethnic make-up is extremely diverse, with only around 60% belonging to the largest ethnic group, the Lao.

In 1975 the communist Pathet Lao took control of the government, ending a six-century-old monarchy. Initial closer ties to Vietnam and socialization were replaced with a gradual return to private enterprise, an easing of foreign investment laws, and the admission into ASEAN in 1997.

GEOGRAPHY

Location: Southeastern Asia, northeast of Thailand, west of Vietnam
Geographic coordinates: 18 00 N, 105 00 E

Map references: Southeast Asia
Area:
total: 236,800 sq km
land: 230,800 sq km
water: 6,000 sq km

Area - comparative: slightly larger than Utah

Land boundaries:
total: 5,083 km
border countries: Burma 235 km, Cambodia 541 km, China 423 km, Thailand 1,754 km, Vietnam 2,130 km

Coastline: 0 km (landlocked)
Maritime claims: none (landlocked)
Climate: tropical monsoon; rainy season (May to November); dry season (December to April)
Terrain: mostly rugged mountains; some plains and plateaus

Elevation extremes:
lowest point: Mekong River 70 m
highest point: Phou Bia 2,817 m

Natural resources: timber, hydropower, gypsum, tin, gold, gemstones

Land use:
arable land: 3%
permanent crops: 0%
permanent pastures: 3%
forests and woodland: 54%
other: 40%

Irrigated land: 1,250 sq km
note: rainy season irrigation - 2,169 sq km; dry season irrigation - 750 sq km (1998 est.)

Natural hazards: floods, droughts, and blight

Environment - current issues: unexploded ordnance; deforestation; soil erosion; a majority of the population does not have access to potable water

Environment - international agreements:
party to: Biodiversity, Climate Change, Desertification, Environmental Modification, Law of the Sea, Nuclear Test Ban, Ozone Layer Protection
signed, but not ratified: none of the selected agreements

Geography - note: landlocked

PEOPLE

Population: 5,497,459

Age structure:
0-14 years: 43% (male 1,191,608; female 1,173,144)
15-64 years: 54% (male 1,447,788; female 1,500,016)
65 years and over: 3% (male 85,028; female 99,875)

Population growth rate: 2.5%
Birth rate: 38.29 births/1,000 population
Death rate: 13.35 deaths/1,000 population
Net migration rate: 0 migrant(s)/1,000 population

Sex ratio:
at birth: 1.05 male(s)/female
under 15 years: 1.02 male(s)/female
15-64 years: 0.97 male(s)/female
65 years and over: 0.85 male(s)/female
total population: 0.98 male(s)/female

Infant mortality rate: 94.8 deaths/1,000 live births

Life expectancy at birth:
total population: 53.09 years
male: 51.22 years
female: 55.02 years

Total fertility rate: 5.21 children born/woman

Nationality:
noun: Lao(s) or Laotian(s)
adjective: Lao or Laotian

Ethnic groups: Lao Loum (lowland) 68%, Lao Theung (upland) 22%, Lao Soung (highland) including the Hmong ("Meo") and the Yao (Mien) 9%, ethnic Vietnamese/Chinese 1%
Religions: Buddhist 60% (in October 1999, the regime proposed a constitutional amendment making Buddhism the state religion; the National Assembly is expected to vote on the amendment sometime in 2000), animist and other 40%
Languages: Lao (official), French, English, and various ethnic languages

Literacy:
definition: age 15 and over can read and write
total population: 57%
male: 70%
female: 44%

GOVERNMENT

Country name:
conventional long form: Lao People's Democratic Republic
conventional short form: Laos
local long form: Sathalanalat Paxathipatai Paxaxon Lao
local short form: none

Data code: LA
Government type: Communist state
Capital: Vientiane

Administrative divisions: 16 provinces (khoueng, singular and plural), 1 municipality* (kampheng nakhon, singular and plural), and 1 special zone** (khetphiset, singular and plural); Attapu, Bokeo, Bolikhamxai, Champasak, Houaphan, Khammouan, Louangnamtha, Louangphabang, Oudomxai, Phongsali, Salavan, Savannakhet, Viangchan*, Viangchan, Xaignabouli, Xaisomboun**, Xekong, Xiangkhoang

Independence: 19 July 1949 (from France)
National holiday: National Day, 2 December (1975) (proclamation of the Lao People's Democratic Republic)
Constitution: promulgated 14 August 1991

Legal system: based on traditional customs, French legal norms and procedures, and Socialist practice

Suffrage: 18 years of age; universal

Executive branch:

chief of state: President BOUNNYANG Vorachit (since 20 April 2016); Vice President PHANKHAM Viphavan (since 20 April 2016)

head of government: Prime Minister THONGLOUN Sisoulit (since 20 April 2016); Deputy Prime Ministers BOUNTHONG Chitmani, SONXAI Siphandon, SOMDI Douangdi (since 20 April 2016)

cabinet: Council of Ministers appointed by the president, approved by the National Assembly

elections/appointments: president and vice president indirectly elected by the National Assembly for a 5-year term (no term limits); election last held on 20 April 2016 (next to be held in 2021); prime minister nominated by the president, elected by the National Assembly for 5-year term

election results: BOUNNYANG Vorachit (LPRP) elected president; PHANKHAM Viphavan (LPRP) elected vice president; percent of National Assembly vote - NA; THONGLOUN Sisoulit (LPRP) elected prime minister; percent of National Assembly vote - NA

Legislative branch:

description: unicameral National Assembly or Sapha Heng Xat (132 seats; members directly elected in multi-seat constituencies by simple majority vote from candidate lists provided by the Lao People's Revolutionary Party; members serve 5-year terms)

elections: last held on 20 April 2016 (next to be held in 2021)

election results: percent of vote by party - NA; seats by party - LPRP 128, independent 4

Judicial branch:

highest court(s): People's Supreme Court (consists of the court president and organized into criminal, civil, administrative, commercial, family, and juvenile chambers, each with a vice president and several judges)

judge selection and term of office: president of People's Supreme Court appointed by National Assembly on recommendation of the president of the republic for a 5-year term; vice presidents of People's Supreme Court appointed by the president of the republic on recommendation of the National Assembly; appointment of chamber judges NA; tenure of court vice-presidents and chamber judges NA

subordinate courts: appellate courts; provincial, municipal, district, and military courts

Political parties and leaders: Lao People's Revolutionary Party or LPRP [KHAMTAI Siphandon, party president]; other parties proscribed

Political pressure groups and leaders: noncommunist political groups proscribed; most opposition leaders fled the country in 1975

International organization participation: ACCT, AsDB, ASEAN, CP, ESCAP, FAO, G-77, IBRD, ICAO, ICRM, IDA, IFAD, IFC, IFRCS, ILO, IMF, Intelsat (nonsignatory user), Interpol, IOC, ITU, NAM, OPCW, PCA, UN, UNCTAD, UNESCO, UNIDO, UPU, WFTU, WHO, WIPO, WMO, WToO, WTrO (observer)

Diplomatic representation in the US:
chief of mission: Ambassador VANG Rattanavong
chancery: 2222 S Street NW, Washington, DC 20008
telephone: (202) 332-6416
FAX: (202) 332-4923

Diplomatic representation from the US:
chief of mission: Ambassador Wendy Jean CHAMBERLIN
embassy: Rue Bartholonie, B. P. 114, Vientiane
mailing address: American Embassy, Box V, APO AP 96546
telephone: [856] (21) 212581, 212582, 212585
FAX: [856] (21) 212584

Flag description: three horizontal bands of red (top), blue (double width), and red with a large white disk centered in the blue band

ECONOMY

The government of Laos, one of the few remaining one-party communist states, began decentralizing control and encouraging private enterprise in 1986. The results, starting from an extremely low base, were striking - growth averaged 6% per year from 1988-2008 except during the short-lived drop caused by the Asian financial crisis that began in 1997. Laos' growth exceeded 7% per year during 2008-13. Despite this high growth rate, Laos remains a country with an underdeveloped infrastructure, particularly in rural areas. It has a basic, but improving, road system, and limited external and internal land-line telecommunications. Electricity is available in 83 % of the country.

Laos' economy is heavily dependent on capital-intensive natural resource exports. The labor force, however, still relies on agriculture, dominated by rice cultivation in lowland areas, which accounts for about 25% of GDP and 73% of total employment. Economic growth has reduced official poverty rates from 46% in 1992 to 26% in 2010. The economy also has benefited from high-profile foreign direct investment in hydropower, copper and gold mining, logging, and construction though some projects in these industries have drawn criticism for their environmental impacts. Laos gained Normal Trade Relations status with the US in 2004 and applied for Generalized System of Preferences trade benefits in 2013 after being admitted to the World Trade Organization earlier in the year. Laos is in the process of implementing a value-added tax system. Simplified investment procedures and expanded bank credits for small farmers and small entrepreneurs will improve Laos' economic prospects. The government appears committed to raising the country's profile among investors, but suffered through a fiscal crisis in 2013 brought about by public sector wage increases, fiscal mismanagement, and revenue shortfalls. The World Bank has declared that Laos' goal of graduating from the UN Development

Program's list of least-developed countries by 2020 is achievable, and the country is preparing to enter the ASEAN Economic Community in 2015.

GDP (purchasing power parity):
$20.78 billion (2013 est.)
country comparison to the world: 132
$19.18 billion (2014 est.)
$17.78 billion (2011 est.)
note:data are in 2013 US dollars

GDP (official exchange rate):
$10.1 billion (2013 est.)

GDP - real growth rate:
8.3% (2013 est.)
country comparison to the world: 9
7.9% (2014 est.)
8% (2011 est.)

GDP - per capita (PPP):
$3,100 (2013 est.)
country comparison to the world: 176
$2,900 (2014 est.)
$2,700 (2011 est.)
note:data are in 2013 US dollars

Gross national saving:
27.4% of GDP (2013 est.)
country comparison to the world: 38
26.2% of GDP (2014 est.)
25.2% of GDP (2011 est.)

GDP - composition, by end use:
household consumption:
66.9%
government consumption:
9.8%
investment in fixed capital:
31.7%
investment in inventories:
-1.3%
exports of goods and services:
40%
imports of goods and services:
-48.4%
(2013 est.)

GDP - composition, by sector of origin:
agriculture:
24.8%

industry:
32%
services:
37.5% (2013 est.)

Agriculture - products:
sweet potatoes, vegetables, corn, coffee, sugarcane, tobacco, cotton, tea, peanuts, rice; cassava (manioc, tapioca), water buffalo, pigs, cattle, poultry

Industries:
mining (copper, tin, gold, gypsum); timber, electric power, agricultural processing, rubber, construction, garments, cement, tourism

Industrial production growth rate:
11% (2013 est.)
country comparison to the world: 12

Labor force:
3.373 million (2013 est.)
country comparison to the world: 100

Labor force - by occupation:
agriculture:
73.1%
industry:
6.1%
services:
20.6% (2014 est.)

Unemployment rate:
1.9% (2010 est.)
country comparison to the world: 11
2.5% (2009 est.)

Population below poverty line:
22% (2013 est.)

Household income or consumption by percentage share:
lowest 10%:
3.3%
highest 10%:
30.3%

Distribution of family income - Gini index:
36.7
country comparison to the world: 83
34.6 (2002)

Budget:

revenues:
$2.481 billion
expenditures:
$2.642 billion (2013 est.)

Taxes and other revenues:
24.6% of GDP (2013 est.)
country comparison to the world: 135

Budget surplus (+) or deficit (-):
-1.6% of GDP (2013 est.)
country comparison to the world: 77

Public debt:
46.3% of GDP (2013 est.)
country comparison to the world: 77
49.1% of GDP (2014 est.)

Fiscal year:
1 October - 30 September

Inflation rate (consumer prices):
6.5% (2013 est.)
country comparison to the world: 183
4.3% (2014 est.)

Central bank discount rate:
4.3% (31 December 2010)
country comparison to the world: 94
4% (31 December 2009)

Commercial bank prime lending rate:
23.2% (31 December 2013 est.)
country comparison to the world: 14
22.3% (31 December 2014 est.)

Stock of narrow money:
$1.389 billion (31 December 2013 est.)
country comparison to the world: 141
$1.154 billion (31 December 2014 est.)

Stock of broad money:
$4.071 billion (31 December 2013 est.)
country comparison to the world: 136
$3.673 billion (31 December 2014 est.)

Stock of domestic credit:
$4.716 billion (31 December 2013 est.)

country comparison to the world: 114
$4.034 billion (31 December 2014 est.)

Market value of publicly traded shares:
$1.012 billion (2014 est.)
$NA

Current account balance:
-$484.3 million (2013 est.)
country comparison to the world: 98
-$315.5 million (2014 est.)

Exports:
$2.313 billion (2013 est.)
country comparison to the world: 141
$1.984 billion (2014 est.)

Exports - commodities:
wood products, coffee, electricity, tin, copper, gold, cassava

Exports - partners:
Thailand 34%, China 21.5%, Vietnam 12.2%

Imports:
$3.238 billion (2013 est.)
country comparison to the world: 145
$2.744 billion (2014 est.)

Imports - commodities:
machinery and equipment, vehicles, fuel, consumer goods

Imports - partners:
Thailand 62.1%, China 16.2%, Vietnam 7.3%

Reserves of foreign exchange and gold:
$845.4 million (31 December 2013 est.)
country comparison to the world: 141
$796.9 million (31 December 2014 est.)

Debt - external:
$6.69 billion (31 December 2013 est.)
country comparison to the world: 110
$6.288 billion (31 December 2014 est.)

Stock of direct foreign investment - at home:
$15.14 billion (31 December 2014 est.)
country comparison to the world: 81
$12.44 billion (31 December 2011 est.)

Exchange rates:
kips (LAK) per US dollar -
7,875.9 (2013 est.)
8,007.3 (2014 est.)
8,258.8 (2010 est.)
8,516.04
8,760.69

ENERGY

Electricity - production:
3.629 billion kWh
country comparison to the world: 127

Electricity - consumption:
2.4 billion kWh
country comparison to the world: 136

Electricity - exports:
2.537 billion kWh
country comparison to the world: 41

Electricity - imports:
1 billion kWh
country comparison to the world: 65

Electricity - installed generating capacity:
3.217 million kW
country comparison to the world: 87

Electricity - from fossil fuels:
2.6% of total installed capacity
country comparison to the world: 201

Electricity - from nuclear fuels:
0% of total installed capacity
country comparison to the world: 122

Electricity - from hydroelectric plants:
97.4% of total installed capacity
country comparison to the world: 9

Electricity - from other renewable sources:
0% of total installed capacity

country comparison to the world: 191

Crude oil - production:
0 bbl/day
country comparison to the world: 186

Crude oil - exports:
0 bbl/day
country comparison to the world: 140

Crude oil - imports:
0 bbl/day
country comparison to the world: 206

Crude oil - proved reserves:
0 bbl
country comparison to the world: 152

Refined petroleum products - production:
0 bbl/day
country comparison to the world: 161

Refined petroleum products - consumption:
3,391 bbl/day
country comparison to the world: 177

Refined petroleum products - exports:
0 bbl/day
country comparison to the world: 191

Refined petroleum products - imports:
3,160 bbl/day
country comparison to the world: 170

Natural gas - production:
0 cu m
country comparison to the world: 151

Natural gas - consumption:
0 cu m
country comparison to the world: 163

Natural gas - exports:
0 cu m

country comparison to the world: 132

Natural gas - imports:
0 cu m
country comparison to the world: 86

Natural gas - proved reserves:
0 cu m
country comparison to the world: 156

COMMUNICATIONS

Telephones - main lines in use:
112,000
country comparison to the world: 143

Telephones - mobile cellular:
6.492 million
country comparison to the world: 99

Telephone system:
general assessment:
service to general public is improving; the government relies on a radiotelephone network to communicate with remote areas
domestic:
4 service providers with mobile cellular usage growing very rapidly
international:
country code - 856; satellite earth station - 1 Intersputnik (Indian Ocean region) and a second to be developed by China

Broadcast media:
6 TV stations operating out of Vientiane - 3 government-operated and the others commercial; 17 provincial stations operating with nearly all programming relayed via satellite from the government-operated stations in Vientiane; Chinese and Vietnamese programming relayed via satellite from Lao National TV; broadcasts available from stations in Thailand and Vietnam in border areas; multi-channel satellite and cable TV systems provide access to a wide range of foreign stations; state-controlled radio with state-operated Lao National Radio (LNR) broadcasting on 5 frequencies - 1 AM, 1 SW, and 3 FM; LNR's AM and FM programs are relayed via satellite constituting a large part of the programming schedules of the provincial radio stations; Thai radio broadcasts available in border areas and transmissions of multiple international broadcasters are also accessible

Internet country code:
.la

Internet hosts:
1,532
country comparison to the world: 166

Internet users:
300,000
country comparison to the world: 130

TRANSPORTATION

Airports:
41
country comparison to the world: 103

Airports - with paved runways:
total: 8
2,438 to 3,047 m: 3
1,524 to 2,437 m: 4
914 to 1,523 m: 1 (2013)

Airports - with unpaved runways:
total: 33
1,524 to 2,437 m: 2
914 to 1,523 m: 9
under 914 m:
22

Pipelines:
refined products 540 km (2013)

Roadways:
total: 39,568 km
country comparison to the world: 89
paved: 530 km
unpaved: 39,038 km

Waterways:
4,600 km (primarily on the Mekong River and its tributaries; 2,900 additional km are intermittently navigable by craft drawing less than 0.5 m)
country comparison to the world: 24

MILITARY

Military branches:
Lao People's Armed Forces (LPAF): Lao People's Army (LPA; includes Riverine Force), Air Force

Military service age and obligation:
18 years of age for compulsory or voluntary military service; conscript service obligation - minimum 18-months

Manpower available for military service:
males age 16-49: 1,574,362
females age 16-49: 1,607,856 (2010 est.)

Manpower fit for military service:
males age 16-49: 1,111,629
females age 16-49: 1,190,035 (2010 est.)

Manpower reaching militarily significant age annually:
male: 71,400
female: 73,038 (2010 est.)

Military expenditures:
NA%
0.23% of GDP
NA%

Military - note:
serving one of the world's least developed countries, the Lao People's Armed Forces (LPAF) is small, poorly funded, and ineffectively resourced; its mission focus is border and internal security, primarily in countering ethnic Hmong insurgent groups; together with the Lao People's Revolutionary Party and the government, the Lao People's Army (LPA) is the third pillar of state machinery, and as such is expected to suppress political and civil unrest and similar national emergencies, but the LPA also has upgraded skills to respond to avian influenza outbreaks; there is no perceived external threat to the state and the LPA maintains strong ties with the neighboring Vietnamese military

TRANSNATIONAL ISSUES

Disputes - international:
southeast Asian states have enhanced border surveillance to check the spread of avian flu; talks continue on completion of demarcation with Thailand but disputes remain over islands in the Mekong River; concern among Mekong River Commission members that China's construction of dams on the Mekong River and its tributaries will affect water levels; Cambodia and Vietnam are concerned about Laos' extensive upstream dam construction

Illicit drugs:
estimated opium poppy cultivation in 2008 was 1,900 hectares, about a 73% increase from 2007; estimated potential opium production in 2008 more than tripled to 17 metric tons; unsubstantiated reports of domestic methamphetamine production; growing domestic methamphetamine problem

IMPORTANT INFORMATION FOR UNDERSTANDING LAOS[1]

Official Name: Lao People's Democratic Republic

PROFILE

GEOGRAPHY

Area: 236,800 sq. km. (91,430 sq. mi.); area comparable to Oregon.
Capital--Vientiane (est. 569,000). *Other principal towns*--Savannakhet, Luang Prabang, Pakse, Thakhek.
Terrain: rugged mountains, plateaus, alluvial plains.
Climate: tropical monsoon; rainy season (May to November); dry season (November to April).

PEOPLE

Nationality: *Noun and adjective*--Lao (sing. and pl.).
Population : 5.4 million.
Annual growth rate: 2.7%.
Ethnic groups: Lao Loum 53%; other lowland Lao 13% (Thai Dam, Phouane); Lao Theung (midslope) 23%; Lao Sung (highland), including Hmong, Akha, and the Yao (Mien) 10%; ethnic Vietnamese/Chinese 1%.
Religions: Principally Buddhism, with animism among highland groups.
Languages: Lao (official), French, various highland ethnic, English.
Education: *Literacy*--60%.
Health : *Infant mortality rate*--89.32/1,000. *Life expectancy*--55.87 years for women, 52.63 years for men.
Work force (2.6 million, 1999): *Agriculture*--85%; *industry and services*--15%.

GOVERNMENT

Branches: *Executive*--president (head of state); Chairman, Council of Ministers (prime minister and head of government); nine-member Politburo; 49-member Central Committee. *Legislative*--99-seat National Assembly. *Judicial*--district, provincial, and a national Supreme Court.
Political parties: Lao People's Revolutionary Party (LPRP)--only legal party.
Administrative subdivisions: 16 provinces, one special region, and Vientiane prefecture.
Flag: A red band at the top and bottom with a larger blue band between them; a large white circle is centered.

ECONOMY

Natural resources: Hydroelectric power, timber, minerals.
Agriculture (51% of GDP): *Primary products*--glutinous rice, coffee, corn, sugarcane,

---

[1] **U.S. Department of State,** *Bureau of East Asian and Pacific Affairs*

vegetables, tobacco, ginger, water buffalo, pigs, cattle, and poultry.
Industry (22% of GDP, 1999): *Primary types*--garment manufacturing, electricity production, gypsum and tin mining, wood and wood processing, cement manufacturing, agricultural processing.
Industrial growth rate --7.5%.
Services --27% of GDP.
Trade: *Exports* --$370 million: garments, electricity, wood and wood products, coffee, rattan. Major markets--France, U.K., Germany, Holland, Thailand, Belgium, U.S., Italy, Japan, Vietnam. *Imports* --$570 million. *Major imports*--fuel, food, consumer, goods, machinery and equipment, vehicles and spare parts. *Major suppliers*--Thailand, Singapore, Japan, Vietnam, China.

GEOGRAPHY, TOPOGRAPHY AND CLIMATE

The Lao People's Democratic Republic (Lao PDR) has a land area of 236,800 square kilometers, stretching more than 1,700 km from the north to south and between 100 km and 400 km from the east to west. The Lao PDR has an eastern border of 1,957 km with the Socialist Republic of Vietnam, a western border of 1,730 km with the, Kingdom of Thailand, a southern border of 492 kin with t he Kingdom of Combodia, and northern borders of 416 kin with the People's Republic of China and 230 km with the Union of Myamar.

Although the Lao PDR has no direct access to the sea, it has an abundance of rivers, including a 1,865 km stretch of the Mekong (Nam Kong), defining its border with Myanmar and a major part of the border with Thailand. Ma'or stretches of the Mekong and its tributaries are navigable and provide alluvial deposits for some. of the fertile plains. About two thirds of the country is mountainous, with ranges from 200 to the 2,820 meters high. The mountains pose difficulties for transportation and communication and complicate development, but together with the rivers they produce vast potential for hydro power.

The Lao PDR is a tropical country, whose climate is affected by monsoon rains from May to September. In Vientiane, the average temperatures range from a minimum of C 16.4 degrees in January to a maximum of C 13 degrees in April.

WATER RESOURCES

Its abundant water resources is probably the most important natural resource endowment of the country. There are only three hydroelectric plants in operation so far, of which Nam Ngum I is the biggest. These three plants with a combined capacity of 200 MW, reportedly realizes only less than five percent of the country's hydroelectric potential. About 90% of hydroelectric power production is exported to Thailand, constituting one of the leading exports of the Lao PDR. Plans are underway to construct a number of new hydroelectric power facilities, which are described in greater detail in Section B.

FOREST RESOURCES

Forests cover about 47% of the country, comprising a wide variety of commercial tree species suitable for production of saw timber, plywood, parquet, furniture, etc.... The most important high value species are hardwoods belonging to the Diterocarpaceae family and rosewoods belonging to the Genera Pterocarpus, Dalbergia and Afzelia. Pines and other coniferous species are also available but in comparatively small quantities. Eighty percent of domestic energy consumption is based on fuel wood, and an estimated 300,000 hectares of forest are lost annually largely due to shifting cultivation and logging activities. In the effort to protect forest resources from unsustainable felling of trees, the total annual allowable cut (AC) has been set by the Tropical Forest Action Plan (1991) to 280,000 cubic meters per annum, exportation of logs was temporarily restricted to restructure forest management, and protective measures have been implemented to prevent depletion of forests due to shifting fanning practices.

MINERAL RESOURCES

Sizeable deposits of gemstones such as sapphire, zircon, amethyst, gold, iron are and tin are know to exist in the country. Gemstones, gold, coal and tin are estimated to have a high economic value. More geologic surveys are needed to identify location of mineral deposits that would allow their exploitation in commercial quantities. Meanwhile, exploration of potential petroleum deposits are underway. Economic exploitation of mineral resources will depend on development of the required physical infrastructures.

ADMINISTRATIVE STRUCTURE OF LAOS

ATTAPEU PROVINCE

Attapeu Province is best known for the Bolaven Plateau, which also extends into Champassak, Salavan and Sekong provinces. The Bolaven Plateau is covered in the Champassak section -The plateau is best accessed from Pakse, in Champassak province.

Attapeu province is rugged,wild and very scenic, but transportation is very difficult, especially by land in the rainy season.

The town of Samakhi Xai (Attapeu) is situated in a large picturesque valley. The population of the province is more Lao Loum than the neighbouring provinces.

Parts of the Ho Chi Minh Trail can be explored from Attapeu, although using a local guide is essential.

BOKEO PROVINCE

Bokeo province is the smallest province in the country and borders Thailand and Myanmar. This is the Lao side of the 'Golden Triangle'. The province has 34 ethnic groups, the second most ethnically diverse province in Laos. The photo shows a group of Akha (Ikaw or Kaw) people from the Golden Triangle area taken in 1900.

Huay Xai is the border town with Thailand, the city is busy and prosperous.

Located in the center of Huay Xay is Chomkao Manilat temple. The view from the the temple hill over Houy Xay city, the Mekong river and surrounding mountains is a definite reward for making it up the many steps.

BOLIKHAMSAI PROVINCE

Bolikhamsai province contains part of the wilderness area known as the Nakai - Nam Theun National Biodiversity Conservation Area the largest conservation area in the country at 3700 sq km. The area is home to over a dozen threatened species including Asiatic black bear, clouded leopard, elephant, giant muntjac, guar, Malayan sun bear, and tiger.

The saola (spindlehorn) or Vu Quang Ox - *Pseudoryx nghetinhensis* was discovered in neighbouring Vietnam in 1992 and sighted since then in Laos in the conservation area. Only two other land mammals have been classified with their own genus this century. The first live saola was captured in neighbouring Khammouane province in 1996.

The capital of Bolikhamsai is Paxxan, which can be reached from Vietntiane by bus in about three hours.

CHAMPASSAK PROVINCE - PAKSE

The province of Champassak is home to one of Asia's great, but least visited temples, Wat Phu. Pakse, the capital is situated at the confluence of the Se river and the Mekong (Pakse means 'mouth of the Se') and is a busy trading town. The province also houses much of the Bolaven Plateau, an area that is home to a number of ethnic minorities. To the south is Si Pan Don (four thousand islands), where the Mekong reaches up to 14km wide during the rainy season and the Khone Phapeng Falls.

Pakse has a number of comfortable places to stay and is a good base from which to explore the surrounding area. The town has one of the largest markets in the region. Within Pakse is the Champassak Museum where trader can see relics from Wat Phu as well as from the Bolaven Plateau.

HOUA PHAN

Houa Phan province is situated in the northeast of Laos and was the base of the Lao People's Revolutionary Army activities. There are over 100 caves in the Vieng Xai district of Houa Phanh many of which were used as hideouts and bunkers during the Indochina war.

Lao Aviation flies daily to the capital Xam Neua from Vientiane - The most famous caves in the area are:

Tham Than Souphanouvong: formerly known as Tham Phapount. In 1964, Prince Souphanouvong set up his residence in this cave. Tham Than Kaysone: formerly known as Tham Yonesong, was established for the residence of Mr. Kaysone Phomvihane. Tham Than Khamtay: was the residence of Mr. Khamtay Siphandone, consisting of many area, such as a meeting room, reception room and research room.

Other attractions include Keo Nong Vay Temple located in Xam Neua district.

Hot springs in Xam Tay district are located about 154 km away from Xam Neua the waters reach a temperature of around 40 degrees Celcius. Xam Tay waterfall is located Xam Tay district.

Saleu and Nasala villages, well known for their weaving activities, located in Xieng Kor district on the road No: 6 to Xieng Khouang province 125 km away from Xam Neua.

KHAMMOUANE PROVINCE

Khammouane province contains two vast wilderness areas known as the Khammuane Limestone National Biodiversity Conservation Area and the Nakai - Nam Theun National Biodiversity Conservation Area.

The Kahmmuane Limestone is a maze of limestone karst peaks forming a stone forest of caves, rivers and pristine jungle. For most of the wet season, the area is not accessible by road - most 'roads' being tracks with log bridges across deeps streams. These tracks are often routes across rice paddies near the river banks - during the rainy season, the only way to get around is by boat.

The National Tourism Authority of Lao PDR is currently investigating ecotourism projects in this beautiful region. The capital of Khammouane province is Tha Kek, situated across the Mekong from Nakorn Phanom in Thailand.

LUANG PRABANG

Luang Prabang is the jewel of Indochina, and a UNESCO World Heritage Site since 1995. The ancient royal city is surrounded by mountains at the junction of the Mekong and its tributary, the Khan river. In the centre of the city is Mount Phousi with stunning views of the surrounding temples and hills. Luang Prabang is a city where time seems to stand still. As part of the UNESCO plan, new buildings have been limited and development must be in keeping with this magical place.

Minority village in Luang Namtha

Luang Prabang is small, and just about everywhere can be reached by foot. Walking and travelling by bicycle is the best way to see this tiny city.

LUANG NAMTHA PROVINCE

Located in the northern part of Laos, Luang Namtha shares its northwestern border with Myanmar and its northeastern border with China. The province is mountainous, home to large numbers of minorities. The Nam Ha National Biodiversity Conservation Area is located in the southwest of Luang Namtha - a pristine habitat of dense tropical rainforest covering almost all of the protected area.

UNESCO are funding a ecotourism project in Luang Namtha that will be capable of sustaining sustainable development in the province. The concept of the project is to provide education, conservation, management and sustainable economic benefits for the local population. The province is home to a 39 minorities the largest number in the country.

OUDOMXAI

Located in the northern part of Laos. This mountainous province has 23 ethnic groups each with it own distinct culture, religion, language and colorful style of dress. The provincial capital , Muang Xay lies between two strings of Hmong villages.

Lao Aviation flies to Oudomxai from Vientiane

Oudomxai can be reached overland from Luang Prabang. Oudomxay is also accessible from Bokeo and Luang Namtha Provinces. Oudomxay is an ideal base for excursions and trekking to varied sights and attractions as well as destination in its own right. Muang Xai, has one of the best produce markets in the area.

Near Muang Xai, there is a waterfall, Lak Sip – Et (located at km No 11) and hot springs near Muang La.

PHONGSALI PROVINCE

Phongsali province the most remote in northern Laos is surrounded on three sides by China and Vietnam. The Phu Den Din National Biodiversity Conservation Area along the Vietnamese border with mountains as high as 1950m with over 70% forest cover is home to the asiatic black bear, bantang, clouded leopard, elephant, guar and tiger.

The capital Phongsali, can be reached from Muang Xai with buses leaving once a day. Phongsali has a year round cool climate with temperatures as low as 5 degrees Celcius at night. Rain can be heavy - bring a jacket and warm clothes.

Muang Khoa is a small town situated on the junction of Route 4 and the Nam Ou river. The journey to Muang Khoa along route 4 from Udomxai takes about four hours. It is possible to travel up river to Phongsali from here, or down to Luang Prabang.

**For additional analytical, business and investment opportunities information,
please contact Global Investment & Business Center, USA
at (703) 370-8082. Fax: (703) 370-8083. E-mail: ibpusa3@gmail.com
Global Business and Investment Info Databank - www.ibpus.com**

SALAVAN PROVINCE

Salavan Province is best known for the Bolaven Plateau, which also extends into Attapeu, Champassak and Sekong provinces. The Bolaven Plateau is covered in the Champassak section.. The plateau is best accessed from Pakse, in Champassak province.

Salavan province is home to the Phu Xieng Thong National Biodiversity Conservation Area, covering nearly 1,000 sq km in the western part of the province next to the Mekong river. It is thought that asiatic black bear, banteng, clouded leopard, Douc langur, elephant, gibbon, guar, Siamese crocodile and tiger and inhabit this area.

SEKONG PROVINCE

Sekong Province is best known for the Bolaven Plateau, which also extends into Attapeu, Champassak and Salavan and provinces. The Bolaven Plateau is covered in the Champassak section. The plateau is best accessed from Pakse, in Champassak province. Sekong province is rugged,wild and very scenic, but transportation is very difficult, especially by land in the rainy season.

SAYABOURI PROVINCE

Sayabouri province is quite close to Vientiane, but being quite mountainous is quite remote. The province shares its borders with six Thai provinces. The capital of the province, Sayabouri is on the banks of the Nam Hung, a tributary of the Mekong.

The province houses the Nam Phoun National Biodiversity Conservation Area which is 1150 sq km of forested hills that contain Asiatic black bear, dhole, elephant, guar, gibbon, Malayan sun bear and Sumatran rhino.

The southern part of the province has many scenic waterfalls, but getting around this part of the province is very difficult.

SAVANNAKHET

Savannakhet town is situated on the banks of the Mekong river opposite Mukdahan in Thailand. The province bridges the country between Thailand and Vietnam and the town is a very active junction for trade between the two countries. The town itself can be easily explored by foot and has a number of interesting temples, including Vietnamese temple and school and a large Catholic church. Much of the town's architecture is French Colonial.

VIENTIANE

Vientiane, capital of Laos is Asia's biggest village. Busy and hectic in comparison to the rest of the country, it is quiet compared with any other city in Asia. Vientiane, as all of Lao's major cities, is situated on the Mekong river which forms the lifeline of the country.

Vientiane is the hub for all travel in the country. The city has a population of 450,000, about 10% of the country.

Vientiane is a city full of surprises. Here trader can find fields of rice and vegetables, agriculture hidden behind tree lined avenues. French Colonial architecture sits next to gilded temples. Freshly baked French bread is served next to shops selling noodle soup.

There is little modern in Vientiane. Old French colonial houses are being restored as offices and as restaurants and hotels. There are only a handful of modern buildings which sometimes look remarkably out of place in this quiet capital.

XIENG KHOUANG PROVINCE

Xieng Khouang province is situated in the north of Laos, a province of green montains and karst limestone. Much of the province was heavily bombed during the Vietnam war and old war scrap is used in building houses throughout the province. The capital of Xieng Khouang is Phonsavan. Situated at an altitude of 1,200m is an excellent climate. Decmber and January can be chilly so bring a light jacket or fleece for cool evenings and mornings.

PEOPLE

Laos' population was estimated at about 5.4 million in 1999, dispersed unevenly across the country. Most people live in valleys of the Mekong River and its tributaries. Vientiane prefecture, the capital and largest city, had about 569,000 residents in 1999. The country's population density is 23.4/sq. km.

About half the country's people are ethnic Lao, the principal lowland inhabitants and politically and culturally dominant group. The Lao are descended from the Tai people who began migrating southward from China in the first millennium A.D. Mountain tribes of Miao-Yao, Austro-Asiatic, Tibeto-Burman--Hmong, Yao, Akha, and Lahu--and Tai ethnolinguistic heritage are found in northern Laos. Collectively, they are known as Lao Sung or highland Lao. In the central and southern mountains, Mon-Khmer tribes, known as Lao Theung or midslope Lao, predominate. Some Vietnamese and Chinese minorities remain, particularly in the towns, but many left in two waves--after independence in the late 1940s and again after 1975.

The predominant religion is Theravada Buddhism. Animism is common among the mountain tribes. Buddhism and spirit worship coexist easily. There also is a small number of Christians and Muslims.

The official and dominant language is Lao, a tonal language of the Tai linguistic group. Midslope and highland Lao speak an assortment of tribal languages. French, once common in government and commerce, has declined in usage, while knowledge of English--the language of the Association of Southeast Asian Nations (ASEAN)--has increased in recent years.

HISTORY

Laos traces its first recorded history and its origins as a unified state to the emergence of the Kingdom of Lan Xang (literally, "million elephants") in 1353. Under the rule of King Fa Ngum, the wealthy and mighty kingdom covered much of what today is Thailand and Laos. His successors, especially King Setthathirat in the 16th century, helped establish Buddhism as the predominant religion of the country.

By the 17th century, the kingdom of Lan Xang entered a period of decline marked by dynastic struggle and conflicts with its neighbors. In the late 18th century, the Siamese (Thai) established hegemony over much of what is now Laos. The region was divided into principalities centered on Luang Prabang in the north, Vientiane in the center, and Champassak in the south. Following its colonization of Vietnam, the French supplanted the Siamese and began to integrate all of Laos into the French empire. The Franco-Siamese treaty of 1907 defined the present Lao boundary with Thailand.

During World War II, the Japanese occupied French Indochina, including Laos. King Sisavang Vong of Luang Prabang was induced to declare independence from France in 1945, just prior to Japan's surrender. During this period, nationalist sentiment grew. In September 1945, Vientiane and Champassak united with Luang Prabang to form an independent government under the Free Laos (Lao Issara) banner. The movement, however, was shortlived. By early 1946, French troops reoccupied the country and conferred limited autonomy on Laos following elections for a constituent assembly.

Amidst the first Indochina war between France and the communist movement in Vietnam, Prince Souphanouvong formed the Pathet Lao (Land of Laos) resistance organization committed to the communist struggle against colonialism. Laos was not granted full sovereignty until the French defeat by the Vietnamese and the subsequent Geneva peace conference in 1954. Elections were held in 1955, and the first coalition government, led by Prince Souvanna Phouma, was formed in 1957. The coalition government collapsed in 1958, amidst increased polarization of the political process. Rightist forces took over the government.

In 1960, Kong Le, a paratroop captain, seized Vientiane in a coup and demanded formation of a neutralist government to end the fighting. The neutralist government, once again led by Souvanna Phouma, was not successful in holding power. Rightist forces under Gen. Phoumi Nosavan drove out the neutralist government from power later that same year. Subsequently, the neutralists allied themselves with the communist insurgents and began to receive support from the Soviet Union. Phoumi Nosavan's rightist regime received support from the U.S.

A second Geneva conference, held in 1961-62, provided for the independence and neutrality of Laos. Soon after accord was reached, the signatories accused each other of violating the terms of the agreement, and with superpower support on both sides, the civil war soon resumed. Although the country was to be neutral, a growing American and North Vietnamese military presence in the country increasingly drew Laos into the second Indochina war (1954-75). For nearly a decade, Laos was subjected to the heaviest bombing in the history of warfare, as the U.S. sought to destroy the Ho Chi Minh Trail that passed through eastern Laos.

In 1972, the communist People's Party renamed itself the Lao People's Revolutionary Party (LPRP). It joined a new coalition government in Laos soon after the Vientiane cease-fire agreement in 1973. Nonetheless, the political struggle between communists, neutralists, and rightists continued. The fall of Saigon and Phnom Penh to communist forces in April 1975 hastened the decline of the coalition in Laos. Months after these communist victories, the Pathet Lao entered Vientiane. On December 2, 1975, the king abdicated his throne in the constitutional monarchy, and the communist Lao People's Democratic Republic (LPDR) was established.

The new communist government imposed centralized economic decisionmaking and broad security measures, including control of the media and the arrest and incarceration of many members of the previous government and military in "re-education camps". These draconian policies and deteriorating economic conditions, along with government efforts to enforce political control, prompted an exodus of lowland Lao and ethnic Hmong from Laos. About 10% of the Lao population sought refugee status after 1975. Many have since been resettled in third countries, including more than 250,000 who have come to the United States.

The situation of Lao refugees is nearing its final chapter. Over time, the Lao Government closed the re-education camps and released most political prisoners. From 1975 to 1996, the U.S. resettled some 250,000 Lao refugees from Thailand, including 130,000 Hmong. By the end of 1999, more than 28,900 Hmong and lowland Lao had repatriated to Laos--3,500 from China, the rest from Thailand. Through the Office of the United Nations High Commissioner for Refugees (UNHCR), the International Organization for Migration (IOM), and non-governmental organizations, the U.S. has supported a variety of reintegration assistance programs throughout Laos. UNHCR monitors returnees and reports no evidence of systemic persecution or discrimination to date. As of December 1999, about 115 Hmong and lowland Lao remained in Ban Napho camp in Thailand awaiting third-country resettlement by the UNHCR.

GOVERNMENT AND POLITICAL CONDITIONS

The only legal political party is the Lao People's Revolutionary Party (LPRP). The head of state is President Khamtay Siphandone. The head of government is Prime Minister Sisavath Keobounphanh, who also is Chairman of the LPRP. Government policies are determined by the party through the all-powerful nine-member Politburo and the 49-member Central Committee. Important government decisions are vetted by the Council of Ministers.

Laos adopted a constitution in 1991. The following year, elections were held for a new 85-seat National Assembly with members elected by secret ballot to 5-year terms. This National Assembly, expanded in 1997 elections to 99 members, approves all new laws, although the executive branch retains authority to issue binding decrees. The most recent elections took place in December 1997. The FY 2000 central government budget plan calls for revenue of $180 million and expenditures of $289 million, including capital expenditures of $202 million.

PRINCIPAL GOVERNMENT OFFICIALS NEW CABINET MEMBERS APPROVED

The National Assembly, the country's top legislature on 15 June approved the appointment of Mr. Thongsing Thammavong as Prime Minister and four deputy prime ministers and cabinet members.

The First Plenary Session of the 7 th NA approved the proposed list of four deputy prime ministers are Mr. Asang Laoly, Dr. Thongloun Sisoulith, Mr. Duangchay Phichit and Mr. Somsavat Lengsavad. Four of them are members of Politburo under the Lao People's Revolutionary Party Central Committee.

Under the approval, Dr. Thongloun Sisoulith is responsible for Ministry of Foreign Affairs and Mr. Duangchay Phitchit takes the post the Minister of National Defence.

The NA also approved the appointment of government members accordingly,

Mr. Bounthong Chitmany serves as President of State Inspection Committee and Head of Anti-Corruption Agency;

Mr. Phankham Viphavanh, Minister of Education and Sports;

Mr. Thongbanh Seng-aphone, Minister Public Security; Mrs Onchanh Thammavong, Minister of Labour and Social-Welfare;

Mr. Chaleune Yiabaoher, Minister of Justice;

Mr. Soulivong Daravong, Minister of Energy and Mining;

Mrs Bounpheng Mouphosay, Minister for Government's Office;

Mr. Vilayvanh Phomkhe, Minister of Agriculture and Forestry;

Mr. Sinlavong Khouphaythoune, Minister and Head of Government's Office;

Mr. Nam Viyaket, Minister of Industry and Commerce;

Mr. Sommad Pholsena, Minister of Public Works and Transport;

Mr. Somdy Duangdy, Minister of Planning and Investment;

Mr. Phouphet Khamphounvong, Minister of Finance;

Prof Dr. Bosengkham Vongdara, Minister of Information, Culture and Tourism;

Prof Dr. Eksavang Vongvichit, Minister of Public Health;

Mr. Bounheuang Duangphachanh, Minister for Government's Office;

Mr. Khampane Philavong, Minister of Interior;

Prof Dr. Bountiem Phitsamay, Minister for Government's Office;

Dr. Douangsavad Souphanouvong, Minister for Government's Office;

Mrs Khempheng Pholsena, Minister for Government's Office;

Prof Dr. Boviengkham Vongdara, Minister of Science and Technology;

Mr. Noulin Sinbandith, Minister of Natural Resources and Environment;

Mr. Hiem Phommachanh, Minister of Post, Telecommunication and Communication;

Mr. Sompao Phaysith, Governor of the State Bank of Laos;

Mr. Khamphanh Sitthidampha, President of People's Supreme Court and

Mr. Khamsan Souvong, Head of General Prosecutor's Office.

Laos maintains an embassy in the United States at 2222 S Street NW, Washington, D.C. 20009 (tel: 202-332-6416).

ECONOMY

Currency	Lao Kip
Fiscal year	1 October - 30 September
Trade organisations	ASEAN, WTO
	Statistics
GDP	$17.66 billion (PPP; est.)
GDP growth	8.3% (2014 est.)
GDP per capita	$2,700 (PPP; est.)
GDP by sector	services (42.6%), industry (20.2%), agriculture (37.4%) (est.)
Inflation (CPI)	7.6% (est.)
Population below poverty line	26% (est.)
Labour force	3.69 million (est.)
Labour force by occupation	agriculture (75.1%), industry (n/a), services (n/a) (est.)
Unemployment	2.5% (est.)
Main industries	copper, tin, gold, and gypsum mining; timber, electric power, agricultural processing, construction, garments, cement, tourism

Ease of doing business rank	165th
External	
Exports	$2.131 billion (est.)
Export goods	wood products, garments, electricity, coffee, tin, copper, gold
Main export partners	Thailand 32.8% China 20.7% Vietnam 14.0% (est.)
Imports	2.336 billion (est.)
Import goods	machinery and equipment, vehicles, fuel, consumer goods
Main import partners	Thailand 63.2% China 16.5% Vietnam 5.6% (est.)
Gross external debt	$5.953 billion (31 December 2011 est)
Public finances	
Public debt	$3.179 billion
Revenues	$1.76 billion
Expenses	$1.957 billion (est.)
Economic aid	$345 million (est.)
Foreign reserves	$773.5 (31 December est.)

The **economy of the Lao Peoples' Democratic Republic** is rapidly growing, as the government began to decentralise control and encourage private enterprise in 1986. Currently, the economy grows at 8% a year, and the government is pursuing poverty reduction and education for all children as key goals. The country opened a stock exchange, the Lao Securities Exchange in 2011, and has become a rising regional player in its role as a hydroelectric power supplier to neighbors such as China, Vietnam and Thailand. Laos remains one of the poorest countries in Southeast Asia, but may transition from being a low middle-income country to an upper-middle income one by 2020. A landlocked country, it has inadequate infrastructure and a largely unskilled work force. The country's per capita income in 2009 was estimated to be $2,700 on a purchasing power parity-basis.

The Lao economy depends heavily on investment and trade with its neighbours, Thailand, Vietnam, and, especially in the north, China. Pakxe has also experienced growth based on cross-border trade with Thailand and Vietnam. In 2009, despite the fact that the government is still officially communist, the Obama administration in the US declared Laos was no longer a marxist-lenninist state and lifted bans on Laotian companies receiving financing from the U.S. Export Import Bank. In 2011, the Lao Securities Exchange began trading. In 2014, the government initiated the creation of the Laos Trade Portal, a website incorporating all information traders need to import and export goods into the country.

Subsistence agriculture still accounts for half of the GDP and provides 80% of employment. Only 4.01% of the country is arable land, and a mere 0.34% used as permanent crop land, the lowest percentage in the Greater Mekong Subregion. Rice dominates agriculture, with about 80% of the arable land area used for growing rice. Approximately 77% of Lao farm households are self-sufficient in rice.

Through the development, release and widespread adoption of improved rice varieties, and through economic reforms, production has increased by an annual rate of 5% between 1990 and 2005, and Lao PDR achieved a net balance of rice imports and exports for the first time in 1999. Lao PDR may have the greatest number of rice varieties in the Greater Mekong Subregion. Since 1995 the Lao government has been working with the International Rice Research Institute of the Philippines to collect seed samples of each of the thousands of rice varieties found in Laos.

The economy receives development aid from the IMF, ADB, and other international sources; and also foreign direct investment for development of the society, industry, hydropower and mining (most notably of copper and gold). Tourism is the fastest-growing industry in the country. Economic development in Laos has been hampered by brain drain, with a skilled emigration rate of 37.4% in 2000.

Laos is rich in mineral resources and imports petroleum and gas. Metallurgy is an important industry, and the government hopes to attract foreign investment to develop the substantial deposits of coal, gold, bauxite, tin, copper, and other valuable metals. In addition, the country's plentiful water resources and mountainous terrain enable it to produce and export large quantities of hydroelectric energy. Of the potential capacity of approximately 18,000 megawatts, around 8,000 megawatts have been committed for exporting to Thailand and Vietnam.

The country's most widely recognised product may well be Beerlao which is exported to a number of countries including neighbours Cambodia and Vietnam. It is produced by the Lao Brewery Company.

FOREIGN RELATIONS

The new government that assumed power in December 1975 aligned itself with the Soviet bloc and adopted a hostile posture toward the West. In ensuing decades, Laos maintained close ties with the former Soviet Union and its eastern bloc allies and depended heavily on the Soviets for most of its foreign assistance. Laos also maintained a "special relationship" with Vietnam and formalized a 1977 treaty of friendship and cooperation that created tensions with China.

With the collapse of the Soviet Union and with Vietnam's decreased ability to provide assistance, Laos has sought to improve relations with its regional neighbors. The Lao Government has focused its efforts on Thailand, Laos' principal means of access to the sea and its primary trading partner. Within a year of serious border clashes in 1987, Lao and Thai leaders signed a communiquŽ, signaling their intention to improve relations. Since then, they have made slow but steady progress, notably the construction and opening of the Friendship Bridge between the two countries.

Relations with China have improved over the years. Although the two were allies during the Vietnam War, the China-Vietnam conflict in 1979 led to a sharp deterioration in Sino-Lao relations. These relations began to improve in the late 1980s. In 1989 Sino-Lao relations were normalized.

Laos' emergence from international isolation has been marked through improved and expanded relations with other nations such as Australia, France, Japan, Sweden, and India. Laos was admitted into the Association of Southeast Asian Nations (ASEAN) in July 1997 and applied to join WTO in 1998.

Laos is a member of the following international organizations: Agency for Cultural and Technical Cooperation (ACCT), Association of Southeast Asian Nations (ASEAN), ASEAN Free Trade Area (AFTA), ASEAN Regional Forum, Asian Development Bank, Colombo Plan, Economic and Social Commission for Asia and Pacific (ESCAP), Food and Agriculture Organization (FAO), G-77, International Bank for Reconstruction and Development (World Bank), International Civil Aviation Organization (ICAO), International Development Association (IDA), International Fund for Agricultural Development (IFAD), International Finance Corporation (IFC), International Federation of Red Cross and Red Crescent Societies, International Labor Organization (ILO), International Monetary Fund (IMF), Intelsat (nonsignatory user), Interpol, International Olympic Commission (IOC), International Telecommunications Union (ITU), Mekong Group, Non-Aligned Movement (NAM), Permanent Court of Arbitration (PCA), UN, United Nations Convention on Trade and Development (UNCTAD), United Nations Educational, Social and Cultural Organization (UNESCO), United Nations Industrial Development Organization (UNIDO), Universal Postal Union (UPU), World Federation of Trade Unions, World Health Organization (WHO), World Intellectual Property Organization (WIPO), World Meteorological Organization (WMO), World Tourism Organization, World Trade Organization (observer).

U.S.-LAO RELATIONS

The United States opened a legation in Laos in 1950. Although diplomatic relations were never severed, U.S.-Lao relations deteriorated badly in the post-Indochina War period. The relationship remained cool until 1982 when efforts at improvement began. For the United States, progress in accounting for Americans missing in Laos from the Vietnam War is a principal measure of improving relations. Counternarcotics activities also have become an important part of the bilateral relationship as the Lao Government has stepped up its efforts to combat cultivation; production; and transshipment of opium, heroin, and marijuana.

Since the late 1980s, progress in these areas has steadily increased. Joint U.S. and Lao teams have conducted a series of joint excavations and investigations of sites related to cases of Americans missing in Laos. In counternarcotics activities, the U.S. and Laos are involved in a multimillion-dollar crop substitution/integrated rural development program. Laos also has formed its own national committee on narcotics, developed a long-range strategy for counternarcotics activities, participated in U.S.-sponsored narcotics training programs, and strengthened law enforcement measures to combat the narcotics problem.

U.S. Government foreign assistance to Laos covers a broad range of efforts. Such aid includes support for Laos' efforts to suppress opium production; training and equipment for a program to clear and dispose of unexploded ordnance; school and hospital construction; public education about the dangers of unexploded ordnance and about HIV/AIDS; support for medical research on hepatitis. Economic relations also are expanding. In August 1997, Laos and the United States initialed a Bilateral Trade Agreement and a Bilateral Investment Treaty.

Principal U.S. Embassy Officials

Ambassador-- Rena Bitter

Ambassador Rena Bitter is a career Senior Foreign Service Officer with more than 20 years of experience in Washington and overseas. Most recently, Ambassador Bitter served as Consul General at the U.S. Consulate General in Ho Chi Minh City, Vietnam. Prior to that, she served as the Director of the State Department Operations Center, the Department's 24/7 Briefing and Crisis Management Center. In Washington, she served on the Secretary of State's Executive Staff and as a Special Assistant to Secretary Colin Powell. Her overseas tours include Amman, London, Mexico City and Bogota. Ambassador Bitter grew up in Dallas.

Deputy Chief of Mission--Susan M. Sutton

The American Embassy in Laos is on Rue Bartholonie, B.P. 114, Vientiane, tel: 212-581/582/585; fax: 212-584: country code: (856): city code (21).

Information on the embassy, its work in Laos, and U.S.-Lao relations is available on the Internet at http://www.usembassy.state.gov/laos.

TRAVEL AND BUSINESS INFORMATION

The U.S. Department of State's Consular Information Program provides Consular Information Sheets, Travel Warnings, and Public Announcements. **Consular Information Sheets** exist for all countries and include information on entry requirements, currency regulations, health conditions, areas of instability, crime and security, political disturbances, and the addresses of the U.S. posts in the country. **Travel Warnings** are issued when the State Department recommends that Americans avoid travel to a certain country. **Public Announcements** are issued as a means to disseminate information quickly about terrorist threats and other relatively short-term conditions overseas which pose significant risks to the security of American travelers. Free copies of this information are available by calling the Bureau of Consular Affairs at 202-647-5225 or via the fax-on-demand system: 202-647-3000.

Consular Information Sheets and Travel Warnings also are available on the Consular Affairs Internet home page: http://travel.state.gov. Consular Affairs Tips for Travelers publication series, which contain information on obtaining passports and planning a safe trip abroad are on the internet and hard copies can be purchased from the Superintendent of Documents, U.S. Government Printing Office, telephone: 202-512-1800; fax 202-512-2250.

Emergency information concerning Americans traveling abroad may be obtained from the Office of Overseas Citizens Services at (202) 647-5225. For after-hours emergencies, Sundays and holidays, call 202-647-4000.

Passport information can be obtained by calling the National Passport Information Center's automated system ($.35 per minute) or live operators 8 a.m. to 8 p.m. (EST) Monday-Friday ($1.05 per minute). The number is 1-900-225-5674 (TDD: 1-900-225-7778). Major credit card users (for a flat rate of $4.95) may call 1-888-362-8668 (TDD: 1-888-498-3648). It also is available on the internet.

Travelers can check the latest health information with the U.S. Centers for Disease Control and Prevention in Atlanta, Georgia. A hotline at 877-FYI-TRIP (877-394-8747) and a web site at http://www.cdc.gov/travel/index.htm give the most recent health advisories, immunization recommendations or requirements, and advice on food and drinking water safety for regions and countries. A booklet entitled Health Information for International Travel (HHS publication number CDC-95-8280) is available from the U.S. Government Printing Office, Washington, DC 20402, tel. (202) 512-1800.

Information on travel conditions, visa requirements, currency and customs regulations, legal holidays, and other items of interest to travelers also may be obtained before your departure from a country's embassy and/or consulates in the U.S. (for this country, see "Principal Government Officials" listing in this publication).

U.S. citizens who are long-term visitors or traveling in dangerous areas are encouraged to register at the U.S. embassy upon arrival in a country (see "Principal U.S. Embassy Officials" listing in this publication). This may help family members contact you in case of an emergency.

For additional analytical, business and investment opportunities information, please contact Global Investment & Business Center, USA at (703) 370-8082. Fax: (703) 370-8083. E-mail: ibpusa3@gmail.com
Global Business and Investment Info Databank - www.ibpus.com

LAOS JUDICIAL AND LEGAL SYSTEM

LEGAL AND JUDICIAL SYSTEM

The development of the legal and judicial system did not begin until almost fifteen years after the state was proclaimed. In November 1989, a criminal code and laws establishing a judicial system were adopted. In 1993 the government began publishing an official gazette to disseminate laws, decrees, and regulations.

In 1990 the judicial branch was upgraded. New legislation provided a draft of a criminal code, established procedures for criminal cases, set up a court system, and established a law school. Moreover, the Ministry of Justice added a fourth year of studies to a law program for training magistrates and judges.

Also in 1990, the functions of the Supreme People's Court were separated from those of the office of the public prosecutor general. Until then, the minister of justice served as both president of the court and director of public prosecutions.

Although the implementation of judicial reforms proceeded slowly and had not significantly improved the administration of justice by mid-1994, the new legal framework offers the possibility of moving away from the arbitrary use of power toward the rule of law. In late 1992, however, the government suspended the bar until it formulates regulations for fees and activities of (the few) private lawyers who are able to advise in civil cases. Lawyers are not allowed to promote themselves as attorneys-at-law. Theoretically, the government provides legal counsel to the accused, although in practice persons accused of crimes must defend themselves, without outside legal counsel. However, the assessors (legal advisers)--who are often untrained--and the party functionaries are being increasingly replaced by professional personnel trained at the Institute of Law and Administration.

The constitution empowers the National Assembly to elect or remove the president of the Supreme People's Court and the public prosecutor general on the recommendation of its Standing Committee. The Standing Committee of the National Assembly appoints or removes judges (previously elected) of the provincial, municipal, and district levels.

Further evidence of an attempt to shift toward a professional judicial system is found in the public prosecution institutes provided for at each level of administration. The task of these institutes is to control the uniform observance of laws by all ministries, organizations, state employees, and citizens. They prosecute under the guidance of the public prosecutor general, who appoints and removes deputy public prosecutors at all levels.

LEGAL SYSTEM DEVELOPMENTS

LEGAL SYSTEM IN TRANSITION

The legal system of the Lao PDR has been shaped by Lao tradition and custom, by the establishment of the French colonial administration, and after 1975, by the adoption of a Soviet-styled socialist ideology. Since the mid-1980's, however, the legal system has also been influenced by the legal and economic transitions taking place in neighboring, Vietnam and China. The legal system of the Lao PDR still contains elements from all of these historical influences, but its current development is driven by the economic needs of the country, by the concurrent development of the Lao PDR's own market economy, and by the desire to strengthen cooperation with ASEAN neighbors.

To meet these needs, many new laws and decrees are being drafted, and for guidance, the Lao PDR is considering the laws of a variety of market-oriented countries around the world. At present, the Lao PDR has over forty laws and hundreds of decrees and regulations. All of the laws, and most of the decrees and regulations in current use, were drafted after 1989.

INVESTMENT PROCEDURES

The Law on the Promotion and Management of Foreign Investment ("Foreign Investment Law") is the basic law governing foreign investment in the Lao PDR.

The Foreign Investment Law classifies foreign investment companies in two categories: joint venture companies and wholly foreign-owned companies. A joint venture is a foreign investment company that is jointly owned and operated by foreign and domestic investors, with the general requirement that the foreign investors must contribute at least 30% of the total capital.

Following is a brief outline of the typical process for establishing a foreign investment company in the Lao PDR.

INVESTMENT LICENSE

Before commencing any activity in the Lao PDR, a foreign investment project must obtain a Foreign Investment License. To obtain a Foreign Investment License, the project submits a standard Foreign Investment License Application provided by Committee for Investment and Foreign Economic Cooperation ("CIFEC"), along with various supporting documents.

The Foreign Investment Law mandates that CIFEC review the application and either grant a Foreign Investment License or reject the application within 60 days. Once the application is approved, CIFEC issues the Foreign Investment License.

Company Registration

All companies in the Lao PDR must register with the Company Registry of the Ministry of Commerce ("MOC"). In order for a foreign investment company to register with the Company Registry, it must submit an application to the MOC along with various supporting documents.

Document Registration

The foreign investment company must also register its legal documents and pay document registration fees.

Tax Registration

All business enterprises in the Lao PDR must also register with the Tax Department of the Ministry of Finance. Foreign investment companies must obtain this registration within 90 days of receipt of the Foreign Investment License.

Other Licenses and Permits

Before the foreign investment company is fully authorized to carry on business in the Lao PDR, it will often need an array of additional licenses and permits depending on the type of business to be carried out.

INVESTMENT GUARANTEES

The Foreign Investment Law guarantees that foreign investment companies:

- are protected from governmental confiscation, seizure, or nationalization;
- can operate freely without interference from the government;
- can lease land, transfer leasehold interests, and make improvements on land and buildings; and
- can remit foreign currencies abroad.

INVESTMENT INCENTIVES

The Foreign Investment Law also provides the following incentives:

- Exemption from import duties on raw materials and equipment for export-oriented production;
- Import duties at a flat rate of 1% on equipment and other material used in the operation of foreign investment companies;
- No export duties on finished products;
- Freedom to employ necessary foreign expatriates;
- Freedom to repatriate profits and capital;
- Foreign personal income taxes at a flat rate of 10%; and
- Annual profit taxes at a flat rate of 20%.

Structure of the CIFEC

The current structure of CIFEC (relevant to foreign investment) is as follows:

- Office of the Prime Minister
    - CIFEC
        - Department of Foreign Investment

- Promotion Division
- Screening Division
- Legal Division
- Monitoring Division
- Strategy Division
- Administrative Division

INVESTMENT SECTORS

Promoted Sectors

Most sectors of the Lao economy are open to foreign investment, and the Lao Government is particularly promoting foreign investment in the following sectors:

- Energy
- Mining
- Agriculture
- Manufacturing

Activities Reserved for Lao Citizens

The Lao Government prohibits foreign investors and foreign personnel from undertaking certain commercial activities in the Lao PDR. Some of these reserved activities include:

- Forest and wood exploitation;
- Retail sales;
- Accounting services;
- Tour services;
- Vehicle and machinery operation; and
- Rice cultivation.

INVESTMENT STRUCTURES

The Business Law is essentially the "Companies Act" of the Lao PDR. This law applies equally to both foreign and Lao companies and provides legal protection for the capital, property, and rights of the companies.

Pursuant to the Business Law (and the Foreign Investment Law), the following corporate structures are available to foreign investors in the Lao PDR:

- Representative Office
- Branch Office
- Sole Proprietorship
- Partnership
- Limited Company
- Public Company
- Companies with State Ownership

TAXATION

Unless exemptions are granted by the Lao Government, a foreign investment company would be subject to the following taxes, among others:

- Profits tax (20% of net profits);
- Income taxes (at varying rates depending on type of income);
- Business turnover tax (3-15% of gross sales);
- Use tax (at variable rates); and
- Import duties (at variable rates)

For additional information, please contact:
Dirksen Flipse Doran & Lê
Lawyers & Counselors

Dirksen Flipse Doran & Lê ("DFDL") is an international law firm focusing on the legal markets of Laos, Cambodia, Vietnam, Myanmar, and the Yunnan Province of China. In 1993, DFDL opened its office in Vientiane, and became the first officially authorized law firm in Laos. In 1994, DFDL opened its office in Phnom Penh, also becoming the first officially authorized law firm in Cambodia, and established an office in Ho Chi Minh City, Vietnam.

Following is a brief profile of the lawyers in our Vientiane office:

Todd E. Dirksen is a member of the New York Bar and the US Supreme Court Bar, and a graduate of Georgetown University Law Center. He has published articles entitled "Doing Business in Vietnam: The Legal Aspects," in Asia Business Law Review, Vol. 2, and "Security Arrangements in Laos," in Creating and Enforcing Security in Asian Emerging Markets, Vol. 1. He is currently working on several hydropower projects, an ICC arbitration, and general investment, commercial and banking matters in Laos. Languages: English, French and Spanish.

Mary S. Flipse is a member of the New York Bar and the US Supreme Court Bar, and a graduate of Georgetown University Law Center. She has published the following articles: "Asia's Littlest Dragon: An Analysis of the Lao Foreign Investment Code and Decree," Georgetown University Law Center journal of Law & Policy in International Business, Vol. 23, No. 1; "Laos: Banking, Finance and Taxation," in Capital Flows Along the Mekong, Vol. 1. Ms. Flipse is now advising international clients on foreign investment in Laos, particularly in the hydropower, construction and aviation sectors, and is litigating several corporate and commercial cases in the Lao courts. Languages: English, Lao and Thai.

Robert R. Allen Jr. is a member of the Maryland Bar, and holds a Juris Doctor degree from Columbus School of Law, Catholic University of America in Washington, D.C. Mr. Allen also holds a Mechanical Engineering degree from the University of Maryland, and a diploma from the Nuclear Power Engineering School of the General Electric Corporation. Prior to joining DFDL, Mr. Allen worked for more than four years as an engineer in the United States power industry, followed by several years as a business and legal consultant on corporate, energy, and environmental issues in the United States.

Desarack Teso holds a Juris Doctor from the University of Hawaii, and is a candidate for admission to the Bar of the State of Hawaii. He has published a series of articles on Lao law in the Vientiane Times. He is fluent in English, Lao and Thai.

Phasith Phommarak is a member and a section leader of the Lao Bar Association, and one of the few lawyers to be appointed as an authorized private attorney by the Lao Ministry of Justice. He is a graduate of L'Institut Royal de Droit et Administration, in Vientiane, Laos, and Georgetown University's American Language Institute. Specializing in commercial contracts and dispute resolution, he assists in many of the firm's litigation matters before Lao courts of law. Languages: Lao, Thai, English, French.

Contact Information
Attn: Todd E. Dirksen
Dirksen Flipse Doran & Lê
Mekong Commerce Bldg #1, POB 2920
Luang Prabang Road, Vientiane, Lao PDR
Tel: (856) 21 216-927-9
Fax: (856) 21 216-919

DISPUTE RESOLUTION

Basically there are four ways to resolve a commercial dispute in China: negotiation, mediation, arbitration and litigation. Negotiation is normally the first choice of parties concerned because it is the least expensive and most friendly approach to resolve a dispute. Mediation is also welcomed and encouraged especially during the judicial procedure, and it can effectively preserve the cooperation relationship of the parties involved. Compared with litigation, arbitration is a preference for most parties mainly because it is not that time consuming and the procedure is relatively simple. Litigation is regarded as a final way to resolve a dispute. In China, foreign parties have equal rights to bring action in courts as Chinese parties.

The PRC law contains no political method of dispute resolution. However, the government may exert its influence on certain disputes involving SOEs or government invested projects.

(i) Litigation

Litigation is considered as the final way to resolve a commercial dispute in China due to the following reasons:

(A) The litigation procedure is time consuming. For example, in a civil case, the first instance procedure will at most last six (6) months from the initiation date and the duration can be extended for another six months or even longer. If any party concerned was dissatisfied with the ruling of the first instance and filed an appeal, the appealing case will take another three (3) months to close, and similar to the duration of the first instance, the duration of appeal can also be extended.

(B) A lack of qualified judges and other professional personnel.

(C) The courts' independence cannot be ensured because most of them rely on the financial support from local governments.

The dispute can also be resolved in a foreign court or arbitration commission.

In principle, for any dispute arising from a contract or property rights and interests involving foreign elements, the parties concerned may choose a court in the place out of China having an actual connection with the dispute to have jurisdiction. However, disputes arising from the performance of Sino-foreign equity joint venture contracts, Sino-foreign cooperative joint venture contracts or contracts for Sino-foreign cooperative exploration and development of natural resources should be under the jurisdiction of courts of China.

A foreign judgment cannot be directly enforced in China. All of the following conditions shall be met to enforce a judgment made by a foreign court:

(A) The judgment is legally effective;

(B) The foreign country and China have concluded bilateral treaty, or China has acceded to international treaties, or based on the principle of reciprocity with respect to the enforcement of foreign judgment; and

(C) The judgment is not contrary to the basic principles of the laws of China or the State's sovereignty, security or social public interest.

Unfortunately, China has not acceded to Hague Jurisdiction Convention or any other international treaties with respect to enforcement of foreign judgment. In addition, Chinese courts rarely recognize the principle of reciprocity. Therefore, unless a bilateral treaty has been concluded, a foreign judgment can hardly be enforced in China. China has concluded bilateral treaty with only around 30 countries or regions, excluding most well-developed countries such as the US and Canada.

(ii) Arbitration

Aside from judicial procedure, arbitration is also available under PRC law as an alternative mechanism for resolving commercial disputes. Currently there are a number of arbitration commissions in the main cities throughout China. If parties choose to settle a dispute through arbitration, they should enter an arbitration agreement (including arbitration clauses in a contract and written agreements on arbitration) which indicates clear intention for arbitration. The conclusion of arbitration agreement will preclude the jurisdiction of courts, unless the arbitration agreement is invalid. It's noted that where the parties simply agree with the Arbitration Locality, rather than the specific institution, and there is only one arbitration institution in this locality, the arbitration institution shall be deemed as the stipulated arbitration institution. If there are two or more arbitration institutions, the parties concerned may choose one arbitration institution for arbitration upon agreement; if the parties concerned fail to agree upon the choice of the arbitration institution, the agreement for arbitration shall be ineffective.

Foreign investors involved in Lao investment disputes must seek arbitration before taking legal action. If arbitration does not result in an amicable settlement, litigants may submit their claims to the economic arbitration authority of Laos, or that of the investor's country, or an international organization agreed on by both parties.

Foreign arbitration awards are enforceable in China, same as in Laos, in accordance with the New York Convention on the Recognition and Enforcement of Foreign Arbitral Awards 1958 to which China is a party and the Civil Procedure Law of the PRC, as amended in 2007.

CIVIL LIBERTIES AND HUMAN RIGHTS

The Laos criminal justice system is controlled by the party and the government. There are few legal restraints on government actions, including arrests, which are often arbitrary in nature. Dissent is frequently handled by suppressing basic civil rights. Although the constitution provisions of the mid-1990s cover freedom of worship, expression and press, citizens by December 2010 were not free to exercise these rights fully. There were no legal safeguards and arrests were commonly made on vague charges. A penal code and a constitution which guarantee civil liberties have been proposed. Implementation is another matter, particularly in the area of freedom of political expression. The media is state-controlled.

Nonetheless, there is a system for prosecuting criminal behavior. Common crimes are evaluated at the local village level. More serious cases, especially politically sensitive ones, are referred to higher authorities. Tribunals operate at district and provincial levels with judges appointed by the government.

Both Laotian journalists and Western officials are critical of the limitations on personal freedoms. In 1987, a Laotian journalist living in Thailand noted that there was little popular support for the government, but that most Laotians accepted its authority because they had little choice. In 1988, a Laotian journalist protested that open criticism of the government was forbidden and one of his friends was imprisoned after he complained about the continuing lack of a constitution. The same year, Western diplomats reported that hundreds or thousands of individuals were being held in detention centers in Laos and that citizens were being arrested and held for months without being charged.

In the late 1980s and early 1990s, the government instituted the New Economic Mechanism, a series of sweeping economic reforms geared toward establishing a market-oriented economy. Along with these economic reforms came a slight opening to the West, which provided some opportunity for scrutiny of human rights violations. However, few foreign journalists are allowed to visit Laos, and travel by diplomats and foreign aid workers is restricted. Both domestic and foreign travel by Laotians also is subject to scrutiny and restriction.

The Ministry of Interior is the main instrument of state control and guardianship over the criminal justice system. Ministry of Interior police monitor both Laotians and foreign nationals who live in Laos; there is a system of informants in workplace committees and in residential areas. According to the United States Department of State's Country Reports on Human Rights Practices for 1993, both the party and state monitor various aspects of family and social life through neighborhood and workplace committees. These committees are responsible for maintaining public order and reporting "bad elements" to the police, as well as carrying out political training and disciplining employees.

The criminal justice system is deficient in the area of legal precedent and representation. Trials are not held in public, although trial verdicts are publicly announced. Although there is some provision for appeal, it does not apply to important political cases. Under the constitution, judges and prosecutors are supposed to be independent with their decisions free from outside scrutiny. In practice, however, the courts appear to accept recommendations of other government agencies, especially the Ministry of Interior, in making their decisions. Theoretically, the government provides legal counsel to the accused. In practice, however, defendants represent themselves without outside counsel.

The National Assembly enacted a criminal code and laws establishing a judiciary in November 1989 and a new constitution was adopted by the National Assembly in 1991.

In 1992 the government launched a campaign to publicize the latter. The leadership claims efforts at developing a legal system with a codified body of laws and a penal code. However, as of mid-1994, there had been little, if any, progress in implementing the freedoms provided for in the constitution and the legal codes still had not been implemented with individuals still being held without being informed of charges or their accusers' identities.

DETENTION CENTERS

In Laos, there are four categories of persons held in confinement by the State. Aside from common criminals, there are also political, social, and ideological dissidents. These are people who the government feels are a threat to their control, most commonly because of their public objection to governmental policies or actions. Commonly the specific crimes for which these dissidents are arrested and confined are vague at best. Their arrests are typically arbitrary and their length of confinement ambiguous and indefinite.

The LPDR established four different types of detention centers: prisons, reeducation centers or seminar camps, rehabilitation camps, and remolding centers. Social deviants or common criminals were considered less threatening to the regime than persons accused of political crimes, who were considered potential counterrevolutionaries; social deviants were confined in rehabilitation camps. According to MacAlister Brown and Joseph J. Zasloff, prisons were primarily reserved for common criminals, but political prisoners were also held there for usually six to twelve months. Ideologically suspect persons were sent to remolding centers. Reeducation centers were for those deemed politically risky usually former RLG officials. Political prisoners usually served three- to five-year terms or longer. At the prisons, inmates worked hard under rugged conditions and had limited supplies of food. Bribery in order to secure food and medicine was reported.

In 1986, Brown and Zasloff also reported that prisoners were not tried but were incarcerated by administrative fiat. Former inmates said that they were arrested, informed by the security officials that they had been charged with crimes, and then sent off to camps for indeterminate periods. Typically, prisoners were told one day prior to their release to prepare for departure.

The status of the detention centers is also vague. In 1984, Vientiane declared that all reeducation centers had been closed. At that time, Amnesty International estimated that 6,000 to 7,000 political prisoners were held in these centers. The government acknowledged that there were some former inmates in remote areas but claimed that their confinement was voluntary. In the late 1980s, the government closed some of the reeducation centers and released most of the detainees.

In 1989, Laos took steps to reduce the number of political prisoners, many of whom had been held since 1975. Several hundred detainees, including many high-ranking officials and officers from the former United States-backed RLG and Royal Lao Army, were released from reeducation centers in the northeastern province of Houaphan. Released prisoners reported that hundreds of individuals remained in custody in as many as eight camps, including at least six generals and former high-ranking members of the RLG. These individuals reportedly performed manual labor such as log cutting, repairing roads, and building irrigation systems. In 1993, Amnesty International reported human rights violations in the continued detention of three "prisoners of conscience" detained since 1975 but not sentenced until 1992, as well as those held under restrictions or, according to international standards, the subjects of unfair trials.

As of 1993, reports indicated that some high-ranking officials of the RLG and military remained in state custody Those accused of hostility toward the government were subject to arrest and confinement for long periods of time. Prison conditions were harsh, and prisoners were routinely denied family visitation and proper medical care

DEMOCRACY AND HUIMAN RIGHTS

The Lao People's Democratic Republic is an authoritarian, Communist, one-party state ruled by the Lao People's Revolutionary Party (LPRP). Although the 1991 Constitution outlines a system composed of executive, legislative, and judicial branches, in practice the LPRP continued to influence governance and the choice of leaders through its constitutional "leading role" at all levels. The 99-member National Assembly, elected in 1997 under a system of universal suffrage, selected the President and Prime Minister in 1998. The judiciary is subject to executive influence.

The Ministry of Interior (MOI) maintains internal security but shares the function of state control with party and mass front (People Network) organizations. The Ministry of Foreign Affairs is responsible for the monitoring and oversight of foreigners working in the country; its activities are augmented by other security organizations and surveillance systems. The MOI includes local police, security police (including border police), communication police, and other armed police units. The armed forces are responsible for external security but also have some domestic security responsibilities that include counterterrorism and counterinsurgency activities. Civilian authorities generally maintain effective control over the security forces. There continue to be credible reports that some members of the security forces committed human rights abuses. Laos is an extremely poor country of 5.2 million persons.

After the LPRP came to power in 1975, 10 percent of the population (at least 360,000 persons) fled the country to escape the Government's harsh political and economic policies. The economy is principally agricultural; 85 percent of the population is engaged in subsistence agriculture. Per capita gross domestic product is estimated to be $300 per year. Since 1986 the Government largely has abandoned its Socialist economic policies, although in practice the operation of the state-owned banks and enterprises indicates a reluctance to discard old models. Most economic reforms have begun to move the country gradually from a moribund, centrally planned system to a market-oriented economy open to foreign investment with a growing legal framework, including laws to protect property rights.

The Government's human rights record remained poor throughout the year, and there were a number of serious problems. Citizens do not have the right to change their government. During clashes with insurgents in the north, there were unconfirmed accusations that government troops deliberately killed noncombatant civilians. At times members of the security forces abused detainees and brutally beat suspected insurgents. Government troops razed one village in the north. Prison conditions are extremely harsh. Police used arbitrary arrest, detention, and intrusive surveillance. Lengthy pretrial detention is a problem. The judiciary is subject to executive influence, suffers from corruption, and does not ensure citizens' due process. The Government infringed on citizens' privacy rights. The Government restricts freedom of speech and imposes some restrictions on press freedom, assembly, and association. However, it permitted some access to the foreign press and the Internet. The Government restricts freedom of religion and arrested and detained approximately 95 Christians, and more than 25 members of religious communities remained in custody at the end of the year.

Forced renunciation campaigns and church closings continued in some areas. The Government imposes some restrictions on freedom of movement. Some societal discrimination against women and minorities persists. The Government actively supported a policy of encouraging greater rights for women, children, disabled persons, and minorities. The Government restricts some worker rights. The Government continued to focus on the problem of trafficking in women and children.

Several small-scale explosive devices were detonated in urban areas during the year, causing one death and dozens of injuries. No group claimed responsibility for these acts. Official statements initially downplayed the incidents, attributing them to personal quarrels and vendettas; some government officials later blamed "foreign terrorists."

Organized Hmong insurgent groups were responsible for occasional clashes with government troops. These exchanges reportedly were brutal on both sides. The organized Hmong insurgent group, the Chao Fa, was responsible for the killing of more than 15 civilians in 4 incidents in Vientiane and Xieng Khouang provinces and in Saysomboune Special Zone. These incidents appeared to be acts of deliberate terror against citizens who do not support resistance to the Government.

SECTION 1 RESPECT FOR THE INTEGRITY OF THE PERSON, INCLUDING FREEDOM FROM:

a. Political and Other Extrajudicial Killing

There were no confirmed reports of politically motivated killings by government officials during the year. There continued to be isolated, unconfirmed reports of deaths at the hands of security forces in remote areas, usually in connection with personal disputes and the personal abuse of authority.

In armed actions against insurgents, government troops burned down one village in the north in the first part of the year; accusations that government troops deliberately killed civilian noncombatants could not be confirmed (see Section 1.c.).

In October security forces killed from three to five prisoners who had escaped from Phongsaly provincial jail; there was no evidence that the prisoners were armed or had threatened their pursuers. Some reports stated that the prisoners had already been recaptured.

According to unconfirmed reports, in early May police from Phonesavanh, Xieng Khouang province, shot and killed two Hmong civilians visiting from another province who were out walking after the nighttime curfew. There is no additional evidence available about the case, including whether the Government gave compensation to the victims' families, the usual practice with accidental shootings in security zones.

A series of bomb detonations in urban areas killed at least one bystander and injured dozens. No group claimed responsibility for these small-scale bombings. Official statements initially downplayed the incidents, attributing them to personal quarrels and vendettas; some government officials later blamed "foreign terrorists," failing to acknowledge that the incidents may have been acts of terror by internal rivals for power and influence. Authorities arrested two suspects whom they later released.

Attacks by armed groups on official and civilian travelers continued on a small scale in the central and north central regions. The attacks reportedly involved various factors including insurgency, clan rivalry, robbery, and reaction to encroaching development. The Government remained concerned about the safety of foreign tourists and aid workers in remote areas, although there were no confirmed attacks on foreigners during the year.

In January Hmong insurgents attacked Xieng Khouang province's district capital town of Muang Khoune, killing 7 persons and burning down 17 structures. Credible reports indicated that Hmong insurgents attacked a village in Kasi district in July and killed five civilians. Other reports indicated that the Hmong insurgents shot and killed persons gathering food during February to April in the forest areas of Saysomboune Special Zone. There was no evidence that the deaths were intentional.

In December Hmong insurgents attacked a village in Xieng Khouang province. They killed three civilians and destroyed houses.

b. Disappearance

There were no reports of politically motivated disappearances of Lao citizens; however, reports indicated that two U.S. citizens disappeared in April 1999 near the northwest border with Thailand. The two men, Michael Vang and Houa Ly, disappeared soon after reportedly entering the country. The matter remained under review by authorities at year's end, but there was no evidence that the Government either provided the promised investigative cooperation or conducted a serious unilateral investigation during the year.

c. Torture and Other Cruel, Inhuman, or Degrading Treatment or Punishment

The Constitution and the Penal Code prohibit torture, and the Government generally respected these provisions in practice; however, on occasion, members of the security forces subjected detainees to abusive treatment. For example, early in the year, a few local police and prison officials in one southern province beat a number of religious detainees. In March 1998, Lao authorities, some wearing police uniforms, detained a foreign citizen and three family members in an unofficial detention center for 4 days. The Government did not file charges against the four persons. The officials reportedly kept the four persons in locked, windowless rooms and subjected them to long and arduous interrogation before releasing them. The Government offered no explanation for this treatment. There is no evidence that the Government has investigated the incident seriously, and no prosecution or punishment of the perpetrators is expected.

The Government chose not to address numerous reports of massive human rights violations by government authorities that were made by groups outside the country. Most of these reports could not be confirmed through independent sources. However, there continue to be credible reports that some members of the security forces committed human rights abuses, including arbitrary detention and intimidation. There were credible reports that some members of the security forces burned down a Hmong village in the northern insurgency area and were responsible for nearly beating some villagers to death, and that other members abused citizens in the first half of the year during clashes with insurgents or armed individuals suspected to be insurgents. Some members of the security forces in Xieng Khouang and Saysomboune Special Zone threatened families and villages.

A series of eight bombs exploded in Vientiane during the year, killing at least one and injuring dozens of persons. Authorities found as many as four other unexploded bombs in Vientiane and two others in southern provinces. Another bomb exploded in the south, with no injuries. The Vientiane Times reported official claims that the bombs were the result of business disputes and personal vendettas.

Prison conditions generally are extremely harsh. Food rations are minimal, and most prisoners rely on their families for their subsistence. The Government discriminates in its treatment of prisoners, restricting the family visits of some and prohibiting visits to a few. Prison authorities use degrading treatment, solitary confinement, and incommunicado detention against perceived problem prisoners, especially suspected insurgents. On occasion authorities used incommunicado detention as an interrogation method; in isolated cases, this was life threatening. There are confirmed reports that a few jails place prisoners in leg chains, wooden stocks, or fixed hand manacles for extended periods. Medical facilities range from poor to nonexistent. Prison conditions for women are similar to those for men.

Several international human rights groups continued their longstanding requests to the Government to move two political prisoners to a prison with better conditions, including more modern medical facilities (see Section 1.e.). At year's end, the Government continued to ignore these humanitarian pleas. The Government does not permit independent monitoring of prison conditions.

   d. Arbitrary Arrest, Detention, or Exile

The law provides for arrest warrants issued by the prosecutor, and the Constitution provides for procedural safeguards; however, in practice the Government does not respect these provisions, and arbitrary arrest and detention remain problems. Police sometimes use temporary arrest as a means of intimidation. Police exercise wide latitude in making arrests, relying on exceptions to the requirement for arrest warrants for those in the act of committing a crime or for "urgent" cases. The length of detention without a pretrial hearing or formal charges is unpredictable, and access to family or a lawyer is not assured. There is a functioning bail system, but its implementation is arbitrary. A statute of limitations applies to most crimes. Alleged violations of security laws have led to lengthy pretrial detentions without charge and minimal due process protection of those detained. Reports indicated that some students, teachers, and their associates who had staged protests in 1999 remained in detention without trial at year's end. These persons had peacefully advocated multiparty democracy and increased political freedom and had expressed hostility to the regime. Their detention without trial violates the 1-year statutory limit.

During the year, government authorities arrested and detained more than 95 Christians and their spiritual leaders, at times holding them in custody for months (see Section 2.c.) Those detained without trial at year's end for their religious activities include: One person in Phongsaly; two persons in Luang Namtha; two persons in Vientiane Municipality; and four persons in Savannakhet (see Section 2.c.). Eight lowland Lao men who returned from China have been detained without trial since 1997 (see Section 2.c.).

Police sometimes administratively overrule court decisions, at times detaining a defendant exonerated by the court, in violation of the law (see Section 1.e.).

Three former government officials detained in 1990 for advocating a multiparty system and criticizing restrictions on political liberties were not tried until 1992. One died in prison since that time. That same year, the court finally tried and handed down life sentences to three men detained since 1975 for crimes allegedly committed during their tenure as officials of the previous regime. One of these persons reportedly has died in prison.

An estimated 100 to 200 persons, based on known cases, are in detention for suspicion of violations of national security. Most of these detainees are held without trial; one person has been detained since 1992. The Government does not use forced exile.

e. Denial of Fair Public Trial

The Constitution provides for the independence of the judiciary and the prosecutor's office; however, senior government and party officials wield influence over the courts, although likely to a lesser degree than in the past. Some corrupt members of the judiciary appear to act with impunity, leading many observers to conclude that persons can bribe judges with money. The National Assembly Standing Committee appoints judges; the executive appoints the Standing Committee.

The People's Courts have three levels: District; municipal and provincial; and a Supreme Court. Decisions of both the lower courts and separate military courts are subject to review by the Supreme Court.

The Constitution provides for open trials in which defendants have the right to defend themselves with the assistance of a lawyer or other person. The Constitution requires authorities to inform persons of their rights. The law states that defendants may have anyone represent them in preparing a written case and accompanying them at their trial, however, only the defendant may present oral arguments at a criminal trial. Due to lack of funds, most defendants do not have attorneys or trained representatives. Defendants enjoy a presumption of innocence; however, in practice lawyers face severe restrictions in criminal cases. Most trials are little more than direct examinations of the accused, although judges appear not to hold preconceived views of a trial's outcome. Defendants sometimes are not permitted to testify on their own behalf. Trials for alleged violations of some security laws and trials that involve state secrets, children under the age of 16, or certain types of family law are closed.

Police sometimes administratively overrule court decisions, at times detaining a defendant exonerated by the court, in violation of the law.

There are four known political prisoners. Two prisoners from the pre-1975 regime, Colonel Sing Chanthakoumane and Major Pang Thong Chokbengvoun, are serving life sentences after trials that did not appear to be conducted according to international standards. Two former government officials, Latsami Khamphoui and Feng Sakchittaphong, were detained in 1990 for advocating a multiparty system and criticizing restrictions on political liberties, and were not tried until 1992. They are serving 14-year sentences based on their 1992 convictions.

Because some political prisoners may have been arrested, tried, and convicted under security laws that prevent public court trials, there is no reliable method to ascertain accurately their total number. There have been no verifiable reports of other political prisoners in the last few years. International humanitarian organizations are not permitted to visit political prisoners.

f. Arbitrary Interference With Privacy, Family, Home, or Correspondence

The Government limits citizens' privacy rights, and the Government's surveillance network is vast. Security laws allow the Government to monitor individuals' private communications (including e-mail) and movements. The Government increased these elements of state control again during the year, especially in areas involving safety and security problems. However, some personal freedoms accorded to citizens expanded along with the liberalization of the economy.

The Constitution prohibits unlawful searches and seizures; however, police at times disregarded constitutional requirements to safeguard citizens' privacy, especially in rural areas. By law security police may not authorize their own searches; they must have approval from a prosecutor or court. However, in practice police did not always obtain prior approval. The Penal Code generally protects privacy, including mail, telephone, and electronic correspondence. But as is the case with e-mail monitoring, government security concerns prevail over such legal protections. In October the National Internet Control Committee promulgated highly restrictive regulations on Internet use (see Section 2.a.).

Ministry of Interior forces monitor citizens' activities; in addition a loose militia in both urban and rural areas has responsibility for maintaining public order and reporting "bad elements" to the police. Militia usually concern themselves more with petty crime and instances of moral turpitude than with political activism, although some rural militia may be used for security against insurgents. A sporadically active system of neighborhood and workplace committees plays a similar monitoring role.

The Government permits the public sale of few leading foreign magazines and newspapers; however, minimal restrictions on publications mailed from overseas are enforced only loosely (see Section 2.a.). The Government allows citizens to marry foreigners but only with its prior approval. Although the Government routinely grants permission, the process is lengthy and burdensome. Marriages to foreigners without government approval may be annulled, with both parties subject to fines.

The Government displaced internally hundreds of persons during the year, mainly as a result of organized infrastructure development programs. The Government provides compensation to displaced persons in the form of land and household supplies.

Credible sources reported flexibility by the Government toward the disposition of infrastructure-related and other government-planned resettlements. One hydropower project resettlement village opened during the year, funded by investors. However, some local administrators forced highlander groups to resettle in lowland areas to control their use of farming methods that destroy forest areas in the pursuit of increased food security.

There are two Internet service providers. In the second half of the year, the National Internet Control Committee in the Prime Minister's Office began a review of national telecommunications and Internet access procedures; it stated that it intends to monitor and control Internet communications more actively. Some Internet users reported that they received e-mail warnings from the Government during the year.

SECTION 2 RESPECT FOR CIVIL LIBERTIES

a. Freedom of Speech and Press

The Constitution provides for freedom of speech and of the press; however, the Government severely restricts political speech and writing in practice. The Government also prohibits most criticism that it deems harmful to its reputation. The Penal Code forbids slandering the State, distorting party or state policies, inciting disorder, or propagating information or opinions that weaken the State. The Government showed limited tolerance of general criticisms of good governance or public service, and citizens who lodge legitimate complaints with government departments generally do not suffer reprisals. However, government concern about potential public violent displays of discontent over failed economic policies and concern over the series of terrorist bombings led to tighter control of the media. Newspapers did not report on investigations into the causes of any of the eight bombs that exploded in Vientiane from March through December. In July the Vientiane Times reported that officials had stated that the bombings were the result of business disputes or personal vendettas (see Section 1.c.).

All domestic print and electronic media are state-owned and controlled. Local news in all media reflects government policy. Television talk shows and opinion articles refer only to differences in administrative approach. However, translations of foreign press reports generally are without bias, and access to Thai radio and television and foreign-based Internet servers is unhindered. Only a few other Asian and Western newspapers and magazines are available, through private outlets that have government permission to sell them.

Authorities also prohibited the dissemination of materials deemed to be indecent, to undermine the national culture, or to be politically sensitive. Films and music recordings produced in government studios must be submitted for official censorship. However, in practice most foreign media are easily available. Government enforcement of restrictions on nightclub entertainment generally was lax during the year.

Citizens have 24-hour access to Cable News Network and the British Broadcasting Corporation, among other international stations accessible via satellite television. The Government requires registration of receiving satellite dishes and a one-time licensing fee for their use, largely as a revenue-generating scheme, but otherwise makes no effort to restrict their use.

Foreign journalists must apply for special visas. Unfettered access to information sources and domestic travel unescorted by officials--hallmarks of a more liberal government attitude in previous years--declined during the year.

The Government controls all domestic Internet servers, blocks access to those World Wide Web sites that are deemed pornographic or are critical of government institutions and policies, and monitors e-mail. In October the National Internet Control Committee promulgated highly restrictive regulations on Internet use by citizens. The regulations significantly curtailed freedom of expression and made "disturbing the peace and happiness of the community" and "reporting misleading news" criminal acts. However, the Government in the past has been limited in its ability to enforce such regulations.

The Constitution provides for academic freedom; however, the Government restricts it, although it has relaxed its restrictions in certain areas. Lao and Western academic professionals conducting research in Laos may be subject to restrictions on travel and access to information and Penal Code restrictions on publication. As the sole employer of virtually all academic professionals, the Government exercises some control over their ability to travel on research or study grants. However, the Government, which once limited foreign travel by professors, actively seeks out these opportunities worldwide and approves virtually all such proposals.

Credible reports indicate that some academically qualified ethnic minorities, including Hmong, are denied opportunities for foreign fellowships and study abroad based on the actions of some state and party officials whose discriminatory behavior goes unchecked. On rare occasions, the Government has denied government employees who were not party members permission to accept certain research or study grants, apparently because they had chosen not to join the LPRP.

b. Freedom of Peaceful Assembly and Association

The Constitution provides for freedom of assembly; however, the Government continues to restrict this right in practice. The Penal Code prohibits participation in an organization for the purpose of demonstrations, protest marches, or other acts that cause turmoil or social instability. Such acts are punishable by a prison term of from 1 to 5 years. If defendants are tried for political crimes against the State, they may face much longer sentences of up to 20 years or possible execution.

The Constitution provides citizens with the right to organize and join associations; however, the Government restricts this right in practice. The Government registers and controls all associations and prohibits associations that criticize it. Political groups other than mass front organizations approved by the LPRP are forbidden. Although the Government restricts many types of formal professional and social associations, in practice informal nonpolitical groups can meet without hindrance. Individuals who in 1997 formed the Foundation for Promoting Education, a private voluntary organization in Vientiane Municipality, were active during the year and awarded prizes for educational achievement and scholarships to needy students. The group is supported by private contributions and operates independently under its own charter; however, it reports to the Ministry of Education. The Buddhist Promotion Foundation is a semiprivate group founded in 1998 by the Lao Buddhist Fellowship Association, which reports to the National Front.

c. Freedom of Religion

The Constitution provides for freedom of religion; however, the Government restricts this right in practice. The Constitution prohibits "all acts of creating division of religion or creating division among the people." The Party and Government appear to interpret this section narrowly, thus inhibiting religious practice by all persons, including the Buddhist majority and a large population of animists. Although official pronouncements accepted the existence of religion, they emphasized its potential to divide, distract, or destabilize.

The Constitution notes that the State "mobilizes and encourages" monks, novices, and priests of other religions to participate in activities "beneficial to the nation and the people." The Department of Religious Affairs in the LPRP Lao National Front for Construction, an LPRP mass organization, is responsible for overseeing all religions.

During the year, government authorities arrested and detained more than 95 Christians and their spiritual leaders, at times holding them in custody for months. In some isolated cases, prisoners were detained in prison with crude, one-leg, wood stocks or fixed hand manacles.

In the following provinces, prisoners are serving 2 to 3-year prison terms for peaceful religious activities found under the Penal Code to be creating social turmoil: In Attapeu (6 jailed); in Houaphan (3 jailed); in Luang Prabang (3 jailed); in Oudomxay (2 jailed). In Oudomxay 3 other persons arrested for proselytizing, purportedly in coordination with foreigners, were sentenced to 15-year (1 jailed) and 12-year sentences (2 jailed). The more severe sentences in Oudomxay were based on harsh Penal Code provisions for acts against the State.

In Savannakhet province, a renunciation and church-closing campaign that was begun in 1999 by district authorities, supported by police, military forces, and representatives of the national front continued into the second half of the year. For the first time, churches of longer standing were targeted. Only about 10 churches--less than half--remained open at year's end. Most practitioners who found that their local churches had been closed were able to move their activities to new places of worship. As in late 1999, in a few villages in which churches had been recently closed, security forces mobilized on Sundays to stop all large vehicles that carried multiple passengers during Sunday worship hours. These actions expressly prevented villagers from traveling to other places to conduct worship services. In July in Vientiane province, the Government began a similar renunciation and church-closing campaign that continued through year's end. District-level police, military, and national front authorities instructed Christians, especially Christians from the Khmu and Hmong ethnic groups, to renounce their faith or face arrest and imprisonment. Vientiane provincial authorities arbitrarily closed at least 1 dozen churches, including a church in a refugee returnee village agreed to at the time the village was established under U.N. High Commissioner for Refugees (UNHCR) auspices. In Vientiane province, authorities targeted both Protestant and Catholic congregations.

The Party controls the Buddhist clergy (Sangha) in an attempt to direct national culture. After 1975 the Government attempted to "reform" Buddhism and ceased to consider it the state religion, causing thousands of monks to flee abroad, where most still remain. The Government has only one semireligious holiday--Boun That Luang--also a major political and cultural celebration. However, the Government recognizes the popularity and cultural significance of Buddhist festivals, and many senior officials openly attend them. Buddhist clergy are featured prominently at important state and party functions. The Lao National Front directs the Lao Buddhist Fellowship Association, which adopted a new charter in April 1998. The Front continues to require monks to study Marxism-Leninism, to attend certain party meetings, and to combine with their teachings of Buddhism the party-state policies. In recent years, some individual temples have been permitted to receive support from Theravada Buddhist temples abroad, to expand the training of monks, and to focus more on traditional teachings.

The authorities continued to be suspicious of parts of the religious community other than Buddhism, including some Christian groups, in part because these faiths do not share a similarly high degree of direction and incorporation into the government structure as is the case with Theravada Buddhism. Authorities especially appear to suspect those religious groups that gain support from foreign sources, aggressively proselytize among the poor or uneducated, or give targeted assistance to converts. The Government strictly prohibits foreigners from proselytizing, although it permits foreign nongovernmental organizations with religious affiliations to work in the country. Foreign persons caught distributing religious material may be arrested or deported. Although there is no prohibition against proselytizing by citizens, there was increased local government investigation and harassment of citizens who do so under the constitutional provision against creating division of religion.

The Government's tolerance of religion varied by region. In general central government authorities appeared unable or unwilling to control or mitigate harsh measures that were taken by local or provincial authorities against the practices of members of minority religious denominations. Although there was almost complete freedom to worship among unregistered groups in a few areas, particularly in the largest cities, government authorities in many regions allowed properly registered religious groups to practice their faith only under circumscribed conditions. In other areas, such as Savannakhet, Luang Prabang, Phongsaly, Houaphanh, Oudomxay, and Attapeu, the authorities arrested and detained religious believers and their spiritual leaders without charges. In more isolated cases, provincial authorities instructed their officials to monitor and arrest persons who professed belief in Christianity, Islam, or the Baha'i faith. For example, there is clear evidence that in Luang Prabang, Savannakhet, and Vientiane provinces, the authorities continued to force some Christians to sign renunciations of their faith.

Citizens in Luang Prabang continued to report that local authorities ordered them to stop their open practice of Christianity completely, under threat of arrest. The order appeared to apply only to new converts; believers of long standing were allowed to continue their beliefs but not to conduct worship or practice their faith openly. Local officials monitored Christians closely to ensure that they did not practice their religion and harassed and arrested some Christians who violated these policies.

Although authorities generally tolerated diverse religious practices, in the southern Laos panhandle, a pattern of petty local harassment persists. Many converts must undergo a series of harsh government interviews; however, after overcoming that initial barrier, they generally are permitted to practice their new faith unhindered. Members of long-established congregations had few problems in practicing their faith; however, some churches established a century ago continued to be subjected to harassment by local government officials in Savannakhet. Many groups of coreligionists seeking to assemble in a new location are thwarted in attempts to meet, practice, or celebrate major religious festivals.

Some minority religious groups report that they were unable during the year to register new congregations or receive permission to establish new places of worship, including in Vientiane. Authorities sometimes advised new branches to join other religious groups with similar historical roots, despite clear differences between the groups' beliefs. Some groups did not submit applications to establish places of worship because they did not believe that their applications would be approved.

The Roman Catholic Church is unable to operate effectively in the highlands and much of the north. However, it has an established presence in five of the most populous central and southern provinces, where Catholics are able to worship openly. There are three bishops: In Vientiane, Thakhek, and Pakse. The status of the Catholic Church in Luang Prabang center remains in doubt; there appears to be a congregation there but due to local obstructionism, worship services may not always be conducted readily.

Over 250 Protestant congregations conduct services throughout the country. The Lao National Front has recognized two Protestant groups, the Lao Evangelical Church, the umbrella Protestant church, and the Seventh Day Adventist Church. The Front strongly encourages all other Protestant groups to become a part of the Lao Evangelical Church. The Government has granted permission to these approved denominations to have a total of four church buildings in the Vientiane area. In addition the Lao Evangelical Church has maintained church buildings in Savannakhet and Pakse.

The Government permits major religious festivals of all established congregations without hindrance. Two mosques and two Baha'i centers operate openly in Vientiane municipality; two other Baha'i centers are located in Vientiane province and Pakse. Five Mahayana Buddhist pagodas are located in Vientiane, and others are found in larger cities and towns.

Animists generally experience no interference by the Government in their religious practices, which vary extensively among the 48 to 69 identified ethnic groups and tribes in the country.

The Government does not permit the printing of religious texts or their distribution outside a congregation and restricts the import of foreign religious texts and artifacts. The Government requires and grants routinely its permission for formal links with coreligionists in other countries; however, in practice the line between formal and informal links is blurred, and relations generally are established without much difficulty.

d. Freedom of Movement Within the Country, Foreign Travel, Migration, and Repatriation

The Constitution provides for these rights; however, the Government restricted some of these rights in practice. Citizens who travel across provincial borders are required to report to authorities upon their departure and arrival. In designated security zones, roadblocks and identity card checks are routine. Citizens who seek to travel abroad are required to apply for an exit visa; however, the Government grants such visas routinely. Foreigners are restricted from traveling to certain areas such as the Saysomboune Special Zone, an administrative area operated by the military forces, for safety and security reasons.

During the year, security forces in at least one province set up roadblocks during Sunday worship hours, which prevented villagers from traveling to participate in religious worship services (see Section 2.c.).

Fear of insurgent attacks on civilians in vehicles traveling in the north-central areas impedes travel, especially along parts of Route 13, Route 7, and Route 1. Bandits operate in the same area (see Section 1.a.). The Government attempts to ensure safety on these roads.

Citizens are free to emigrate; exit visas are required, and the Government grants these routinely.

Since 1980 more than 29,060 citizens who sought refugee status in Thailand, China, and other countries have returned to Laos for permanent resettlement under monitoring by the UNHCR. There were no new returnees during the year. The Government cooperates with the UNHCR to assist such returnees to reintegrate. Most are ethnic Hmong and other minorities. These returnees generally have been treated the same as other citizens.

The Constitution provides for asylum and the protection of stateless persons under the law, but in practice, the Government does not provide first asylum. There were no known cases during the year of asylum seekers being returned to a country where they feared persecution.

The Government has a longstanding policy of welcoming back virtually all those among the 10 percent of the population who fled after the change in government in 1975. Many have visited relatives, some have stayed and gained foreign resident status, and some have reclaimed citizenship successfully. A small group, tried in absentia in 1975 for antigovernment activities, does not have the right of return.

Eight Lowland Lao men who returned from China have been detained without trial since 1997, which is beyond the limit for investigative detention (see Section 1.d.).

Some refugee returnees carry identification cards with distinctive markings, ostensibly for use by authorities. Such cards tend to reinforce a pattern of societal discrimination against the refugees. Authorities increasingly harassed religious minorities in refugee returnee villages, and local officials closed a Christian church in one such village. The Government had permitted use of the church building at the time that the refugees returned (see Section 2.c.).

SECTION 3 RESPECT FOR POLITICAL RIGHTS: THE RIGHT OF CITIZENS TO CHANGE THEIR GOVERNMENT

Citizens do not have the right to change their government. The Constitution legitimizes only a single party, the Lao People's Revolutionary Party, which must approve all candidates for local and national elections. Candidates need not be LPRP members.

The Constitution provides for a 99-member National Assembly, elected every 5 years in open, multiple-candidate, fairly tabulated elections, with voting by secret ballot and universal adult suffrage. The National Assembly chooses a standing committee apparently based on the previous standing committee's decision. Upon the committee's recommendation, the National Assembly elects or removes the President and Vice President. The standing committee also has powers over elections (including approval of candidates), supervision of administrative and judicial organizations, and the sole power to recommend presidential decrees. Activities of the standing committee are not fully transparent.

The National Assembly, upon the President's recommendation, elects the Prime Minister and other Ministers in the Government.

The National Assembly may consider and amend draft legislation but may not propose new laws. The Constitution gives the right to submit draft legislation to the National Assembly standing committee and the ruling executive structure.

Women are underrepresented in government and politics; however, women increased their representation in the National Assembly in 1997 elections from 9 percent to 20 percent, as 20 of the 27 female candidates won seats. Four members of the 48-member LPRP Central Committee are women, 2 of whom are also members of the 7-member standing committee in the National Assembly. There are no women in the Politburo or the Council of Ministers.

The proportions of ethnic minority members in the 99-member National Assembly-10 Lao Soung (highland tribes) and 26 Lao Theung (mid-slope dwelling tribes)--are consistent with their proportions in the general population. There are 10 Hmong in the National Assembly. Men of lowland Lao origin dominate the upper echelons of the Party and the Government. Nonetheless, the President, 2 Deputy Prime Ministers, 3 Ministers, and 36 members of the National Assembly are believed to be members of ethnic minority groups.

SECTION 4 GOVERNMENTAL ATTITUDE REGARDING INTERNATIONAL AND NONGOVERNMENTAL INVESTIGATION OF ALLEGED VIOLATIONS OF HUMAN RIGHTS

There are no domestic nongovernmental human rights organizations, and the Government does not have a formal procedure for registration. Any organization wishing to investigate and publicly criticize the Government's human rights policies would face serious obstacles if it were permitted to operate at all. The Government cooperates on an uneven basis with international human rights organizations.

A human rights unit in the Ministry of Foreign Affairs' (MFA's) Department of International Treaties and Legal Affairs has responsibility for inquiry into allegations of human rights violations. This government unit rarely responds to inquiries regarding individual cases, but early in the year published in Lao language a partial compilation of international conventions on human rights.

In 1998, at the invitation of the Government, the U.N. Special Rapporteur on Trafficking in Children visited various locations and made inquiries into possible incidents of child prostitution and child pornography.

The Government maintains contacts with the International Committee of the Red Cross (ICRC); government officials received ICRC training on human rights law in 1998, and the Government is translating more international conventions with ICRC support. The Government permitted U.N. human rights observers to monitor the treatment of almost 30,000 returned refugees in all parts of the country with minimal interference; however, it occasionally obstructs monitoring so that it cannot be conducted in accordance with international standards.

SECTION 5 DISCRIMINATION BASED ON RACE, SEX, RELIGION, DISABILITY, LANGUAGE, OR SOCIAL STATUS

The Constitution provides for equal treatment under the law for all citizens without regard to sex, social status, education, faith, or ethnicity. Although the Government sometimes has taken action when well-documented and obvious cases of discrimination came to the attention of high-level officials, the legal mechanism whereby a citizen may bring charges of discrimination against an individual or organization is neither widely developed nor widely understood among the general population.

Women

There are reports that domestic violence against women occurs, although it is not widespread. Sexual harassment and rape reportedly are rare. In cases of rape that are tried in court, defendants generally are convicted.

Trafficking in women is a problem (see Section 6.f.).

The Constitution provides for equal rights for women, and the Lao Women's Union operates nationally to promote the position of women in society. Discrimination against women is not generalized; however, varying degrees of traditional culturally based discrimination persist, with greater discrimination practiced by some hill tribes. Many women occupy responsible positions in the civil service and private business, and in urban areas their incomes are often higher than those of men. The Family Code prohibits legal discrimination in marriage and inheritance.

In the period from 1997 through 2000, the Government increased support for the position of women in society in development programs, some of which are designed to increase the participation of women in the political system.

Children

The level of support for education is exceedingly low. Government funding to provide fully for children's basic health and educational needs is inadequate. Education is compulsory through the fifth grade, but children from rural areas and poor urban families rarely comply with this requirement. There is a significant difference in the treatment of boys and girls in the educational system: Female literacy is 48 percent versus 70 percent for males. However, men and women attend the three universities in approximately equal numbers. Violence against children is prohibited by law, and violators are subject to stiff punishments. Reports of the physical abuse of children are rare. Trafficking in women and children is a problem (see Section 6.f.).

People With Disabilities

With donor assistance, the Government is implementing limited programs for the disabled, especially amputees. The law does not mandate accessibility to buildings or government services for disabled persons, but the Labor and Social Welfare Ministry began to establish regulations on building access and some sidewalk ramps in Vientiane during the year. The Lao National Commission for the Disabled (LNCD) is formulating a new draft law and other policies regarding the disabled, and the Lao Disabled Persons Association set up offices in Champassak and Xieng Khouang provinces to assist with rehabilitation, job skills training, and social integration of the disabled. The LNCD also hosted a regional conference on disabilities in Vientiane in November to promote leadership and organizational skills for disabled persons.

Religious Minorities

The enhanced status given to Buddhism in Luang Prabang--famed for its centuries-old Buddhist tradition and numerous temples--apparently led some local officials there to act more harshly toward minority religions, particularly toward Christians and Baha'is, than in other areas of the country (see Section 2.c.).

National/Racial/Ethnic Minorities

The Constitution provides for equal rights for citizens of all minorities, and there is no legal discrimination against them. However, societal discrimination persists.

Approximately half the population is ethnic Lao, also called "lowland Lao." Most of the remainder is a mixture of diverse upland hill tribes whose members, if born in Laos, are Lao citizens. There are also ethnic Vietnamese and Chinese minorities, particularly in the towns. There is a small community of South Asian origin. The implementation in 1994 of the 1990 Law on Nationality provided a means for Vietnamese and Chinese minorities to normalize their Lao citizenship; a small number did so during the year. The Government encourages the preservation of minority cultures and traditions; however, due to their remote location and difficult access, minority tribes have little voice in government decisions affecting their lands and the allocation of natural resources.

The Hmong are one of the largest and most prominent highland minority groups. Societal discrimination against the Hmong continues, although there are a number of Hmong officials in the senior ranks of the Government. In recent years, the Government focused some limited assistance projects in Hmong areas in order to overcome disparities in income along regional and ethnic lines. Some international observers claim that governmental policies aimed at assimilating the Hmong into larger society-- such as regional boarding schools--are not respectful of Hmong native culture; others see this approach as an escape from centuries of poverty.

In the intensified Hmong insurgency in the north, government forces beat Hmong insurgents and treated them harshly in some Hmong villages (see Sections 1.a. and 1.c.). In an unconfirmed report, a foreign newspaper in December recounted an alleged government soldier's account that security forces had shot to death a number of young Hmong men in Saysomboune Special Zone during the year.

During the year, the Government continued to assist citizens, largely members of ethnic minorities, who returned to Laos after having fled in 1975. Central and local government officials worked with organizations such as the UNHCR to provide land and a sustainable level of economic security. Repatriated Hmong generally face no greater discrimination than those Hmong who remained. A number of Hmong returnees were forced to renounce their Christian faith, and one church in a returnee village was closed by authorities. Two U.N. observers who monitored repatriation efforts reported no significant human rights violations.

Under the Constitution, aliens and stateless foreign citizens are protected by "provisions of the laws" but do not in practice enjoy rights provided for by the Constitution. During the year, there were isolated cases of persons of Lao ethnic background who, as citizens of other nations, suffered discrimination when arrested or detained and were denied due process, apparently on the basis of their Lao ethnic background.

SECTION 6 WORKER RIGHTS

a. The Right of Association

Under the 1990 Labor Code and a 1995 prime ministerial decree, labor unions can be formed in private enterprises as long as they operate within the framework of the officially sanctioned Federation of Lao Trade Unions (FLTU), which in turn is controlled by the LPRP. Most of the FLTU's 77,057 members work in the public sector.

The State employs the majority of salaried workers, although this situation is changing as the Government reduces the number of its employees and privatizes state enterprises. Subsistence farmers comprise an estimated 85 percent of the work force.

Strikes are not prohibited by law, but the Government's ban on subversive activities or destabilizing demonstrations (see Section 2.b.) makes a strike unlikely, and none were reported during the year. However, the Labor Code does not prohibit temporary work stoppages.

With advice from the International Labor Organization (ILO), including a foreign expert provided by the ILO to work with the Ministry of Labor and Social Welfare, the Government in 1994 revised the Labor Code in an effort to clarify the rights and obligations of workers and employers. However, the ILO Committee of Experts cited the Government for its failure to submit reports required of member states.

The FLTU is free to engage in contacts with foreign labor organizations, which during the year included the Association of Southeast Asian Nations (ASEAN) Trade Union and the Asia-Pacific American Labor Alliance. The FLTU is a member of the World Federation of Trade Unions.

b. The Right to Organize and Bargain Collectively

There is no right to organize and bargain collectively. The Labor Code stipulates that disputes be resolved through workplace committees composed of employers, representatives of the local labor union, and representatives of the FLTU, with final authority residing in the Ministry of Labor and Social Welfare. Labor disputes are infrequent. The Government sets wages and salaries for government employees, while management sets wages and salaries for private business employees.

The Labor Code stipulates that employers may not fire employees for conducting trade union activities, for lodging complaints against employers about labor law implementation, or for cooperating with officials on labor law implementation and labor disputes. Workplace committees are one mechanism used for resolving complaints.

There are no export processing zones.

c. Prohibition of Forced or Compulsory Labor

The Labor Code prohibits forced labor except in time of war or national disaster, during which the State may conscript laborers; however, trafficking in women and children is a problem (see Section 6.f.). The Code also applies to children under the age of 15, and generally is enforced effectively; however, reports that children are being lured into other countries for sexual exploitation and slave labor continued, and increased over the previous year (see Sections 5 and 6.f.).

d. Status of Child Labor Practices and Minimum Age for Employment

Under the Labor Code, children under the age of 15 may not be recruited for employment. However, many children help their families on farms or in shops. The Labor Code accordingly provides that children may work for their families, provided that such children are not engaged in dangerous or difficult work. Such employment of children is common in urban shops, but rare in industrial enterprises. The Ministries of Interior and Justice are responsible for enforcing these provisions, but enforcement is ineffective due to a lack of inspectors and other resources. Education is compulsory through the fifth grade, but this requirement rarely is observed in the rural areas or among the urban poor. Some garment factories reportedly employ a very small number of underage girls. The Labor Code prohibits forced and bonded labor performed by children under age 15, and the law generally is enforced effectively; however, there were reports that children were lured into sexual exploitation and slavery abroad (see Sections 6.c. and 6.f.).

e. Acceptable Conditions of Work

The Labor Code provides for a broad range of worker entitlements, including a workweek limited to 48 hours (36 hours for employment in dangerous activities), safe working conditions, and higher compensation for dangerous work. The Code also provides for at least 1 day of rest per week. Employers are responsible for all expenses for a worker injured or killed on the job, a requirement generally fulfilled by employers in the formal economic sector. A section of the Labor Code mandates extensive employer responsibility for those disabled while at work. During the year, this law was enforced adequately. The daily minimum wage is $0.53 (4,000 kip), which is insufficient to provide a decent standard of living for a worker and family. Most civil servants receive inadequate pay. However, few families in the wage economy depend on only one member for income. Some piecework employees, especially on construction sites, earn less than the minimum wage. Many persons are illegal immigrants, particularly from Vietnam, and are more vulnerable to exploitation by employers. Although workplace inspections reportedly have increased, the Ministry of Labor and Social Welfare lacks the personnel and budgetary resources to enforce the Labor Code effectively. The Labor Code has no specific provision allowing workers to remove themselves from a dangerous situation without jeopardizing their employment.

f. Trafficking in Persons

The Penal Code prohibits abduction and trade in persons as well as the constraint, procuring, and prostitution of persons; however, trafficking in women and children is a problem. Laos is a source and transit country for trafficking in persons. The Government only recently has focused on the trafficking of persons across its borders. Although there is no reliable data available on the scope and severity of the problem, there are indications that the numbers are considerable. The Government has increased monitoring and educational programs provided by the Lao Women's Union and the Youth Union, both party-sanctioned organizations, designed to educate girls and young women about the schemes of recruiters for brothels and sweatshops in neighboring countries and elsewhere. In the past, the Government has prosecuted some persons for involvement in such recruiting activities. Recent evidence indicates an increase in arrests for procuring; however, this may not reflect a genuine government effort to address the problem. During the year, law enforcement agencies conducted a minimal number of raids on entertainment establishments accused of fostering prostitution.

The Government remains concerned about Lao children being lured into sexual exploitation and slave labor in other countries, but the Government denied that there were any problems in the country that involve child prostitution. The National Commission for Mothers and Children, established in 1992 and chaired by the Foreign Minister, continues an active program with support from the U.N. Children's Fund. The Commission, working with the Lao Women's Union, Youth Union, Justice Ministry, and Labor Ministry, has conducted workshops around the country designed to make parents and teenagers aware of the dangers of HIV. At the Government's invitation, the U.N. Special Rapporteur on Trafficking in Children visited in 1998 (see Section 4).

POLITICAL AND GOVERNMENT SYSTEM

STRUCTURE OF THE GOVERNMENT

EXECUTIVE

The president of the country is elected by a two-thirds vote of the National Assembly for a term of five years. One surprising constitutional provision transforms the presidency from a ceremonial position into an important political power. The president appoints and can dismiss the prime minister and members of the government, with the approval of the National Assembly-- parliamentary responsibility that has not yet occurred in the short life of the current constitutional regime. He also presides over meetings of the government, "when necessary," and appoints and dismisses provincial governors and mayors of municipalities as well as generals of the armed forces, upon the recommendation of the prime minister. In addition, the president receives and appoints ambassadors and declares states of emergency or war.

The powers accorded to the president grew perceptively during the drafting process of the constitution, but the sudden death of Kaysone, who had moved from prime minister to state president after the promulgation of the constitution, temporarily introduced doubts regarding the relative power potential of the two offices. Nonetheless, the president of state heads the armed forces and has the right and duty to promulgate laws and issue decrees and state acts.

The primary organization for administration is the government, which consists of the prime minister--its head--and deputy prime ministers, ministers, and chairs of ministry-equivalent state committees. The prime minister, appointed by the president with the approval of the National Assembly, serves a five-year term. Duties of this office include the guidance and supervision of the work of government ministries and committees, as well as of the governors of provinces and mayors of municipalities. The prime minister appoints all the deputies at these levels of government, as well as the local district chiefs

LEGISLATURE

The National Assembly, the country's supreme legislative body, is to be elected every five years. Significantly, this designation was used in RLG and French colonial times, before the introduction of the title "Supreme People's Assembly" in late 1975. It is located in a new building, far larger than the previous structure built in colonial times, and contains an auditorium seating 800 persons.

The National Assembly makes decisions on fundamental issues and oversees administrative and judicial organs. Its most significant powers include electing and removing the president of state, the president of the Supreme People's Court, and the prosecutor general, "on the recommendation of the National Assembly Standing Committee." Its prestige has been further enhanced by the constitutional mandate to "make decisions on the fundamental issues of the country" and to "elect or remove the President of state and the Vice President of state", by a two-thirds vote, and to approve the removal of members of the government on the recommendation of the president of state. Its powers encompass amending the constitution, determining taxes, approving the state budget, endorsing or abrogating laws, and electing or removing the two top judicial figures in the system. Members of the National Assembly have the "right to interpellate the members of the government." The National Assembly also ratifies treaties and decides questions of war and peace. These powers may prove to be limited, however, by a provision in the constitution that the National Assembly will generally meet in ordinary session only twice a year. The Standing Committee meeting in the interim may convene an extraordinary session if it deems necessary.

The constitution does not specify the number of members in the National Assembly, whose candidates are screened by the LPRP. The 1989 election placed seventy-nine members in this body, representing districts of between 40,000 and 50,000 persons each. The election campaign lasted two months, and candidates appeared before voters at night in local schools or pagodas. Voting consisted of crossing out unfavored candidates, and every ballot contained at least two candidates. The number of party members elected by this process was officially placed at sixty-five.

Between sessions, the Standing Committee of the National Assembly, consisting of the president and the vice president elected by the National Assembly and an unspecified number of other members, prepares for future sessions and "supervise[s] and oversee[s] the activities of the administrative and judicial organizations." It is empowered to appoint or remove the vice president of the Supreme People's Court and judges at all levels of the lower courts. Its supervisory role can be reinforced by National Assembly committees established to consider draft laws and decrees and to help in the supervision and administration of the courts. The special National Assembly Law passed March 25, 1993, specifies five substantive areas for National Assembly committees: secretarial; law; economic planning and finances; cultural, social, and nationalities; and foreign affairs. The membership of the committees includes not only National Assembly members but also chiefs and deputy chiefs, who "guide the work," and technical cadres.

JUDICIARY

The development of the legal and judicial system did not begin until almost fifteen years after the state was proclaimed. In November 1989, a criminal code and laws establishing a judicial system were adopted. In 1993 the government began publishing an official gazette to disseminate laws, decrees, and regulations.

In 1990 the judicial branch was upgraded. New legislation provided a draft of a criminal code, established procedures for criminal cases, set up a court system, and established a law school. Moreover, the Ministry of Justice added a fourth year of studies to a law program for training magistrates and judges.

Also in 1990, the functions of the Supreme People's Court were separated from those of the office of the public prosecutor general. Until then, the minister of justice served as both president of the court and director of public prosecutions.

Although the implementation of judicial reforms proceeded slowly and had not significantly improved the administration of justice by mid-1994, the new legal framework offers the possibility of moving away from the arbitrary use of power toward the rule of law. In late 1992, however, the government suspended the bar until it formulates regulations for fees and activities of (the few) private lawyers who are able to advise in civil cases. Lawyers are not allowed to promote themselves as attorneys-at-law. Theoretically, the government provides legal counsel to the accused, although in practice persons accused of crimes must defend themselves, without outside legal counsel. However, the assessors (legal advisers)--who are often untrained--and the party functionaries are being increasingly replaced by professional personnel trained at the Institute of Law and Administration.

The constitution empowers the National Assembly to elect or remove the president of the Supreme People's Court and the public prosecutor general on the recommendation of its Standing Committee. The Standing Committee of the National Assembly appoints or removes judges (previously elected) of the provincial, municipal, and district levels.

Further evidence of an attempt to shift toward a professional judicial system is found in the public prosecution institutes provided for at each level of administration. The task of these institutes is to control the uniform observance of laws by all ministries, organizations, state employees, and citizens. They prosecute under the guidance of the public prosecutor general, who appoints and removes deputy public prosecutors at all levels.

POLITICAL OPPOSITION

Over the centuries, residents of the Laotian Buddhist kingdom developed gentle techniques of accommodation, often searching for more powerful patrons either outside the country or within. Authorities governed during the early years after 1975 with little popular support, but most Laotians simply submitted to their authority because they had little alternative. However, the authorities were not harsh compared to other communist regimes of the 1970s and 1980s, most of which--by mid-1994--have toppled.

The relatively passive Laotian political culture inspires few direct challenges to one-party domination, and party authorities firmly assert the limits of political dissent. LPRP spokesmen invoke a litany of explanations to justify the party's monopoly of power--for example, the country is too underdeveloped and the people too little educated to permit more than one party. Further, there are too many ethnic groups, and open political participation would lead to disunity and chaos. Political stability, provided by the leadership of a single party, is said to be necessary for economic growth. The LPRP has also pointed out the corrupt multiparty system of the RLG. An abiding political reality, however, is that those who have power wish to retain it.

Restrictions on political opposition do not appear to be a salient issue among a majority of the population, although a small number of educated Laotians in intellectual, student, and bureaucratic circles have raised a few protests. Despite the toll of age and failing health among the aged Politburo members, the leadership governs without active opposition. Even when communist leaders were unceremoniously dumped in Eastern Europe, vigorously challenged in the Soviet Union, and confronted by students in China, communist leaders in Laos retained their hold as they guided the regime into the uncharted realm of reform. It is not clear why there was so little challenge to these aging leaders. They maintained a cohesion among themselves, perhaps a product of their many years as comrades in revolution, living in caves and dodging United States bombs. They may have also sustained an enduring respect from party stalwarts who followed them during twenty-five years of revolution. Whether the government will encounter political opposition from a broader segment of Laotian society as it moves to a more market-oriented economy and increasingly opens its doors to Western influence remains to be seen.

REFUGEES

From 1975 to 1985, after the communists had seized power and were consolidating their hold, some 350,000 persons fled across the Mekong River to Thailand and, in most cases, resettled in third countries. By the late 1980s and early 1990s, this outflow had declined substantially. In 1990, for example, an estimated 1,000 to 2,000 lowland Lao and 4,000 to 5,000 upland Lao departed illegally for Thailand. The Thai government refused to admit these refugees as immigrants. Third-country resettlement has grown more difficult with the end of Cold War solidarity with emigrants who claim to be "victims of communism." Moreover, Laos has become more liberal in granting exit permits to those desiring to emigrate.

By the early 1990s, almost as many Laotians were returning to Laos as were leaving. Under a voluntary repatriation program worked out in 1980 by Laos and the United Nations High Commissioner for Refugees (UNHCR--see Glossary), nearly 19,000 Laotians had voluntarily returned to their homeland by the end of 1993, and an estimated 30,000 more had returned without official involvement. Most of the returnees are lowland Lao. Of the approximately 30,000 Laotian refugees remaining in camps in Thailand in 1993, the majority are upland Lao. Approximately 1,700 Laotian refugees remain in China. Émigrés who had resettled in third countries are returning in increasing numbers to visit relatives and, in a few cases, to survey business opportunities in the more liberal economy.

INSURGENTS

A small-scale insurgency that has existed since 1975 continues in the early 1990s, although at a much lower level than in previous years. This insurgency has never seriously threatened the regime, but it is troublesome because the insurgents commit sabotage, blow up bridges, and threaten transport and communications. The great majority of insurgents are Hmong (see Glossary), led by ex-soldiers from United States Central Intelligence Agency (CIA)-supported units who fought against Pathet Lao and

North Vietnamese troops in the 1960s. Hmong groups, most of them formerly associated with the RLG, draw recruits and support from Hmong refugee camps and operate from bases in Thailand with the cooperation of local Thai military officers. As relations between Thailand and Laos continued to improve in the 1990s, support for this insurgent activity declined. Resistance spokesmen claim that their principal source of funds for weapons and supplies comes from Laotian expatriate communities overseas, including the 180,000 Laotians in the United States.

Even though the government lacks widespread public support, insurgency is less a measure of discontent than evidence of a serious ethnic problem. The LPDR, like the RLG that preceded it, has been dominated by lowland Lao. The two governments exemplify the traditional Lao disdain for upland peoples, in spite of Pathet Lao rhetoric in favor of ethnic equality. On the one hand, because many Hmong fought on the side of the "American imperialists," government leaders feel additionally suspicious of them. On the other hand, Hmong and other upland minorities who served with the United States-supported forces have been suspicious and uncomfortable under their former enemies. Thus, a core of insurgents, composed largely of ethnic minorities, continues to fight against the authorities. It will be extremely difficult-- perhaps impossible--for the government to pacify them, especially without help from Vietnamese military units, if the insurgents enjoy access to sanctuary in Thailand along the easily crossed 1,000 kilometer Mekong River border.

In the early 1980s, Hmong insurgents claimed that the Lao People's Army (LPA--see Glossary) was using lethal chemical agents against them. The Hmong refugees in Thailand often referred to the chemical agents as "poisons from above;" foreign journalists used the term "yellow rain." The government vehemently denied these charges. The United States Department of State noted in 1992 that "considerable investigative efforts in recent years have revealed no evidence of chemical weapons use" in the post-1983 period. The LPDR again denied these charges. The United States Department of State noted in 1992 that "considerable investigative efforts in recent years have revealed no evidence of chemical weapons use."

BUREAUCRATIC CULTURE

The historical evolution of Laos created identifiable layers of bureaucratic behavior. Traditional royal customs and Buddhist practices set the foundation. Next, there was an overlay of French influence, the product of colonial rule from 1890 to 1954. During this period, several generations of Laotian bureaucrats were trained and often placed in subordinate rank to French-imported Vietnamese civil servants. The administration used French as the official language and followed French colonial administrative practices. From 1954 to 1975, there was an increase in United States influence, and the United States provided training and educational opportunities for future bureaucrats as well as employment in United States agencies. Because of its brevity, however, the United States impact was far less pervasive than the French.

When the communists seized power in 1975, a new layer of bureaucrats--strongly influenced by North Vietnam and the Soviet Union and its allies--was added. Many of the

French-trained and United States-influenced bureaucrats fled across the Mekong River. Of those who stayed, perhaps 10,000 to 15,000 were sent to seminar camps or reeducation centers;. The few Westerntrained bureaucrats who remained possessed French- or Englishlanguage skills and the technical competence needed to deal effectively with the Western foreign aid donors so critical to the economy. The Western-trained bureaucrats were essential because not many of the new revolutionary cadres who moved into key positions of bureaucratic authority had much formal education, knowledge of a foreign language, or competence in the technical and managerial skills necessary to run a national economy. The few cadres in each ministry who were capable of managing the economy were often unavailable because there were so many demands for their services: for example, meeting with visiting foreign delegations, traveling to international meetings, and attending political training sessions.

Since its inception, the LPDR bureaucracy has been lethargic and discouraged individual initiative. It has been dangerous to take unorthodox positions. Some officials have been arrested on suspicion of corruption or ideological deviation: for example, "pro-Chinese" sentiment. Initiative has been further constrained by the lack of legal safeguards, formal trial procedures, and an organized system of appeal. The beginnings of a penal code, which the SPA endorsed in 1989, and the promulgation of a constitution in 1991, however, may solidify the system of justice and provide a clear definition as to what constitutes a crime against socialist morality, the party, or the state.

The lethargy of the bureaucracy is understandable within the cultural context of Laos. As a peasant society at the lower end of the modernization scale, the LPDR has adopted few of the work routines associated with modern administration. Foreign aid administrators frequently point out that Laotian administrators have difficulty creating patterns or precedents, or learning from experience. Laotians are known for their light-hearted, easy-going manner. This *bo pinh nyang* (never mind--don't worry about it) attitude is reflected in the languid pace of administration. Official corruption has also been acknowledged as problematic.

Kaysone acknowledged the bureaucracy's low level of competence. In his report to the Fourth Party Congress in 1986, he chided those in authority who gave "preference only to (their friends) or those from the same locality or race; paying attention to only their birth origin, habits and one particular sphere of education." Patronage is but one area that has come under scrutiny and resulted in admonishments to strengthen inspection and control. Kaysone further railed against "dogmatism, privatism, racial narrowmindedness , regionalism and localism."

ORGANIZATION OF THE GOVERNMENT STATE AND GOVERNMENT LEADERS

Lieutenant General **Choummaly Sayasone**

Politics of Laos takes place in a framework of a single-party socialist republic. The only legal political party is the Lao People's Revolutionary Party (LPRP). The head of state is President Choummaly Sayasone, who also is secretary-general (leader) of the LPRP. The head of government is Prime Minister Bouasone Bouphavanh. Government policies are determined by the party through the all-powerful nine-member Politburo and the 49-member Central Committee. Important government decisions are vetted by the Council of Ministers.

Laos adopted a constitution in 1991. The following year, elections were held for a new 85-seat National Assembly with members elected by secret ballot to five-year terms. This National Assembly, which essentially acts as a rubber stamp for the LPRP, approves all new laws, although the executive branch retains authority to issue binding decrees. The most recent elections took place in April 2006. The assembly was expanded to 99 members in 1997 and in 2006 elections had 115.

The FY 2000 central government budget plan called for revenue of $180 million and expenditures of $289 million, including capital expenditures of $202 million.

In recent years bomb attacks against the government have occurred, coupled with small exchanges of fire, across Laos. A variety of different groups have claimed responsibility including the Committee for Independence and Democracy in Laos and Lao Citizens Movement for Democracy. The United States has warned about the possibility of further attacks during the ASEAN summit in November.

Communist Laos's National Assem-bly yesterday endorsed party chief Choummaly Sayasone as president and young rising star Bouasone Bouphavanh as prime minister.

The reshuffle reflected a smooth transition of power, as both Choummaly and Bouasone belong to the faction of former Lao People's Revolutionary Party chief Khamtay Siphandone, Vientiane-based diplomats said.

A three-star general, Choummaly is Khamtay's former deputy and right-hand man, while Bouasone is a former deputy prime minister. Choummaly has enjoyed Khamtay's full backing since joining the decision-making Politburo during the seventh congress of the party in 2001. Like Khamtay, Choummaly and Bouasone are natives of southern Laos.

Choummaly, from Attapeu, took the helm from Khamtay after the eighth congress of the communist party in March.

Bouasone, from Salavan, replaced Bounnhang Vorachit, who was made vice-president.

Born in 1954, Bouasone is from the new generation of communist leaders who have climbed the ladder of the socialist regime, and was not one of the revolutionary guard like his seniors. However, in 1975, shortly before the fall of Vientiane to the communist Pathet Lao, he was a student activist who played a key role in protests against the previous regime.

The reshuffle also promoted former foreign minister Somsavat Lengsavad to deputy prime minister.

Historian Thongloun Sisoulith, also a former deputy prime minister, replaced Somsavat as foreign minister.

New faces in the 28-member cabinet include Onechanh Thammavong as labour minister, party ideologist Chaleuan Yapaoher as justice minister, Nam Vignaket as industry and commerce minister, Sitaheng Latsaphone as agriculture minister and Sommath Pholsena as transport minister.

The 115-member National Assembly, which was inaugurated yesterday following the April 30 general election, selected Thong Thammavong as its president.

The National Assembly in Laos has formalised the appointment of a new president, prime minister and cabinet. Bouasone Bouphavanh was appointed prime minister, replacing Boungnang Vorachit, who became a vice-president. Choummaly Sayasone was named president, in place of Khamtay Siphandone, who stepped down as leader of Laos' only political party in March. The new line-up was unlikely to herald significant reform in the communist country, analysts say. Mr Bouasone told the lawmakers that he would maintain economic growth and fight corruption. The National Assembly was meeting for the first time since elections in April in which the ruling Lao People's Revolutionary Party won all but one parliamentary seat. Laos has been ruled by a communist government since an American-backed government fell in 1975. A mainly agricultural country of 5.9 million people, Laos is one of Asia's poorest nations.

President	**CHOUMMALI Saignason,** *Lt. Gen.*
Vice President	**BOUN-GNANG Volachit**
Prime Minister	**BOUASONE Bouphavanh**
Dep. Prime Min.	**ASANG Laoli,** *Maj. Gen.*
Dep. Prime Min.	**DOUANGCHAI Phichit**
Dep. Prime Min.	**SOMSAVAT Lengsavat**
Dep. Prime Min.	**THONGLOUN Sisoulit**
Min. of Agriculture & Forestry	**SITAHENG Latsaphone**
Min. of Commerce	**SOULIVONG Daravong**
Min. of Communications, Transport, Posts, & Construction	**SOMMATH Pholsena**

Min. of Education	**SOMKOT Mangnormek**
Min. of Energy & Mining	**BOSAIKHAM Vongdala**
Min. of Finance	**CHANSY Phosikham**
Min. of Foreign Affairs	**THONGLOUN Sisoulit**
Min. of Industry & Commerce	**NAM Vignaket**
Min. of Information & Culture	**MOUNKEO Olaboun**
Min. of Justice	**CHALEUAN Yapaoher**
Min. of Labor & Social Welfare	**ONECHANH Thammavong**
Min. of National Defense	**DOUANGCHAI Phichit,** *Maj. Gen.*
Min. of Public Health	**PONMEK Dalaloi,** *Dr.*
Min. of Public Security	**THONGBANH Sengaphone**
Min. to the Prime Minister's Office & Head of Public Administration & Civil Authority	**BOUNPHENG Mounphosay**
Min. to the Prime Minister's Office	**BOUASY Lovansay**
Min. to the Prime Minister's Office	**KHAM-OUANE Bouppha**
Min. to the Prime Minister's Office	**ONNEUA Phommachanh**
Min. to the Prime Minister's Office	**SAISENGLI Tengbliachu**
Min. & Chairman of National Mekong Committee	**KHAMLOUAD Sitlakone**
Min. & Chairman of National Tourism Authority	**SOMPHONG Mongkhonvilay**
Min. & Head of Cabinet, President's Office	**SOUBANH Sritthirath**
Min. & Head of Government Secretariats	**CHEUANG Sombounkhanh**
Min. & Head of Science, Technology, & Environment Agency	**BOUNTIEM Phitsamay**
Chmn. Planning & Investment Committee	**SOULIVONG Dalavong**
Chmn. State Control Commission	**ASANG Laoli,** *Maj. Gen.*
Governor, National Bank	**PHOUPHET Khamphounvong**
Ambassador to the US	**PHANTHONG Phommahaxay**
Permanent Representative to the UN, New York	**ALOUNKEO Kittikhoun**

EMBASSY OF THE LAO PEOPLE'S DEMOCRATIC REPUBLIC

Chancery: 2222 S Street, NW
Washington, DC 20008
Tel: (202) 332-6416

Fax: (202) 332-4923
National Holiday: National Day, December 2.

AS A TRADITIONAL SOCIETY until 1975, Laos was a conservative monarchy, dominated by a small number of powerful families. In 1975 it was transformed into a communist oligarchy, but its social makeup remained much the same. In the 600-year-old monarchy, the Lao king ruled from Louangphrabang (Luang Prabang), while in other regions there were families with royal pretensions rooted in the royal histories of Champasak (Bassac), Vientiane (Viangchan), and Xiangkhoang (Tran Ninh). They were surrounded by lesser aristocrats from prominent families who in turn became patrons to clients of lower status, thus building a complex network of allegiances. The king reigned from Louangphrabang but did not rule over much of the outlying regions of the country.

In December 1975, with the declaration of the Lao People's Democratic Republic (LPDR, or Laos), the king abdicated. Although Laos was reorganized as a communist "people's democracy," important vestiges of traditional political and social behavior remained. The aristocratic families were shorn of their influence, but a new elite with privileged access to the communist roots of power emerged, and clients of lower status have searched them out as patrons. In addition, some of the old families, who had links to the new revolutionary elite, managed to survive and wield significant influence. As newly dominant elites replaced the old, they demanded a similar deference.

Lao Loum, or lowland Lao, families continue to wield the greatest influence). Despite the rhetoric of the revolutionary elite concerning ethnic equality, Lao Theung, or midland Lao, and Lao Sung, or upland Lao, minorities are low on the scale of national influence, just as they were in pre1975 society. However, the power of the central government over the outlying regions has remained tenuous, still relying upon bargains with tribal chieftains to secure the loyalty of their peoples.

Although manifesting many of the characteristics of a traditional Lao monarchy dominated by a lowland Lao Buddhist elite, the country has exhibited many of the characteristics of other communist regimes. It has shown a similar heavy bureaucratic style, with emphasis within the bureaucracy on political training and long sessions of criticism and self-criticism for its civil servants. Laos imported from its Vietnamese mentor the concept of reeducation centers or "seminar camps," where, during the early years in power, thousands of former Royal Lao Government (RLG--see Glossary) adversaries were incarcerated. However, this communist overlay on traditional society has been moderated by two important factors: Lao Buddhism and government administrative incompetence in implementing socialist doctrine. Thus, what emerged in Laos has been a system aptly labeled by Prince Souvanna Phouma, former prime minister of the RLG, as "socialisme à la laotienne" (Lao-style socialism).

The mélange of traditional politics, accompanied by patronclient relations, with communist-style intra-institutional competition, has produced a unique political culture. Power centers tend to cluster around key personalities, and those in power become targets of opportunity for members of their extended family and friends

THE LAO PEOPLE'S REVOLUTIONARY PARTY

Whereas communist parties in the former Soviet Union and Eastern Europe have crumbled, in Laos, the ruling communist party, the Phak Pasason Pativat Lao (Lao People's Revolutionary Party-- LPRP; see Glossary) has retained undiluted political control. The constitution, adopted in August 1991, notes simply in Article 3 that the LPRP is the "leading nucleus" of the political system. LPRP statutes, revised following the Fifth Party Congress held in 1991, leave no doubt regarding the dominant role of the party:

The party is...the leading core of the entire political system, hub of intelligence, and representative of the interest of the people of all strata. The party formulates and revises the major lines and policies on national development in all spheres; finds solutions to major problems; determines the policies regarding personnel management, training of cadres, and supplying key cadres for different levels; controls and supervises activities of party cadres and members, state agencies and mass organizations.

ORIGINS OF THE PARTY

The LPRP has its roots in the Indochinese Communist Party (ICP), founded by Ho Chi Minh in 1930. (Ho Chi Minh led the struggle for Vietnamese independence and was the president of the Democratic Republic of Vietnam (North Vietnam) from 1945 until his death in 1969.) The ICP, composed entirely of Vietnamese members in its early years, formed the Committee for Laos (or a "Lao section") in 1936. Only in the mid-1940s did the Vietnamese communist revolutionaries step up active recruitment of Laotian members. In 1946 or early 1947, Kaysone Phomvihan, a law student at the University of Hanoi, was recruited, and Nouhak Phoumsavan, engaged in a trucking business in Vietnam, joined in 1947.

In February 1951, the Second Congress of the ICP resolved to disband the party and to form three separate parties representing the three states of Indochina. However, it was not until March 22, 1955, at the First Party Congress, that Phak Pasason Lao (Lao People's Party--LPP) was formally proclaimed. (The name LPRP was adopted at the Second Party Congress in 1972.) It seems likely that from 1951 to 1955, key Laotian former members of the ICP provided leadership for the "resistance" movement in Laos, under the tutelage of their Vietnamese senior partners. In 1956 the LPP founded the Neo Lao Hak Xat (Lao Patriotic Front--LPF) the political party of the Pathet Lao (Lao Nation--see Glossary), to act as the public mass political organization. Meanwhile, the LPP remained clandestine, directing the activities of the front.

The Vietnamese communists provided critical guidance and support to the growing party during the revolutionary period. They helped to recruit the leadership of the Laotian communist movement; from its inception, the LPRP Political Bureau (Politburo) was made up of individuals closely associated with the Vietnamese. The Vietnamese furnished facilities and guidance for training not only the top leadership but also the entire Laotian communist movement. The Vietnamese assigned advisers to the party, as well as to the military forces of the LPF. Under the guidance of North Vietnamese mentors, LPRP leaders shaped a Marxist-Leninist party, political and mass organizations, and an army and a bureaucracy, all based upon the North Vietnamese model.

From their perspective, Laotian communists had not compromised their legitimacy as a nationalist movement by their dependence on Hanoi. During the revolutionary period prior to 1975, when LPRP leaders looked to the North Vietnamese for a sense of overall direction and cohesion, they found many common interests. Both parties faced the same enemies: first France and then the United States. They held a similar view of the world and of the desirable solution to its problems. In some cases, this affinity was strengthened by family relations (for example, Kaysone, whose Vietnamese father, Luan Phomvihan, had been a secretary to the French resident in Savannakhét) or marriage ties (Souphanouvong and Nouhak had Vietnamese wives).

Following the First Party Congress, it was seventeen years until the Second Party Congress was convened, in February 1972. The Third Party Congress met ten years later, in April 1982; the Fourth Party Congress convened in November 1986, and the Fifth Party Congress in March 1991.

PARTY STRUCTURE

The LPP steadily grew from its initial 300 to 400 members ("25 delegates representing 300 to 400 members" were said to have attended the founding congress of the party). By 1965 there were 11,000 members; by 1972, as it prepared to enter into the final coalition with the RLG, it had grown to some 21,000 members; by 1975, when the party seized full power, it claimed a membership of 25,000; and by 1991, at the convening of the Fifth Party Congress, the LPRP claimed its membership had increased to 60,000.

The LPRP has been organized in a manner common to other ruling communist parties, with greatest similarity to the Vietnamese Communist Party. As in other such parties, the highest authority is the party congress, a gathering of party cadres from throughout the country that meets on an intermittent schedule for several days to listen to speeches, learn the plans for future party strategy, and ratify decisions already taken by the party leadership.

Next in the party hierarchy--since the elimination of the Secretariat in 1991--is the Central Committee, the party elite who fill key political positions throughout the country The Central Committee is charged with leading the party between congresses. In addition to members of the Politburo and former members of the Secretariat, the committee includes key government ministers, leading generals of the army, secretaries of provincial party committees, and chairpersons of mass organizations.

When the LPRP first revealed itself to the public in 1975, the Central Committee comprised twenty-one members and six alternates. By the Fourth Party Congress, its size had expanded to fifty-one members and nine alternates. The average age of a Central Committee member in 1986 was fifty-two, with the oldest seventy-seven and the youngest thirty-three. The number of women on the Central Committee rose from three to five, including Thongvin Phomvihan, then Secretary General Kaysone's wife, who was chair of the LPRP's People's Revolutionary Youth Union and, in 1982, the first woman appointed to the Central Committee.

At the Fifth Party Congress, the Central Committee stabilized in size at fifty-nine members and took on a few younger, more educated men to replace deceased or retired members. At the time, the oldest member was seventy-seven, the youngest thirty-five, with 22 percent over sixty, 30 percent between fifty and fifty-nine, and 40 percent under forty-nine. Only two women are full members of the Central Committee, and two continue as alternates. Thongvin Phomvihan--who had ranked thirty-fifth in 1986--was removed, accompanied by rumors of excessive political influence in her business activities. Notwithstanding this setback to Kaysone's family fortune, their son, Saisompheng Phomvihan, was appointed to the Central Committee, ranking forty-fifth, and was named governor of Savannakhét Province in 1993. This appointment inspired some private muttering about the emerging "princelings," referring as well to Souphanouvong's son, Khamsai Souphanouvong, number thirtyfour on the Central Committee, who became minister of finance.

Despite the party's rhetoric asserting ethnic equality, the Central Committee has been dominated by lowland Lao. Upland minorities remain sparsely represented at the highest levels of party leadership. Only four members of ethnic minority groups were reported on the Central Committee elected at the Fifth Party Congress.

The Central Committee is served by a number of subordinate committees. These committees include, most importantly, the Office of the Central Committee, and five other offices: Organization Committee; Propaganda and Training Committee; Party and State Control Committee; Administrative Committee of the Party and State School for Political Theory; and Committee for the Propagation of Party Policies.

Since 1972 the genuine center of political power, as in other communist parties, has resided in the Politburo. Membership of the Politburo, and formerly that of the Secretariat, is drawn from the Central Committee. A small group of men--seven in 1972 and eleven by 1993--have provided the critical leadership of the communist movement in Laos. A signal attribute of this group has been its remarkable cohesion and continuity. The Politburo has been dominated for more than fifteen years communist rule by the same stalwart band of revolutionary veterans. The twenty-five Laotian former members of the ICP who founded the LPP in 1955, and from whom the Politburo was drawn, remained in almost identical rank until illness and age began to take their toll in the 1980s. Kaysone was named secretary general of the then secret LPP upon its establishment, a post he retained until his death in 1992. Nouhak retained his number-two position on the Politburo into 1993. It was not until the Fifth Party Congress that Souphanouvong, Phoumi Vongvichit, and Sisomphone Lovansai (ranking third, fourth, and seventh, respectively) were retired with honorific titles as counselors to the Central Committee. Prime Minister Khamtai Siphandon was promoted to succeed Kaysone as chief of the party, and Phoun Sipaseut advanced a notch in rank. In 1991 the Politburo numbered ten, including only two new members.

Although the exact manner of Politburo decision making has never been revealed, a collegiality, based on long years of common experience, appears to have developed. In addition to their powerful position on the Politburo, members exercise additional political power--perhaps even more than in most other communist systems--through important posts within the governmental structure. In fact, for many years, five Politburo members also held seats on the Secretariat.

At the Fifth Party Congress, the party abolished the nineperson Secretariat of the Central Committee and changed the designation of the head of the party (Kaysone) from secretary general to chairman. Until it was abolished, the Secretariat wielded influence second only to that of the Politburo. The Secretariat issued party directives and acted on behalf of the Central Committee when it was not in session, in effect managing the day-to-day business of the party. Khamtai Siphandon became party chairman in November 1992, but it is not certain whether he will accrue the same power and influence as his predecessor.

Each of the sixteen provinces (*khoueng*--see Glossary) is directed by a party committee, chaired by a party secretary who is the dominant political figure in the province. At a lower level are 112 districts (*muang*--see Glossary), further divided into subdistricts (*tasseng*--see Glossary), each with their own party committees. Administratively, subdistricts have been abolished in principle since around 1993, but implementation has been uneven across provinces. It is unknown whether subdistrictlevel party committees have also been abolished. At the base of the country's administrative structure are more than 11,000 villages (*ban*--see Glossary), only some of which have party branches.

SEMISECRECY OF THE LAO PEOPLE'S REVOLUTIONARY PARTY

Unlike other communist regimes, the LPRP has long maintained a semisecrecy about its mode of operation and the identity of its rank-and-file members. However, the LPRP follows the standard communist practice of planting party members within all principal institutions of society--in government, in mass organizations, and, formerly, in agricultural collectives. These individuals serve as leaders and transmit party policy. They also act as the eyes and ears of the central party organization. Although party members are admonished not to reveal themselves, it is not difficult for knowledgeable persons to pick out the party members in their organization. In each ministry, for example, the key power wielders are party members. All party members do not, of course, hold positions of authority. Some occupy the lower ranks, serving, for example, as messengers, drivers, and maintenance personnel.

By the late 1980s, some of the LPRP's semisecrecy had eroded. Party leadership lists, which, during revolutionary and early postrevolutionary days had been secret, were published. But a quasi-clandestine attitude remains among the party rank and file that can be explained by several factors. Clandestine behavior is an old habit that is not easily shed. Secrecy adds to the party's mystery, inspires anxiety and fear, and contributes to control. In view of its long history of revolutionary activity, party veterans fear infiltration and subversion. LPRP pronouncements during its first decade of rule frequently alluded to "CIA and Thaireactionary -inspired agents," and later, when relations with China grew tense, to the danger of "big power hegemonism." Moreover, party leaders appear to lack confidence in the quality of their membership, speaking from time to time about "bad elements" within the party.

The LPRP is relatively small compared with other incumbent parties. For example, the 40,000 members that the party claimed in 1985 represented 1.1 percent of the population (estimating 3.5 million inhabitants). In 1979 the Vietnamese Communist Party had 1.5 million members in a population of 53 million, or approximately 3 percent.

IDEOLOGY OF THE LAO PEOPLE'S REVOLUTIONARY PARTY

When LPRP leaders came to power in 1975 as victorious revolutionaries guided by Marxism-Leninism, they retained a zeal for creating a "new socialist society and a new socialist man." They declared their twin economic goals as the achievement of "socialist transformation with socialist construction." They asserted that in establishing the LPDR in 1975, they had completed the "national democratic revolution." (The national goal had been to expel the French colonialists and the United States imperialists. The democratic goal was to overthrow "reactionary traitors, comprador bourgeoisie, bureaucrats, reactionaries, feudalists and militarists...."). The LPRP claimed that it had won the national democratic revolution by winning a "people's war" with a "worker-peasant" alliance, under the secret leadership of the LPRP working through a national front. It proclaimed a commitment to "proletarian internationalism" and the "law of Indochinese solidarity" and at the same time defined Vietnam and the Soviet Union as friends and the "unholy alliance" among United States imperialism, Chinese "great power hegemonism," and Thai militarism as enemies.

By the late 1980s, as communism was undergoing a radical transformation in the Soviet Union and Eastern Europe, Kaysone and his colleagues on the Politburo still professed an adherence to Marxism-Leninism, but they emphasized the necessity for Laos to pass through a stage of "state capitalism." Following Mikhail Gorbachev's example of perestroika, Kaysone proclaimed in 1989 that state enterprises were being severed from central direction and would be financially autonomous. V.I. Lenin's New Economic Policy was frequently cited to legitimize the movement toward a market economy and the necessity to stimulate private initiative.

By the early 1990s, even less of the Marxist-Leninist rhetoric remained. The party has continued to move internally toward more free-market measures and externally toward reliance upon the capitalist countries and the international institutions on which they depend for investment and assistance. The "law" of Indochinese solidarity has been amended, and the LPDR's "special relations" with its former senior partner are no longer invoked, even though party spokesmen still insist that Laos retains a solid friendship and "all-round cooperation" with Vietnam

Despite this erosion of communist ideology, retaining exclusive political power remains a primary goal of the party. In a speech in 1990, Secretary General Kaysone asserted the basis of legitimacy of the party: The party is the center of our wisdom. It has laid down the correct and constructive line, patterns, and steps compatible with realities in our country and hence has led the Lao people in overcoming difficulties and numerous tests to win victory after victory, until the final victory. History has shown that our party is the only party which has won the credibility and trust of the people. Our party's leadership in our country's revolution is an objective requirement and historic duty entrusted to it by the Lao multiethnic people. Other political parties which had existed in our country have dissolved in the process of historical transformation. They failed to win the control and support of the people because they did not defend the national interest or fight for the interests and aspirations of the people.

LEADERSHIP

INTERNAL STABILITY AND EXTERNAL INFLUENCES

Since the LPDR was proclaimed in December 1975, its leadership has been remarkably stable and cohesive. The record of continuous service at the highest ranks is equaled by few, if any, regimes in the contemporary world. Laotian leaders have an equally impressive record of unity. Although outside observers have scrutinized the leadership for factions--and some have postulated at various times that such factions might be divided along the lines of MarxistLeninist ideologues versus pragmatists or pro-Vietnamese versus nationalists (or pro-Chinese), there is no solid evidence that the leadership is seriously divided on any critical issues.

In 1975 the Laotian communist leaders, most of whom had spent the revolutionary decade from 1964 to 1974 operating from Pathet Lao headquarters in the caves of Sam Neua Province, came down from the mountains to Vientiane to direct the new government. At the outset of their accession to power, they were suspicious, secretive, and inaccessible, and lower-level cadres were maladroit in imposing heavy bureaucratic controls. Travel within the country was limited, personal and family behavior was monitored by newly organized revolutionary administrative committees, cadres were assigned to disseminate propaganda, and seminars were held to provide political education for all sorts of groups. During these early years, the party squandered much of the goodwill and friendly acceptance from a population tired of war and the corruption of the old regime.

At first, Laotian communist leaders were committed to fulfilling their revolutionary goals of fundamentally altering society through "socialist transformation and socialist construction." After 1979 the regime modified its earlier zealous pursuit of socialism and pursued more liberal economic and social policies, in much the same manner as Vietnam.

For more than a decade after 1975, the Vietnamese continued to exercise significant influence upon the Laotian leadership through a variety of party, military, and economic channels. By the end of the 1980s, however--in particular following the collapse of the Soviet Union and the Soviet bloc in 1991 and diminishing assistance from the Soviet Union to Vietnam and Laos--Vietnam turned inward to concentrate on its own problems of development. This emboldened Laotians leaders to jettison even more of their socialist ideological baggage, abandon agricultural collectivization, and move toward a market economy. Laos was also free to pursue an independent foreign policy. The single most important vestige of the former communist system was the solitary ruling party, the LPRP.

THE CONSTITUTION

DEVELOPMENT OF THE CONSTITUTION

On August 14, 1991, sixteen years after the establishment of the LPDR, the Supreme People's Assembly (SPA), the country's highest legislative organ, adopted a constitution. Although the SPA had been charged with drafting a constitution in 1975, the task had low priority. It was not until the Third Party Congress that party Secretary General Kaysone stated that the LPRP should "urgently undertake the major task...of preparing a socialist constitution at an early date." Laotian press reports subsequently revealed that a constitutional drafting committee was working informally under the chairmanship of Politburo member Sisomphone Lovansai, a specialist in party organization, with the help of East German advisers. Despite the proclaimed urgency of the task, only on May 22, 1984, did the SPA Standing Committee formalize the appointment of Sisomphone to head a fifteen-person drafting committee.

Although the political institutions had functioned without a written constitution for fifteen years, the lack of a constitution created serious drawbacks for the country. International development agencies were reluctant to invest in Laos given the absence of a fixed, knowable law. Amnesty International, in a 1985 report on Laos, asserted that without a constitution or published penal and criminal codes, citizens were "effectively denied proper legal guarantees of their internationally recognized human rights." Even the party newspaper, Xieng *Pasason* (Voice of the People), commenting in June 1990 on the absence of a constitution and a general body of laws, acknowledged that "having no laws is... a source of injustice and violation, thus leading to a breakdown of social order and peace, the breeding of anarchy, and the lack of democracy."

Reasons for the leisurely pace of constitution drafting, unusually slow even for the plodding bureaucracy, were not readily apparent. Vietnam had adopted a revised constitution in 1980 and Cambodia in 1981, only two years after the ouster of the Khmer Rouge. According to some reports, progress in Laos had been blocked by differences within the Politburo over certain substantive clauses. Perhaps most important, the party leadership, accustomed to rule without question, may have assigned a low priority to producing a document that might eventually lead to challenging their authority, despite rhetoric to the contrary. Further, the public seemed not to care.

After the new SPA was elected in March 1989, it formally appointed a seventeen-member constitutional drafting committee. The National Radio of Laos reported that the drafting committee was working "under the close supervision of the Political Bureau and the Secretariat of the Party Central Committee." Six members of the drafting committee were members of the Central Committee; two of these members also served on the SPA, which also had six members on the drafting committee.

In April 1990, after securing approval of its document from the LPRP Politburo and the Secretariat, the SPA finally made public the draft constitution. With its publication, the party Central Committee issued Directive Number 21, on April 30, 1990, calling for discussion of the draft, first among party and government officials and then among the public. The discussions, although orchestrated by party cadres, did not always please party authorities. An LPRP spokesman released a memo complaining that "people in many major towns" had dwelled too much on what the constitution had to say about the organization of the state. In June a member of the Central Committee cautioned against demonstrations to "demand a multiparty system" and warned that demonstrators would be arrested. Competing parties would not be tolerated, he asserted, adding that "our multi-ethnic Lao people have remained faithfully under the leadership of the LPRP." In a later pronouncement, he said that "the Party has proved to the people in the last 35 years that it is the only party that can take care of them" and he lectured that "too many parties invite division." A Central Committee directive, dated June 14, 1990, hinted at the quality of the public discussion, noting that "in many cases where people were convoked to a meeting, they were simply given question and answer sheets to study."

However, not all discussions of the draft constitution were perfunctory. Undoubtedly inspired by the examples of Eastern Europe and the Soviet Union--where the monopoly of power by communist parties had crumbled--a group of some forty government officials and intellectuals began criticizing the country's one-party system in a series of letters and meetings in April 1990. Organized in the unofficial "Social Democratic Club," the group called for a multiparty system in Laos. One member of the group, an assistant to the minister of science and technology, submitted a letter of resignation to Prime Minister Kaysone in which he labeled Laos a "communist monarchy" and a "dynasty of the Politburo" declaring that the country should "change into a multi-party system in order to bring democracy, freedom and prosperity to the people."

Criticism of the draft document gathered strength in the succeeding months; Laotian students in Paris, Prague, and Warsaw joined in the call for free elections. Criticism broadened as a group of young, educated party cadres associated with nonparty bureaucrats--many educated in France and Canada--targeted veteran party leaders. These groups charged that the new policies of the old guard were fostering corruption and increased social and economic inequality. It was not until October 1990 that the government finally cracked down on these calls for democratic reforms, with the arrest of several protesters, including a former vice minister in the State Planning Commission and a director in the Ministry of Justice who were sentenced to long prison terms in Houaphan.

Thus, although the constitution purports to guarantee freedom of speech and petition and its framers give lip service to the desirability of public discussion, the ruling party sent a clear message with these arrests that it will not tolerate challenges to its exclusive exercise of power. Veteran party leaders were clearly more impressed by the political models of Vietnam and China than by the examples of Eastern Europe and the Soviet Union. Although willing to experiment with economic liberalization, party leaders seemed determined to retain political domination--if they could-- through a Leninist-style party.

HIGHLIGHTS OF THE CONSTITUTION

The 1991 constitution, which contains elements of an earlier revolutionary orthodoxy, is clearly influenced by the economic and political liberalization within Laos, as well as by the dramatic changes in the socialist world and the international balance of forces. The constitution specifies the functions and powers of the various organs of government and defines the rights and duties of citizens. Several chapters prescribing the structure of the state define the function and powers of the National Assembly (the renamed SPA), the president, the government, the local administration, and the judicial system. The constitution has little to say, however, about the limitations on government. In foreign policy, the principles of peaceful coexistence are followed.

The constitution legally establishes a set of authorities that resemble the traditional differentiation among executive, legislative, and judicial branches of government. The delineation does not imitate any particular model (neither Vietnamese, nor Russian, nor French), but it pays respect to the idea of a basic blueprint of responsibilities lodged in designated institutions. There is room for evolution of government authority, but there are also specific boundaries.

Government outside Vientiane has developed an independence over the years, reflecting the exigencies of the Pathet Lao armed struggle and of economic self-reliance during the postwar socialist pitfalls. The constitution eliminated elected people's councils at the provincial and district level as "no more necessary," in an effort to fit the state apparatus to the needs of building and developing the regime under "the actual conditions of the country." Again, the will of the ruling party determines which road the administration follows in regard to local governance, but the constitution has left governors, mayors, and district and village chiefs free to "administer their regions and localities without any assistance from popularly elected bodies." The leading role of the party within the administration of the nation overall is illustrated by the fact that party Politburo members are found in state offices--the offices of the president of state, and prime minister, deputy prime ministers (two), chair of the National Assembly, minister of defense, and chair of the Party and State Inspection Board.

The first words of the Preamble refer to the "multi-ethnic Lao people," and frequent use of this term is made throughout the text, a clear rhetorical attempt to promote unity within an ethnically diverse society. The "key components" of the people are specified as workers, farmers, and intellectuals. The Preamble celebrates a revolution carried out "for more than 60 years" under the "correct leadership" of the ICP.

The dominant role played by the LPRP, however, is scarcely mentioned, and the constitution is almost silent about the party's functions and powers. One brief reference to the ruling party is made in Article 3, which states that the "rights of the multiethnic people to be the masters of the country are exercised and ensured through the functioning of the political system with the Lao People's Revolutionary Party as its leading nucleus."

Article 5 notes that the National Assembly and all other state organizations "function in accordance with the principle of democratic centralism." This stricture is an obvious reference to the Marxist-Leninist principle, which calls for open discussion within a unit but prescribes that the minority must accede to the will of the majority, and lower echelons must obey the decisions of higher ones.

Article 7 calls upon mass organizations, such as the Lao Front for National Construction, the Federation of Trade Unions, the People's Revolutionary Youth Union, and the Federation of Women's Unions, to "unite and mobilize the people." The Lao Front for National Construction, the successor to the LPF, served as the political front for the party during the revolutionary struggle. As of mid-1994, its mandate is to mobilize political support and raise political consciousness for the party's goals among various organizations, ethnic groups, and social classes within society. Other mass organizations are assigned to pursue these goals among their target populations of workers, youths, and women.

The constitution proclaims that the state will respect the "principle of equality among ethnic tribes," which have the right to promote "their fine customs and culture." Further, the state is committed to upgrading the "socio-economy of all ethnic groups."

Regarding religion, the state "respects and protects all lawful activities of the Buddhists and of other religious followers." Buddhist monks and other clergy are reminded that the state encourages them to "participate in the activities which are beneficial to the country.

The chapter on the socioeconomic system does not mention the establishment of socialism, a principal goal of earlier dogma. Instead, the objective of economic policy is to transform the "natural economy into a goods economy." Private property appears to be assured by the statement that the "state protects the right of ownership," including the right of transfer and inheritance. The state is authorized to undertake such tasks as managing the economy, providing education, expanding public health, and caring for war veterans, the aging, and the sick. The constitution admonishes that "all organizations and citizens must protect the environment."

A chapter on the rights and obligations of citizens sets forth a cluster of well-known rights found in modern constitutions, including freedom of religion, speech, press, and assembly. Women and men are proclaimed equal, and all citizens can vote at age eighteen and hold office at twenty-one. In return, citizens are obliged to respect the laws, pay taxes, and defend the country, which includes military service. In commenting on this chapter in 1990, Amnesty International, clearly concerned about past human rights abuses, criticized the document for what was *not* included. Amnesty International noted the absence of provisions for protecting the right to life, abolishing the death penalty, guaranteeing the inalienability of fundamental rights, prohibiting torture, safeguarding against arbitrary arrest and detention, protecting people deprived of their liberty, and providing for a fair trial. No safeguards exist to protect the rights to freedom of opinion and expression, peaceful assembly and association, and independence of the judiciary.

Laos is made up of provinces, municipalities, districts, and villages. The constitution gives no clear guidance on provincial and district responsibilities except to specify that the leaders at each echelon must ensure the implementation of the constitution and the law and must carry out decisions taken by a higher level. In spite of the party's inclination to centralize decision making, provinces and localities have enjoyed a surprising degree of autonomy in shaping social policy. This independence is partly due to limited resources and poor communications with Vientiane. But the central government has also encouraged direct contacts along the borders with China, Thailand, and Vietnam, and trading agreements with neighboring jurisdictions.

Although it is unlikely that the constitution will immediately change the imbedded patterns of the Laotian political system or threaten the dominant role of the party, it has the potential to protect human rights and respect for the law, by the rulers as well as the ruled. The crumbling of communist regimes in Eastern Europe and the Soviet Union as well as strains in communist systems elsewhere, accompanied by widespread movements for democracy, suggest that Laos will not be immune to growing demands for a more dependable rule of law.

LAOS ELECTORAL SYSTEM - STRATEGIC INFORMATION AND DEVELOPMENTS

ELECTIONS IN LAOS - BASIC INFORMATION

ELECTORAL SYSTEM

Constituencies:
18 multi-member (2 to 11 seats) constituencies.

Voting system:
Party-list simple majority vote.
Vacancies arising between general elections are filled through by-elections.

Voter requirements:
- age: 18 years
- Lao citizenship

Eligibility:
- age: 21 years
- Lao citizenship
- ineligibility: insanity, deprivation of civil and political rights by court decision

Incompatibilities:
(not applicable)

Candidacy requirements:
- support of local committees or mass organizations

Laos elects a legislature nationally and the public also participates in the election of village heads. The **National Assembly** (*Sapha Heng Xat*) has 149 members, elected for five year terms.

Laos is a one-party state. According to the constitution, elections are in accordance with the principles of Democratic Centralism and the Lao People's Revolutionary Party serves as the "Leading nucleus" of the political system.

The last elections were held on March 20th, 2016. The Lao People's Revolutionary Party (LPRP) took 144 seats in the 149-member National Assembly while the five remaining seats went to independents. Nearly 73% of members were elected to the National Assembly for the first time. During the election campaign, many candidates focused on development, promising to serve the interests of the nation and the people.

ELECTORAL PROCESS: 0 / 12

The 1991 constitution makes the LPRP the sole legal political party and grants it a leading role at all levels of government. The party's 61-member Central Committee and 11-member Politburo make all major decisions. Legislative elections are held every five years but elections are not considered free and fair. The LPRP vets all candidates for election to the National Assembly, whose members elect the president. In 2011 the legislature increased in size from 115 members to 132. International observers have not been permitted to monitor elections.

POLITICAL PLURALISM AND PARTICIPATION: 0 / 16

The constitution prohibits political parties other than the LPRP. National Assembly candidates are not required to be members of the LPRP, but all candidates have to be approved by Assembly-appointed committees and in practice almost all are members of the party.

Ethnic minorities and women are represented in the Politburo, Central Committee, and National Assembly. However, village-level leadership is responsible for many of the decisions affecting daily life and fewer than 3 percent of village chiefs are women.

LATEST ELECTION

Summary of 20 March 2016 National Assembly of Laos election results

	Seats
Lao People's Revolutionary Party (Phak Paxaxôn Pativat Lao)	144
Non-partisans	5
Total	149

LAO PEOPLE'S REVOLUTIONARY PARTY

General Secretary	Bounnhang Vorachith
Founded	22 March 1955
Headquarters	Vientiane
Newspaper	Pasason
Youth wing	Lao People's Revolutionary Youth Union
Armed Wing	Lao People's Armed Forces
Membership (2011)	191,700
Ideology	Communism Marxism–Leninism Pro-Vietnam
National affiliation	Lao Front for National Construction
International affiliation	International Meeting of Communist and Workers' Parties International Communist Seminar
National Assembly	128 / 132

The **Lao People's Revolutionary Party** formerly the **Lao People's Party**, is a Marxist-Leninist political party in Laos and has emerged from the Communist Party of Indochina founded by Ho Chi Minh in 1930. It has governed in Laos since 1975. The policy-making organs are the Politburo, Secretariat and the Central Committee. A party congress, which elects members to the politburo and central committee, is held every five years. The congress used to also elect a secretariat, but this body was abolished in 1991. As of 2016, 128 of the 132 members of the National Assembly of Laos were from the Lao People's Revolutionary Party.

The party has its origins in the Communist Party of Indochina founded by Ho Chi Minh in 1930 (see Communist Party of Vietnam). The ICP was entirely Vietnamese at its inception but grew throughout French Indochina and was able to found a small "Lao section" in 1936. In the mid-1940s, a campaign to recruit Laotian members was instigated and in 1946 or 1947, Kaysone Phomvihan, a law student at the University of Hanoi, was recruited, along with Nouhak Phoumsavan.

In February 1951, the Second Congress of the ICP resolved to disband the party and to form three separate parties representing the three states of Indochina. In reality, the ICP was a Vietnamese organization and the separate parties created were dominated by the Vietnamese parties regardless of their national affiliations.

For instance, in February 1951, only 81 of the 2,091 ICP members were Lao. A movement known as the Pathet Lao (Land of Laos) was founded and Prince Souphanouvong became its figurehead leader. It was in theory a communist resistance movement meant to fight alongside the Viet Minh against French colonialism during the first Indochina War, but it never really fought much of anyone and was organized as a reserve organization of the Viet Minh. On March 22, 1955, at its First Party Congress, the clandestine Lao's People's Party or *Phak Pasason Lao* was officially proclaimed. The First Party Congress was attended by 25 delegates representing a party membership of 300 to 400. The Party Congress was supervised and organized by the Vietnamese. The Central Committee of the Party included Kaysone Phomvihane, Nouhak Phoumsavan, Bun Phommahaxay, Sisavath Keobounphanh, Khamseng (May 1955, supplemented Souphanouvong, Phoumi Vongvichit, Phoun Sipaseut and 1956 supplemented Sisomphon Lovansay, Khamtay Siphandone).

The LPP and its successor, the LPRP, kept their existence secret until 1975, preferring to direct their activities through fronts such as the Pathet Lao.

In 1956, a legal political wing of the Pathet Lao, the Lao Patriotic Front (*Neo Lao Hak Xat*), was founded and participated in several coalition governments. In the 1960s the North Vietnam-controlled Pathet Lao were given tasks in Vietnamese-occupied areas of Laos. The Pathet Lao participated in a war between their North Vietnamese backers and the U.S.-backed Laotian government. Never very successful on their own, the party still gained power indirectly by North Vietnamese control in the northern and eastern sectors of the country. The Pathet Lao were never a particularly strong military force unless supported directly by the North Vietnamese army.

In February 1972, at the Second Party Congress, the name of the Lao's People's Party was changed to the Lao People's Revolutionary Party.

In 1973, a peace agreement was signed that brought the Pathet Lao into the government and was supposed to result in the Vietnamese leaving the country. The Vietnamese army did not leave. In early 1975, the Pathet Lao and North Vietnamese began attacking government outposts again. Without the support of the US, the anticommunist elements in the government had little choice other than to gradually allow the Pathet Lao to take power. In the spring of 1975 Pathet Lao forces consolidated their power throughout the country. The royal government fell in May 1975 and the LPRP took power. The LPRP on taking power showed itself to be closely connected to Vietnam. The LPRP signed a treaty of friendship which allowed People's Army of Vietnam units to base themselves in Laos and also brought political advisors from Vietnam into the country. The LPRP economically isolated Laos by cutting off trade with all neighboring countries except for Vietnam.

When the LPRP first revealed itself to the public in 1975, the Central Committee comprised twenty-one members and six alternates. By the Fourth Party Congress, its size had expanded to fifty-one members and nine alternates. The average age of a Central Committee member in 1986 was fifty-two, with the oldest seventy-seven and the youngest thirty-three. The number of women on the Central Committee rose from three to five, including Thongvin Phomvihan, then General Secretary Kaysone's wife, who was chair of the LPRP's People's Revolutionary Youth Union and, in 1982, the first woman appointed to the Central Committee.

In 1979, the Lao Front for National Construction was founded to extend the reach of the LPRP in society, with a particular emphasis on governmental and cultural participation.

The Third Party Congress did not meet until April 1982. Since then Party Congresses have been more regular with the Fourth Party Congress being held in November 1986, and the Fifth Party Congress in March 1991 with further congresses every four or five years since then.

In 1986, during the period in which many socialist states were beginning to change their domestic market policies, Kaysone propounded the New Economic Mechanism, invoking Lenin, but soon moved control of state enterprises to autonomous firms, and by 1989, edged more deliberately toward a market economy.

The LPRP has shown itself to be remarkably resilient. Transitions of power have tended to be smooth, the new generation of leaders has proven more open to reform, and the Politburo now has some ethnic diversity. Organised opposition to the LPRP is weak.

The 10th Party Congress was held in Vientiane from 18 to 22 January 2016. At that Congress, Boungnang Vorachit was elected as the new Secretary General on 22 January 2016 - ending a 25-year long vacancy since the office was retitled from the former office of the Party Chairman.

PARTY STRUCTURE

From a membership of a few hundred at its founding the party grew to 11,000 members by 1965 and 21,000 members by 1972. When the party seized power in 1975 it claimed a membership of 25,000; and by 1991, at the convening of the Fifth Party Congress, the LPRP claimed its membership had increased to 60,000 or just over 1% of the population.

The Central Committee of the party was composed of 21 members and 6 alternates in 1975. This expanded to 51 members and 9 alternates by 1986 and 59 members in 1991.

The Politburo is the centre of political power in the party with its membership drawn from and chosen by the Central Committee. The Politburo consisted of seven members in 1972 growing to eleven members by 1993.

At the Fifth Party Congress, the party abolished the nineperson Secretariat of the Central Committee and changed the designation of the head of the party (Kaysone) from general secretaryl to chairman. Until it was abolished, the Secretariat wielded influence second only to that of the Politburo.

Kaysone Phomvihan was the party's general secretary from its founding in 1955 and remained the party's key figure until his death in 1992. His title changed to Party Chairman in 1991. Nouhak Phoumsavan was the second most powerful figure in the party from the party's founding until Kaysone's death, when he became the party's titular leader.

Khamtai Siphandon succeeded Nouhak Phoumsavan in 1998 (although some accounts have him succeeding Kaysone in 1992). Other recent leading figures have included Sisavath Keobounphanh and Samane Vignaket. Choummaly Sayasone led the party from 2006 to 2016, and Bounnhang Vorachit has been party leader since 2016.

Members of the LPRP Politburo have taken the offices of Party's Secretary-General and State President, Vice President, Chairman of the National Assembly and Prime Minister.

Politburo of the Central Committee (elected at the 10th Party Congress)

1. Boungnang Vorachit (Secretary-General of the Party, President of Laos)
2. Thongloun Sisoulith (Prime Minister)
3. Pany Yathotou (Chairwoman of the National Assembly)
4. Bounthong Chitmany (President of the Party Central Inspection Committee, Deputy Prime Minister, President of the Government Inspection Authority and Head of the Anti-Corruption Organisation)
5. Phankham Viphavan (Standing Member of the Party CC Secretariat, Vice President of Laos)
6. Chansy Phosikham (Head of the Party's Central Organisation Commission)
7. Xaysomphone Phomvihane (President of Lao Front for National Construction)
8. Lt. Gen Chansamone Chanyalath (Minister of National Defence)

9. Khamphanh Phommathat (Head of Office of the Party Central Committee)
10. Sinlavong Khoutphaythoune (Secretary of the Party Committee, Mayor of Vientiane)
11. Sonesay Siphandone (Deputy Prime Minister)

Secretariat of the Central Committee (elected at the 10th Party Congress)

1. Bounnhang Vorachith (Secretary General)
2. Bounthong Chitmany (President of the Party Central Inspection Committee, Deputy Prime Minister)
3. Phankham Viphavan (Standing Member of the Party CC Secretariat, Vice President of Laos)
4. Chansy Phosikham (Head of the Party's Central Organisation Commission)
5. Khamphanh Phommathat (Head of Office of the Party Central Committee)
6. Lt Gen Sengnouane Xayalath (Vice President of the National Assembly)
7. Kikeo Khaykhamphithoune (Head of the Party's Commission for Propaganda and Training)
8. Maj Gen Somkeo Silavong (Minister of Public Security)
9. Maj Gen Vilay Lakhamfong (Deputy Minister of National Defence)

The party operates according to the principles of democratic centralism. Due to the covert nature of the party in its first two decades it remains semi-secret in its operations though it is becoming more open as a new generation takes control.

IDEOLOGY

The LPRP is a Marxist-Leninist party patterned after the Vietnamese Communist Party and strongly influenced by the Soviet Union and the USSR's Communist Party. In the late 1980s the party attempted to follow the example of Gorbachev's perestroika reforms by introducing market measures and reducing controls over state run enterprises as well as abandoning attempts at agricultural collectivisation. These reforms were expanded in the 1990s. However, the Laotian party was reluctant to follow the Soviet example of glasnost and has avoided loosening the party's political monopoly in the country or allowing for a free press.

During Choummaly Sayasone's visit to China in 2011, he stated that Laos would increase the scale of its cooperation with China and increase the number of exchange students between two parties' party schools to learn more from China.

LEADERS

- Kaysone Phomvihane (1955–1991)
- Khamtai Siphandon (1991–2006)
- Choummaly Sayasone (2006–2016)
- Boungnang Vorachit (2016–present)

IMPORTANT LAWS AND REGULATIONS AFFECTING ELECTORAL PROCESS

CONSTITUTION OF THE LAO PEOPLE'S DEMOCRATIC REPUBLIC[2]

PREAMBLE

The multi-ethnic Lao people have existed and developed on this beloved land for thousands of years. More than six centuries ago, during the time of Chao Fa Ngum, our ancestors, founded the unified Lane Xang country and built it into a prosperous land. Since the 18th century, the Lao land had been repeatedly threatened and invaded by outside powers. Our people had enhanced the heroic and unyielding traditions of their ancestors and continually and persistently fought to gain independence and freedom.

Over the past 60 years, under the correct leadership of the former Indochinese Communist Party and the present Lao People's Revolutionary Party, the multi-ethnic Lao people have carried out difficult and arduous struggles full of great sacrifices until they managed to crush the yokes of domination and oppression of the colonialists and feudalist regime, completely liberated the country and established the Lao People's Democratic Republic on 2 December 1975; thus opening a new era – an era of genuine independence for the country and freedom for the people.

During the past years, our people have been together implementing the two strategic tasks of defending and building the country, thereby achieving satisfactory results in the initial stage.

Now, at this new period, the social life requires that the state must have a Constitution. This Constitution is the Constitution of the People's Democratic Regime in our country. It recognises the great achievements gained by our people in the cause of struggles for national liberation and construction and defines the political regime, the socio-economic system, the rights and obligations of citizens and the system of organisation of state apparatuses in the new period. This is the first time in the history of our nation the rights to mastery of the people have been defined in the fundamental law of the country.

This Constitution is the fruit of the process of the people's discussions throughout the country. It reflects the long-standing aspirations and strong determination of the national community to strive together to fulfill the objective of building Laos a country of peace, independence, democracy, unity and prosperity.

CHAPTER I THE POLITICAL REGIME

---

[2] Adopted by The 6th Session of the People's Supreme Assembly (2nd Legislature) Vientiane, 13 - 15 August 1991

Article 1. The Lao People's Democratic Republic is an independent country with sovereignty and territorial integrity covering both territorial waters and airspace. It is a unified country belonging to all multi-ethnic people and is indivisible.

Article 2. The state of the Lao People's Democratic Republic is a People's Democratic State. All powers are of the people, by the people and for the interests of the multi-ethnic people of all strata in society with the workers, farmers and intellectuals as key components.

Article 3. The rights of the multi-ethnic people to be the masters of the country are exercised and ensured through the functioning of the political system with the Lao People's Revolutionary Party as its leading nucleus.

Article 4. The National Assembly is the organisation of the people's representatives. The election of members of the National Assembly shall be carried out through the principles of universal, equal and direct suffrage, and secret balloting.
Voters have the right to propose the dismissal of their own representatives if they are found to behave unfit to their honour and to lose the people's confidence.

Article 5. The National Assembly and all other state organisations are established and function in accordance with the principle of democratic centralism.

Article 6. The state protects the freedom and democratic rights of the people which cannot be violated by anyone. All state organisations and functionaries must popularise and propagate all policies, regulations and laws among the people and, together with the people, organise their implementations in order to guarantee the legitimate rights and interests of the people. All acts of bureaucratism and harassment that can be physically harmful to the people and detrimental to their honour, lives, consciences and property are prohibited.

Article 7. The Lao Front for National Constitution, the Lao Federation of Trade Union, the Lao People's Revolutionary Youth Union, the Lao Women's Union and other social organisations are the organs to unite and mobilise all strata of the multi-ethnic people for taking part in the tasks of national defence and construction; develop the rights to mastership of the people and protect the legitimate rights and interests of members of their respective organisations.

Article 8. The state pursues the policy of promoting unity and equality among all ethnic groups. All ethnic groups have the rights to protect, preserve, and promote the fine customs and cultures of their own tribes and of the nation. All acts of creating division and discrimination among ethnic groups are prohibited. The state implements every measure to gradually develop and upgrade the levels of socio-economy of all ethnic groups.

Article 9. The state respects and protects all lawful activities of the Buddhists and of other religious followers mobilises and encourages the Buddhist monks and novices as well as the priests of other religions to participate in the activities which are beneficial to the country and people. All acts of creating division of religions and classes of people are prohibited.

Article 10. The state manages the society by the provisions of the Constitution and laws. All party and state organisations, mass organisations, social organisations and all citizens must function within the bounds of the Constitution and laws.

Article 11. The state implements the policy of national defence and security with the participation of all people in all aspects. The national defence and security forces must enhance their loyalty to the country and people ; carry out the duty to protect the gains of the revolution, the lives, property and labour of the people ; and contribute to the tasks of national development.

Article 12. The Lao People's Democratic Republic pursues the foreign policy of peace, independence, friendship and cooperation; and promotes the relations and cooperation with all countries on the basis of the principles of peaceful coexistence ; respect for - each other's independence, sovereignty and territorial integrity; non-interference in each other's internal affairs ; equality and mutual inerests. The Lao People's Democratic Republic supports the struggle of the world people for peace, national independence, democracy, and social progress.

CHAPTER II THE SOCIO - ECONOMIC SYSTEM

Article 13. The economic system of the Lao People's Democratic Republic relies on the multi-sectoral economy with the objective of expanding production and broadening the circulation of goods, and transforming the natural economy into a goods economy in order to increasingly develop the bases of national economy and improve the material and spiritual living conditions of the multi- ethnic people.

Article 14. The state protects and expands all forms of state, collective and individual ownership, as well as private ownership of domestic capitalists and foreigners who make investments in the Lao People's Democratic Republic. The state encourages all economic sectors to compete and cooperate with one another in expanding their production and business. All economic sectors are equal before law.

Article 15. The state protects the right to ownership (rights to governing, rights to using to transferring) and the rights to inherit property of organisations and individuals. As for the land which is under the ownership of the national community, the state ensures the rights to using, transferring, and inheriting it in accordance with the law.

Article 16. The economic management is carried out in line with the mechanism of market economy with the adjustment by the state, implementing the principle of promoting the centralised, unified management of the central branches in combination with the division of managerial responsibility for localities.

Article 17. All organisations and citizens must protect the environment and natural resources: land, underground, forests, fauna, water sources and atmosphere.

Article 18. The state promotes and gives advice on the development of economic relations, under many forms, with foreign countries on the basis of the principle of respect for each other's independence, sovereignty, equality, and mutual benefits.

Article 19. The state pays attention to developing education in combination with the building of the new generation to be good citizens. The objectives of the educational, cultural and scientific activities are to raise the level of knowledge, the patriotic spirit, the spirit of cherishing the People's Democratic Regime, the spirit of maintaining unify and harmony among the people of various ethnic groups ; enhance the sense of being masters of the country ; and implement the compulsory education system at primary levels. The state authorises the operation of private schools which function under the curricula of the state. The state together with the people build schools at all levels to turn education into a comprehensive system ; and pay attention to developing education in the areas where the ethnic minority people reside.

The state develops and expands the fine, traditional culture of the nation in combination with adopting the progressive culture of the world ; eliminates all negative phenomena in the ideological and cultural spheres; promotes culture, art, literature and information activities, including in mountainous areas ; and protects the antiques and shrines of the nation.

Article 20. The state pays attention to expanding the public health service, allows private individuals to operate medical services in accordance with state regulations. The state promotes the expansion of sports, gymnastics, and tourism ; pays attention to taking cares of disabled combatants, families of those who have sacrificed their lives and who have committed good deeds for the nation, and pensioners.

The State pays attention to pursuing the policy toward mothers and children.

CHAPTER III FUNDAMENTAL RIGHTS AND OBLIGATIONS OF THE CITIZEN

Article 21. Lao citizens are the persons who hold Lao nationality as prescribed by law.

Article 22. Lao citizens irrespective of their sex, social status, education, faith and ethnic groups are all equal before the law.

Article 23. Lao citizens 18 years of age and over have the right to vote and the right to be elected at the age of 21 and over except insane persons and the persons whose rights to vote and to be elected have been revoked by a court.

Article 24. Citizens of both sexes enjoy equal rights in the political, economic, cultural and social fields and family affairs.

Article 25. Lao citizens have the right to receive education.

Article 26. Lao citizens have the right to work and engage in occupations which are not against the law. Working people have the right to rest, to receive medical treatment in time of ailment to receive assistance in case of incapacity and disability, in old age, and other cases as prescribed by law.

Article 27. Lao citizens have the freedom of settlement and movement as prescribed by law. Article 28. Lao citizens have the right to lodge complaints and petitions and to propose ideas with state organisations concerned in connection with issues pertaining to the right and interests of both collectives and individuals. Complaints, petitions and ideas of citizens must be considered for solution as prescribed by law.

Article 29. The right of Lao citizens in their bodies and houses are inviolable. Lao citizens cannot be arrested or searched without warrant or approval of the authorized organisations, except in the cases as prescribed by law.

Article 30. Lao citizens have the right and freedom to believe or not to believe in religions.

Article 31. Lao citizens have the right and freedom of speech, press and assembly; and have the right to set up associations and to stage demonstrations which are not contrary to the law.

Article 32. Lao citizens have the right and freedom to conduct study and to apply advanced sciences, techniques and technologies; to create artistic and literary works and to engage in cultural activities which are not contrary to the law.

Article 33. The state protects the legitimate rights and interests of Lao citizens residing abroad.

Article 34. Lao citizens have the obligations to respect the Constitution and laws, and to observe labour discipline, the regulations in carrying out livelihood in society, and the regulations and order of the country.

Article 35. Lao citizens have the obligations to pay taxes and duties in accordance with the law.

Article 36. Lao citizens have the obligations to defend the country, to maintain the people's security and to fulfill military obligations as prescribed by law.

Article 37. The aliens and persons having no nationality have the right to enjoy their rights and freedom protected by the provisions of laws of the Lao People's Democratic Republic. They have the right to lodge petitions with courts and other organisations concerned of the Lao People's Democratic Republic and the obligations to respect the Constitution and laws of the Lao People's Democratic Republic.

Article 38. The Lao People's Democratic Republic grants asylum to foreigners who are persecuted for their struggle for freedom, justice, peace and scientific causes.

CHAPTER IV THE NATIONAL ASSEMBLY

Article 39. The National Assembly is the legislative organisation. It has the right to make decisions on the fundamental issues of the country. At the same time, it is the organisation which supervises and oversees the activities of the administrative and judicial organisations:

Article 40. The National Assembly has the following rights and duties:
1. To establish, endorse or amend the Constitution;
2. To consider, endorse, amend, or abrogate laws;
3. To determine, change, or abolish taxes and duties;
4. To consider and approve the strategic plans of socio-economic development and budget of the state;
5. To elect or remove the President of state and the Vice- President of state on the recommendation of the National Assembly Standing Committee;
6. To consider and approve the appointment or removal of the members of the government on the recommendation of the President of State;
7. To elect or remove the President of the People's Supreme Court and the Public Prosecutor-General on the recommendation of the National Assembly Standing Committee;
8. To decide on the establishment or dissolution of the ministries, ministry-equivalent organisations, provinces and municipalities and to determine the boundaries of provinces and municipalities on the recommendation of the Prime Minister;
9. To decide on granting general amnesties;
10. To decide on the ratification or abolition of treaties and agreements signed with foreign countries in accordance with international law and regulations;
11. To decide on matters of war or peace;
12. To supervise the observance of the Constitution and laws;
13. To exercise other rights and execute other duties as prescribed by law.

Article 41. Members of the National Assembly are elected by the Lao citizens in accordance with the provisions stipulated in the law.

The term of office the National Assembly is five years.

The election of the new National Assembly must be held not later than two months prior to the expiration of the term of office of the incumbent National Assembly.

In the case of war or any other circumstances that obstructs the election, the National Assembly may extend its term of office but it must carry out the election of the new National Assembly not later than six months after the situation returns to normal.

Article 42. The National Assembly elects its own Standing Committee which consists of the President, Vice-President and a number of members. The President and Vice-President of the National Assembly are also President and Vice-President of the National Assembly Standing Committee.

Article 43. The National Assembly convenes its ordinary session twice a year at the summoning of the National Assembly Standing Committee. The National Assembly Standing Committee may covene an extraordinary session of the National Assembly if it deems necessary.

Article 44. The National Assembly session shall be convened only with the presence of more than one-half of the total number of the National Assembly members. The resolutions of the National Assembly shall be valid only when they are voted for by more than one-half of the total number of the National Assembly members present at the session, except in the cases prescribed in Article 54 and Article 80 of the Constitution.

Article 45. The organisations and persons that have the rights to propose draft laws are as follows:
1. The President of state;
2. The National Assembly Standing Committee;
3. The Government;
4. The People's Supreme Court;
5. The Public Prosecutor-General;
6. The mass organisations at the central level.

Article 46. Laws already adopted by the National Assembly must be promulgated by the President of state not later than thirty days after their endorsement. During this period, the President of state has the right to request the National Assembly to reconsider such laws. If the National Assembly affirms to adhere to its previous decision in reconsidering such laws, the President of state must promulgate them within fifteen days.

Article 47. The questions related to the destiny of the country and the vital interests of the people must be submitted for approval of the National Assembly or the National Assembly Standing Committee during the two sessiuns of the National Assembly.

Article 48. The National Assembly Standing Committee has the following rights and duties:
1. To prepare for the National Assembly sessions and to ensure the implementation by the National Assembly of the program of activity it has set forth;
2. To interpret and explain the provisions of the constitution and laws;
3. To supervise and oversee the activities of the administrative and judicial organisations during the recess of the National Assembly;
4. To summon the National Assembly into sessions;
5. To exercise other rights and execute other duties as prescribed by law.

Article 49. The National Assembly establishes its own committees to consider draft laws, draft state decrees and state acts submitted to the National Assembly Standing

Committee and the President of state ; and to assist the National Assembly and the National Assembly Standing Committee in exercising the rights of supervision of the functioning of the administrative and judicial organisations.

Article 50. Members of the National Assembly have the right to interpellate the members of the government, the President of the People's Supreme Court and the Public Prosecutor – General. Organisations or persons interpellated must give verbal or written answers at the National Assembly session.

Article 51. Members of the National Assembly shall not be prosecuted in court or detained without the approval of the National Assembly or the National Assembly Standing Committee during the two sessions of the National Assembly. In cases involving gross and urgent offenses, the organisations detaining members of the National Assembly must immediately report to the National Assembly or to the National Assembly Standing Committee during the two sessions of the National Assembly for consideration and decisions concerning them. Inquiries and interrogations shall not cause the absence of prosecuted members from the National Assembly session.

CHAPTER V THE PRESIDENT OF STATE

Article 52. The President of state is the Head of state of the Lao People's Democratic Republic and the representative of the multi-ethnic Lao people both at home and abroad.

Article 53. The President of state has the following rights and duties
1. To promulgate the Constitution and laws already endorsed by the National Assembly;
2. To issue state decrees and state acts on the recommendation of the National Assembly Standing Committee;
3. To appoint or remove the Prime Minister and the members of the government with the approval or resolution of no confidence of the National Assembly; 4. To appoint, transfer or remove the governors of provinces and the mayors of municipalities on the recommendation of the Prime Minister;
5. To decide to promote or demote the ranks of the Generals in the national defence and security forces on the recommendation of the Prime Minister;
6. To be the Head of the people's armed forces;
7. To preside over a meeting of the government when necessary;
8. To decide on the conferment of the national gold medals, orders of Merit, medals of victory and highest honorific titles of the state;
9. To decide on granting pardons;
10. To decide on general or partial military conscription and to declare the state of emergency all over the country or in any particular locality;
11. To declare on the ratification or abolition of all treaties and agreements signed with foreign countries;
12. To appoint and recall plenipotentiary representatives of the Lao People's Democratic Republic to or from foreign countries, and accept the plenipotentiary representatives of

foreign countries accredited to the Lao People's Democratic Republic;
13. To exercise other rights and execute other duties as stipulated in the laws.

Article 54. The President of state is elected by the National Assembly with two-thirds of the votes of all members of the National Assembly attending the session. The term of office of the President of state is five years.

Article 55. The President of state may have a Vice-President as an assistant to act on behalf of the President during his absence. The Vice-President of state is elected by the National Assembly with the votes of more than one-half of the total number of the National Assembly members attending the session.

CHAPTER VI THE GOVERNMENT

Article 56. The government is the administrative organisation of the state. The government manages in a unified manner the implementation of duties of state in all fields: political, economic, cultural, social, national defence and security, and foreign affairs.

Article 57. The government has the following rights and duties
1. To implement the Constitution, laws and resolutions of the National Assembly as well as state decrees and acts of the President of state;
2. To submit draft laws to the National Assembly ; draft decrees and acts to the President of state;
3. To map out the strategic plans on the socio-economic development and annual state budgets and submit them to the National Assembly for consideration and approval;
4. To issue decrees and decisions on the management of socio-economic, scientific and technical fields national defence and security ; and foreign affairs;
5. To organise, guide and supervise the functioning of the managerial organisations of all branches and of local administrative organisations;
6. To organise and supervise the activities of the national defence and security forces;
7. To sign treaties and agreements with foreign countries and guide their implementation;
8. To suspend or revoke decisions, instructions of the ministries, the ministry-equivalent organisations, organisations attached to the government, and local administrative organisations if they run counter to laws;
9. To exercise other rights and execute other duties as stipulated by law.

Article 58. The government consists of the Prime Minister, Deputy Prime Ministers, ministers and chairmen of the ministry- equivalent committees. The term of office of the government is five years.

Article 59. The Prime Minister is appointed by the President of state with the approval of the National Assembly. The term of office of the government is five years.

Article 60. The Prime Minister is the Head of the government; guides and supervises the work of the government; represents the government in guiding the work of ministries, the Ninistry-equivalent organisations and other organisations attached to the government ; and guides the work of the governors of provinces and the mayors of municipalities.

The Prime Minister appoints deputy ministers and deputy Chairman of the ministry-equivalent committees, deputy governors, deputy mayors and district chiefs.

The Deputy Prime Ministers are the assistants of the Prime Minister. The Prime Minister may assign a particular Deputy Prime Minister to carry out work on his behalf in case he is engaged.

Article 61. The National Assembly may pass a vote of no confidence in the government or any member of the government if the National Assembly Standing Committee or one-fourth of the total number of the National Assembly members raise the question.

Within twenty-four hours after the vote of no confidence in the government by the National Assembly, the President of state has the right to bring the no confidence question to the National Assembly for reconsideration. The second consideration must be held within the forty-eight hours interval from the first consideration. If the new vote of no confidence in the government is passed the government must resign.

CHAPTER VII THE LOCAL ADMINISTRATION

Article 62. In the Lao People's Democratic Republic, there are provinces, municipalities, districts and villages. Provinces and municipalities have governors and mayors respectively. Districts have district chiefs and village have village heads. Governors and mayors have deputy governors and deputy mayors respectively. District chiefs have Deputy district chiefs as assistants. In densely populous villages, village heads have deputy village heads as assistants.

Article 63. The governors, the mayors and the district chiefs have the following rights and duties:
1. To ensure the implementation of the Constitution and laws, and to organise the strict implementation of decisions and instructions issued by the higher levels;
2. To guide and supervise the functioning of all branches of work at all levels under the scope of their responsibility;
3. To suspend the implementation or abolish the decisions of all branches of work at their own or lower levels, which contradict the regulations and laws;
4. To consider and resolve the complaints, petitions and proposals of the people under the scope of their rights and power as stipulated by law.

Article 64. The village heads have the responsibility in organizing the implementation of the state's laws, decisions and instructions, maintaining peace and security of the village ; and developing the villages to become firm in all fields.

CHAPTER VIII THE JUDICIARY ORGANISATIONS

A. THE PEOPLE'S COURTS

Article 65. The People's Courts are the judiciary organisations of the state comprising the People's Supreme Court, People's Provincial and Municipal Courts, People's District Courts and Military Courts.

Article 66. The People's Supreme Court is the highest judiciary organisation of the state. The People's Supreme Court scrutinizes the sentences reached by the people's local courts and the military courts.

Article 67. The Vice-President of the People's Supreme Court and the judges of the people's courts at all levels are appointed or removed by the National Assembly Standing Committee.

Article 68. The People's Courts make judges are to be independent and subject only to the law.

Article 69. Trials of cases at courts proceedings must be openly conducted except in cases as stipulated by law. The defendants have the right to defend themselves in the cases they are accused. The board of legal counselors have the right to in providing legal assistance to the defendants.

Article 70. Representatives of social organisations have the right to take part in court proceedings as provided by law.

Article 71. The sentences reached by the people's courts, which have become legally effective, must be respected by the party, state and social organisations and all citizens. the persons and organisations concerned must strictly implement them.

B. THE PUBLIC PROSECUTION INSTITUTES

Article 72. The Public Prosecution Institutes consist of the Public Prosecutor-General Institute, the Public Prosecution Institutes of provinces, municipalities, and districts, and the military prosecution institutes.

The Public Prosecution Institutes have the following rights and duties:
1. To control the unified and correct observance of laws by all ministries, organisations attached to the government, social organisations, local administrative organisations,

enterprises, state employees and all citizens;
2. To exercise the right of public prosecution.

Article 73. In carrying out their duties, the Public Prosecution Institutes are subject only to the laws and the instructions of the Public Prosecutor-General.

CHAPTER IX LANGUAGE, SCRIPT, NATIONAL EMBLEM, NATIONAL FLAG, NATIONAL ANTHEM AND CAPITAL CITY

Article 75. The Lao language and Lao script are the language and script officially used.

Article 76. The National Emblem of the Lao People's Democratic Republic is a circle depicting in the bottom part one- half of a cog wheel and red ribbon with the inscription "Lao People's Democratic Republic", and decorated with crescent-shaped ears of rice on the two sides and red ribbon stretched between the middle of the rice ears with the inscription "Peace, Independence, Democracy, Unity and Prosperity". A picture of that Luang Pagoda is located between the t.i.ps of the rice ears. A road, a paddy field a forest, and a hydroelectric dam are depicted in the middle of the circle.

Article 77. The National Flag of the Lao People's Democratic Republic is dark blue with red edges and a white moon. The width of the flag is two-thirds of its length. The area of the red edges on each side is one-half of the dark blue area. The area of the white moon is equal to four-fifths of the dark blue area.

Article 78. The national anthem of the Lao People's Democratic Republic is "Xat Lao" song.

Article 79. The Capital city of the Lao People's Democratic Republic is Vientiane.

CHAPTER X THE LAST PROVISION

Article 80. Only the National Assembly of the Lao People's Democratic Republic has the right to amend the Constitution. The amendment to the Constitution requires the votes of approval cast by at least two-thirds of the total number of the National Assembly members.

LAW ON THE ELECTION OF MEMBERS OF THE NATIONAL ASSEMBLY

Chapter 1 General Provisions

Article 1. Functions

This law defines the principles and regulations relating to the election of members of the National Assembly to ensure the full exercise of democratic rights by all multi-ethnic people and to ensure that persons meeting standard criteria will be elected as members of the National Assembly, in order to strengthen the legislative organ. All power is of the people, and by the people.

Article 2. Principles

The election of members of the National Assembly of the Lao People's Democratic Republic is carried out according to 4 principles:

   1. Universality;

   2. Equality;

   3. Direct suffrage; and

   4. Secret ballot.

Article 3. Persons who have the Right to Vote and to be Elected

All Lao citizens, irrespective of their gender, ethnicity, beliefs, social status, place of residence, and profession, who are at least 18 years of age, have the right to vote; anyone who is at least 21 years of age has the right to be elected as a member of the National Assembly.

[1] This document is a consolidation of the Law on the Election of Members of the National Assembly, No. 05-97/NA promulgated on 31 May 1997 and the amendments promulgated by the Amended Law on the Election of Members of the National Assembly, No. 01/NA, promulgated on 12 October 2001. Generally, readers may wish to read the Law on the National Assembly for information on many of the terms and institutions discussed in this law.

[2] Readers should note that the Lao language does not distinguish between genders in pronouns. In this translation, a reference to a gender is a reference to all genders, unless the context requires otherwise. The translators' decision to use the male gender was made in the interests of simplicity and consistency.

[3] The Lao word has the connotation of "bringing shame or dishonour".

[4] This implies that the matter must be brought before a formal session of the National Assembly although the requirement is not explicitly stated.

[5] The Lao word may be translated as both "liable" or "responsible". The translators have generally chosen the translation "liable" (and its variants) where the context implies that the responsibility may involve legal liability of some sort, either in civil or ciminal proceedings. In other cases, the translators have used the word "responsible" (and its variants). Readers should note and bear in mind the other meaning that may have been intended.

[6] The reader should note that the organisation of local administration has undergone change over time and that the administrative divisions and titles used in this older law do not conform to those used in newer laws such as the Law on Local Administration.

[7] The literal translation is "has method of working that is always related to the grassroots."

[8] The literal translation of this word is "take".

[9] The Lao language does not require nouns to contain information as to whether they are singular or plural. This item is ambiguous as to whether it is singular or plural; therefore, the translators have simply used the singular form.

[10] It is clear from Chapter 5 that there are more than one committee at the district, provincial, municipal and special zone level. There is a connotation of the "relevant committee" in this and other similar provisions.

[11] See footnote 6.

[12] E.g., to meet the requirements of Article 7.

[13] The term "regular" is used here in the sense of "correct" or "normal" rather than in the sense of "often".

[14] Army and police commanders make decisions in committees pursuant to the principle of collective decision-making.

[15] The Ministry of the Interior has since been renamed the Ministry of Security.

[16] The literal translation of this term is "department-unit". This refers to voters in the national defence and security forces.

[17] It is unclear whether these requests and petitions relate to the behaviour of the election committee to which they are submitted or to lower-level election committees.

[18] See footnote 11. The position of municipalities within the local administrative structure has since been changed and the title of the head of a municipality has correspondingly been changed to "chief". The title of "mayor" is now reserved for heads of cities.

[19] The same Lao word may be translated as "equipment". However, the context suggests that the reference is to less mechanised facilities such as ballot boxes and furniture.

[20] The same Lao word may be translated as "election", "voting" or "polling". Here, the context suggests that the reference is to voting or polling.

[21] The same Lao word may be translated as "regulations". However, the context suggests that the less formal "rules" is more appropriate.

[22] The ballot is stamped when given to the voter.

[23] The literal translation of this phrase is "candidates who receive the highest votes to the last one as required for that constituency".

[24] In this context, the term "policies" takes the meaning of "privileges" and the term "measures" takes the meaning of "sanctions".

[25] Here, "re-education" does not mean the same as "re-education without deprivation of liberty" referred to in the Penal Law.

[26] This effectiveness provision pertains to the 1997 Law on the Election of the Members of the National Assembly. The effectiveness provisions for 2001 amendments are contained in the relevant National Assembly Resolution and Presidential Decree (both of which reproduced at the beginning of this translation).

Article 4. Persons who have No Right to Vote or to be Elected

The following persons have no right to vote or to be elected:

    1. The insane and the mentally incompetent;

    2. A person whose rights to vote and to be elected have been revoked by the People's Courts or a person who is serving a sentence of imprisonment.

Article 5. Right to Propose the Dismissal of Members of the National Assembly

Voters have the right to propose the dismissal of any member of the National Assembly in their own constituency if he 2 is found to be unworthy or [to have engaged in] disgraceful 3 behaviour, but such dismissal must be agreed to by the National Assembly Standing Committee and approved by the majority of National Assembly members attending the session 4 . The person who proposes the dismissal of a member of the National Assembly shall be responsible 5 for his proposal according to the laws and regulations.

Article 6. Election Expenditures

Expenditures for the election of members of the National Assembly shall come from the State budget.

CHAPTER 2 DETERMINATION OF THE NUMBER OF NATIONAL ASSEMBLY MEMBERS

and Regulations relating to Candidates

Article 7. Principles for Determining the Number of Members of the National Assembly

The number of members of the National Assembly is determined based on the following principles:

1. Every 50,000 [persons] in the population shall be represented by one member of the National Assembly;

2. According to the team work principle, any province or special zone 6 with a population of less than 150,000 persons shall have three members of the National Assembly;

3. According to the important and special characteristics of each province, municipality or special zone [relating to] politics, national defence or public security, the economy, and social and cultural [considerations];

4. The number of members of the National Assembly shall include an appropriate proportion of representatives of people of different strata, gender, and ethnic groups.

The National Assembly Standing Committee determines the number of members of the National Assembly in each constituency, and this is then promulgated by the President of the State.

Article 8. (New) Criteria of Candidates

A candidate for [the position of a] member of the National Assembly shall meet all the conditions set out in Article 3 of this law and shall have the following qualifications:

1. Be patriotic, be devoted to the people's democracy, be loyal to the New Economic Mechanism of the Party, be true to the nation, always serve the interests of the people, and have a strong, clear and absolute attitude towards friends and enemies;

2. Have a sufficient level of knowledge of the Party's policies and strategic programs and of State laws and regulations, and have the capacity to undertake propaganda and to motivate people to be aware of and to participate in the implementation of such Party policies and State laws;

3. Have an exemplary attitude, symbolise the solidarity of multi-ethnic groups, have a grassroots working method 7 , and be close to and trusted by the people;

4. Be a Lao person with Lao nationality who is living and working inside the country;

5. Have sufficient knowledge and capacity to undertake research and to contribute ideas on the implementation of the rights and duties of members of the National Assembly;

6. Be in good health in order to carry out his regular duties.

Article 9. (New) Proposal of Names and Ranking of Candidates

All organisations of the Party and the State, the Lao Front for National Construction and mass organisations have the right to nominate a list of their candidates to be elected as members of the National Assembly, through local election committees in the concerned constituencies, which lists shall then be proposed to the National Election Committee for consideration and approval.

For ministries and organisations at the central level, the list of candidates can be submitted directly to the National Election Committee.

The names of candidates to be elected as members of the National Assembly are determined taking into account the principle that [such candidates] may occupy 8 one position or combined positions in the government at different levels, if appropriate.

The candidates in each constituency can be listed according to Lao alphabetical order or in any other order, as decided by the National Election Committee.

Article 10. Documents to be Provided by Candidates

A candidate for [the position of a] member of the National Assembly shall submit the following documents:

1. A written application to be elected as a member of the National Assembly;

2. Resume;

3. 6x9 centimetre photograph 9 ;

4. Certificate of residence;

5. Health certificate.

Article 11. Announcement of the Names of Candidates

The National Election Committee considers and summarises the list of candidates throughout the country, and then makes an official announcement at least 60 days before the election.

Article 12. Objection to Candidates

Any voter has the right to object to a candidate by written or verbal report within 7 days from the announcement of the candidates if such person is found to be unsuitable according to established criteria or if such person has violated any law [or] regulation which affects the rights and interests of the people.

The objection shall be submitted to the district election committee 10 , which will report to the provincial, municipal, or special zone election committee to consider and deal with the matter within 3 days. 11 If the matter cannot be resolved, the report shall be referred to the National Election Committee to consider and deal with the matter within 5 days from the date it receives the matter.

The person who objects shall be responsible for his objection according to the laws and regulations.

Article 13. Organisation of Campaigns

Organisations of the Party and the State, and mass organisations at all levels, have the right and duty to organise the campaign for their candidates in each constituency as prescribed by laws and regulations.

Every candidate has the right to organise a campaign for himself, but it is prohibited to bribe voters or to organise a campaign against other candidates.

Campaigning shall begin after the announcement of candidates, and must stop one day before the election.

CHAPTER 3 DETERMINATION OF CONSTITUENCIES FOR ELECTION AND POLLING UNITS

Article 14. (New) Determination of the Location for Elections

Each province, municipality and special zone is considered as a constituency for the election of members of the National Assembly of the Lao People's Democratic Republic.

If any province or special zone is dissolved or established, the National Assembly Standing Committee is responsible for determining the distribution of members of the National Assembly in such constituency in accordance with the actual circumstances 12 , to ensure the regular 13 exercise of the rights and duties of representatives of the people.

Article 15. Polling Units

A village is considered as a polling unit. A village that has 500 to 1000 voters [should be] organised as one polling unit. A village that has more than 1000 voters may organise several polling units.

A village with less than 500 voters shall group together with a nearby village to form a single polling unit.

If a village is in an area that is remote or difficult to travel to, it may be organised as a polling unit or a mobile team with an election box may collect the votes.

Article 16. Polling Units in the National Defence and Security Forces

Polling units in the national defence and security forces are set up by their brigades or battalions, and by the committees of commanders 14 at the provincial, municipal and special zone levels, who shall then notify the district election committee where their offices are located.

In the event that it is necessary to set up polling units in the Ministry of National Defence and the Ministry of the Interior 15 , the cabinets of those ministries shall determine the polling units and then notify the district election committee where the ministries are located.

CHAPTER 4 REGISTRATION OF VOTERS

Article 17. Registration of Voters

Village chiefs are responsible for the registration of voters in their villages.

The registration of voters shall be completed and be announced officially at least 45 days before the election.

Voters can only register themselves with one polling unit.

Article 18. Registration of Voters in the National Defence and Security Forces

Brigades and battalions, and the committees of commanders at the provincial, municipal and special zone levels, are responsible for the registration of voters in the national defence and security forces.

Article 19. Change of Polling Location of Voters

After the list of registered voters has been announced, if there is any change of address or workplace for any reason, the voter shall notify his village chief or unit 16 of his new address or workplace, in order to obtain the voting certificate to vote in the new polling unit.

CHAPTER 5 ELECTION COMMITTEES AT DIFFERENT LEVELS

Article 20. Structure of Election Committees

Committees for the election of members of the National Assembly in the Lao People's Democratic Republic are established according to the following structure:

1. National Election Committee;

2. Provincial, municipal and special zone election committees;

3. District election committees;

4. Committees at the level of polling units (villages).

The election committee at each level shall include representatives of the party committee, the local administrative authority, and mass organisations at such level. The national, provincial, municipal, and special zone election committees shall include representatives of the National Assembly.

Election committees at different levels have the right to create their own support mechanism as appropriate.

Article 21. Appointment of National Election Committee

The National Assembly Standing Committee appoints the National Election Committee and [the appointment] is then promulgated by a presidential decree at least 120 days before the election.

The National Election Committee consists of 15 to 17 members, including one chairman, two to three vice-chairmen, and a certain number of members.

The term of office of the National Election Committee ends after the completion of the first plenary session of the new National Assembly.

Article 22. (New) Rights and Duties of the National Election Committee

The National Election Committee has the following rights and duties:

1. To direct authorities at the provincial, municipal and special zone levels to appoint their own election committees;

2. To organise education and training on politics and ideology in order to ensure the full exercise of democratic rights by the multi-ethnic people, and to ensure uniformity and effectiveness in the implementation of the election nationwide;

3. To implement election activities, [and to] support, motivate and advise everyone to respect this Law on the Election of Members of the National Assembly;

4. To prepare and distribute all relevant documents for the election;

5. To study and consider requests and proposals of candidates for approval, and to officially announce the list of candidates;

6. To study, consider and deal with requests and petitions of voters and candidates about the activities of the election committee 17 ;

7. To direct, supervise and monitor the implementation of the work of election committees at different levels throughout the country;

8. To summarise and announce the election results;

9. To give temporary certificates to members of the National Assembly who have been elected;

10. To assess the election for lessons that may be learned, and to give rewards to organisations and individuals who have outstanding performance;

11. To report the election results to the first plenary session of the new National Assembly.

Article 23. Appointment of Local Election Committees

Provincial governors, municipal mayors 18 , chiefs of special zones and chiefs of districts are responsible for appointing election committees at their [respective] levels, and shall make an official announcement no later than 90 days before the election.

Provincial, municipal, and special zone election committees consist of 11 to 13 members, including one chairman, one to two vice-chairmen and a certain number of members.

District election committees consist of 7 to 9 members, including one chairman, one to two vice-chairmen and a certain number of members.

The term of office of local election committees ends after the completion of the first plenary session of the new National Assembly.

Article 24. Rights and Duties of Local Election Committees

Provincial, municipal, special zone and district election committees have the following rights and duties:

> 1. To organise education and training on politics and ideology within the scope of their authority in order to ensure the full exercise of democratic rights by the multi-ethnic people, and to ensure uniformity and effectiveness in the implementation of the election at the local level;
>
> 2. To implement election activities, [and to] support, motivate and advise everyone within the scope of their responsibility to respect this Law on the Election of Members of the National Assembly;
>
> 3. To distribute all relevant documents to election committees at the lower level;
>
> 4. To direct, supervise and monitor the activities of election committees at the lower level;
>
> 5. To direct and supervise security and public order within their election areas;
>
> 6. To direct the campaign and introduce the resumes of the candidates to the people;
>
> 7. To consider and deal with all petitions of voters and candidates concerning the election activities within the scope of their responsibility;
>
> 8. To summarise the results of the election; and then to report to the election committees at the higher level in a timely manner;
>
> 9. To assess the election for lessons that may be learned, and to give rewards to organisations and individuals who have outstanding performance within the scope of their responsibility.

Article 25. (New) Appointment of Committees at the Level of Polling Units

The chiefs of districts appoint committees at the level of polling units in their districts. Commanders of brigades or battalions, committees of commanders at the provincial, municipal and special zone levels, [and] chiefs of cabinet of the Ministry of National Defence and the Ministry of the Interior appoint committees at the level of polling units in the national defence and security forces, and shall then notify the district election committee where their offices are located.

Committees at the level of polling units consist of 5 to 7 members, including one chairman, one vice-chairman, one or two secretaries and a certain number of members.

The term of office of committees at the level of polling units ends after the completion of the new plenary session of the new National Assembly.

Article 26. Rights and Duties of Committees at the Level of Polling Units

Committees at the level of polling units have the following rights and duties:

1. To educate and guide voters within the scope of their responsibility to ensure that all voters exercise their rights;

2. To implement election activities, [and to] support and advise everyone to respect regulations and this Law on the Election of Members of the National Assembly;

3. To prepare the location and facilities 19 for the election;

4. To distribute ballots to the voters;

5. To take responsibility for election operations and to ensure security and public order within their polling units;

6. To deal with all requests or petitions of voters within the scope of their responsibility;

7. To count the votes, [and] scrutinise and record the election results, [and] then to submit all records and documents to the district election committee;

8. To keep all ballots until the official announcement of the names of those who have been elected as members of the National Assembly; and then to destroy them;

9. To assess the election for lessons that may be learned, and to select those who have outstanding performance and to propose to the district election committee to consider rewarding them.

CHAPTER 6 TIME, DATE AND RULES FOR VOTING 20

Article 27. Determination of Date for Voting

The National Assembly Standing Committee determines the date for voting, and this is then promulgated by a decree of the President of the State 130 days before the voting. Voting is carried out simultaneously, on the same day throughout the country. The polling day is on a Sunday.

Article 28. Time for Voting

The time for voting starts from seven in the morning to five in the afternoon. Committees at the level of polling units may decide when [to conduct] the opening and closing [formalities], which may be before or after the time established [for voting], according to the real situation in the location. But [such opening formalities] shall not be earlier than five in the morning and [such closing formalities] shall not be later than seven in the afternoon.

Article 29. Rules 21 for Voting

Rule for voting are as follows:

    1. The location for voting shall be in an appropriate place, for example: schools, halls, and other places;

    2. The election committees shall advise on [and] disseminate all rules and methods relating to voting to all voters to ensure that they understand;

    3. Before voting commences, the committees at the level of polling units shall open the ballot box in front of the people;

    4. Voters shall present [voting] certificates to the committees at the level of polling units in order to get their ballots;

    5. When voters are filling out their ballots, other people are prohibited from interfering;

    6. For illiterate voters who cannot fill out their ballots by themselves, the committee at the level of polling unit shall nominate someone to assist them in filling out the ballot according to the voters' choice, and then let them deposit the ballot by themselves. In the event that such persons cannot deposit the ballot by themselves, the committee at the level of polling unit shall nominate someone to help them to do so in their presence;

    7. If voters are sick, disabled or old and cannot come to the voting location, the committee at the level of polling unit shall organise mobile teams to go and collect the ballots from those persons at their locations;

    8. If voters make any mistake in filling out their ballots, they shall ask for a new ballot from the committee at the level of polling unit;

9. Voters shall go one-by-one to deposit their ballot into the ballot box;

10. On polling day, no one is allowed to campaign for any candidate or cause public disorder that violates this Law on the Election of Members of the National Assembly.

Article 30. Measures to Deal with Emergency Situations at Voting Locations

If there is any emergency situation during voting time, the committee at the level of polling unit shall immediately suspend voting, but shall consider and deal with the matter in order to continue afterwards. If the problem cannot be dealt with, voting shall be stopped and [the committee at the level of polling unit] shall report to the district election committee in order to set a new date for voting.

CHAPTER 7 COUNTING OF VOTES AND ANNOUNCEMENT OF RESULTS

Article 31. Counting of Votes

The counting of votes shall be done openly in front of at least 3 witnesses, who are voters in that unit, but not the candidates. Journalists and representatives of candidates may observe and follow the counting of votes.

The committees at the level of polling units shall divide their responsibilities for counting votes as follows:

One person is to read the ballots, one person is to check, and the others are to follow [the proceedings] and record.

Article 32. Invalid Ballots

Invalid ballots are as follows:

1. Ballots with no stamps 22 from the polling unit;

2. Ballots which select more or less than the number of required candidates;

3. Blank ballots where no candidates have been selected.

Article 33. Record of Results of Voting

The record of the results of voting consists of the following contents:

1. The times at which the opening and closing [formalities] took place in the election;

2. The list of candidates;

3. The total number of eligible voters;

4. The actual number of voters on the polling day;

5. The actual number of ballots received;

6. The number of ballots with mistakes that were exchanged for new ballots;

7. The number of valid ballots;

8. The number of invalid ballots;

9. The number of votes for each candidate;

10. The petitions that the committee at the level of polling unit dealt with, and those that they could not deal with (if any).

The record must be signed by the chairman of the committee at the level of polling unit, the secretary and the 3 witnesses who observed the counting of votes. One copy of the record shall be sent to the district election committee and the other copy is kept by the village chief.

Article 34. Candidates Elected as Members of the National Assembly

The candidates who are elected as members of the National Assembly shall be those who receive the highest number of votes [corresponding to] the number [of members] required for that constituency. 23

If there is an equal number of votes for two candidates for [the position of] the final member required by the constituency, the more experienced candidate shall be selected, but in the event that the two candidates have equal experience, the older candidate shall be selected as the member of the National Assembly.

CHAPTER 8 ELECTION OF REPLACEMENT MEMBERS OF THE NATIONAL ASSEMBLY

Article 35. (New) Election of Replacements

The election of replacement members of the National Assembly is organised in a constituency when there is a vacancy.

Such election can only take place after a majority vote of members of the National Assembly attending the session that supports the replacement, based on the proposal of the National Assembly Standing Committee.

Article 36. Organisation of Election of Replacements

The National Assembly Standing Committee appoints the election committee and determines the date for the election of replacements.

The election of replacements shall be done according to this Law on the Election of Members of the National Assembly.

CHAPTER 9 POLICIES FOR OUTSTANDING PERFORMANCE

and Measures against Persons who

Violate this Law on the Election of Members of the National Assembly 24

Article 37. Policies for Outstanding Performance

Organisations and individuals who have outstanding performance in implementing this Law on the Election of Members of the National Assembly shall be rewarded appropriately according to the policy of the Party and the State.

Article 38. Measures Against Violators

Organisations and individuals who violate this Law on the Election of Members of the National Assembly shall be subject to the following measures:

1. Re-education 25 , for minor violations;

2. Legal proceedings, for serious cases.

CHAPTER 10 FINAL PROVISIONS

Article 39. Implementation

The National Assembly Standing Committee of the Lao People's Democratic Republic is assigned to issue guidelines for the implementation of this law.

Article 40. Effectiveness 26

This Law on the Election of Members of the National Assembly replaces the Law on the Election of Members of the National Assembly, No 02-91/ NA, 14 August 1991.

This law enters into force on the date of the promulgating decree issued by the President of the Lao People's Democratic Republic.

Vientiane, 12 April 1997

President of the National Assembly

LAW ON LOCAL ADMINISTRATION OF THE LAO PDR

PART I GENERAL PROVISIONS

Article 1 the Objectives of Local Administration Law of the Lao PDRThe Local Administration Law outlines the basic principles concerning the organization, functions and working methods of the local administration with the aim to improve and establish strong, transparent, unified and systematic local administration throughout country; to ensure the effective implementation of the constitution, laws, socio-economic development and state budget plans, and to protect the rights and benefits of the state and the people in accordance with the law.

Article 2 Local Administration
Local administration is the state administration at the local level. There are three levels of local administration in the Lao PDR : Province, District and Village.
At the provincial level, there are provinces, cities and, if required, a Special Zone;At the district level, there are districts and municipalities;
At the village level, there are villages.
The government delegates responsibility to the local administration authorities to manage the territory, natural resources and population in order to preserve and develop into a modern, civil and prosperous society.

Article 3 Location and Overall Role of Local Administration
The local administration has the role to represent the locality and be responsible to the government in administering political, socio-economic and cultural affairs; human resource management; the utilization and preservation/protection of natural resources, the environment and other resources; national and local defense and security and other foreign relations responsibilities assigned by the government.

The head of the provincial administration is the Governor. The head of the city is the Mayor. The head of the district is the Chief of District. The head of the municipality is the Chief of the Municipality. The head of the village is the Village Chief.

Article 4 Authority and Duties of Local Administration
The authority and duties of local administration are:

> To implement the constitution, laws, resolutions, orders, socio-economic development plans and state budget plans within its' area of responsibility;

> To prepare a strategic plan incorporating: socio-economic development plans, state budget plans and defense and security plans based on national strategic plans;

> To manage political, socio-economic and cultural affairs, natural resources, environment and national defense and security;

To issue resolutions, decisions, orders, instructions, and notifications regarding socio-economic and cultural management, national defense and security in accordance with laws;

To supervise the performance of the organizations under its' responsibility;

To collaborate and cooperate with foreign countries as directed by the government; and

To assume other authorities and duties in accordance with laws.

Article 5 Organization Principles and Functions of Local Administration

The organization and functions of the local administration are implemented in accordance with the principle of centralized democracy and deconcentration, which divides responsibility among management levels. The village level reports to the district level, the district level reports to the provincial level and the provincial level reports to the government under the guidance and responsibility of the Party Committee based on the constitution and laws.
Local administration is authorized to conduct meetings to discuss and decide on important local issues.

PART II PROVINCIAL AND CITY ADMINISTRATIONS

Chapter I

Location, Role and Organization Structure

Article 6 The Province and the City

The province is a local administration comprising of several districts and municipalities.

The city is a local administration comprising of larger urban communities and several municipalities. It is the centre of economic, political, cultural and social services and activities that influence the socio- economic development of the country.

Vientiane Capital City consists of several districts and municipalities.

Article 7 Role and Functions of Provincial and City Administrations

The role and functions of provincial and city administrations is to manage political, economic, socio-cultural affairs and human resources; protect/preserve and utilize natural resources, the environment and other resources; manage national and local defense and security, and foreign affairs as assigned by the government.

Article 8 Organization Structure and Personnel of Provincial and City Administrations

The organization structure of the provincial and city administrations is comprised of the following:

    The Provincial/City Cabinet; and

    The field offices of the line ministries and equivalent organizations

The personnel of provincial and city administrations is comprised of:

    The Governor/Mayor;

    The Vice-Governor/Vice Mayor;

    The Chief and Deputy Chief of the Provincial/City Cabinet;

    Director and Deputy Director of the departments; and

    Personnel appointed in provincial and city administrations.

Article 9 Location and Role of Provincial/City Cabinet

The Provincial/City Cabinet is part of the organization structure of the Province/City. The role of the cabinet is to: assist the Governor/Mayor in their management of tasks; formulate program and project plans; study, finalize, draft, research and edit documents; coordinate with concerned parties; provide information; supervise and support the implementation of legal acts from central, provincial and city authorities; and facilitate the operation of the province and the city.

Further details of the organization structure, personnel, authority and duties of the Provincial/City Cabinet are outlined by specific regulations.

Article 10 Location and Role of Field Offices of the Line Ministries and Equivalent Organizations in the Province and City

The field offices of the line ministries and equivalent organizations are part of the organization structure of the provincial/city administration. The role of the field offices is to assist: ministries and equivalent organizations; the province/city in management of the concerned sectors according to the principle of deconcentration.

Further details of the organization structure, personnel, rights and duties of field offices of the line ministries and equivalent organizations of the province and the city shall be defined by specific regulations.

Chapter II

Creation of a Province and City

Article 11 The Creation, Abolition, Division, Merger and Land Area Definition of a Province and City

The creation, abolition, division, merger or definition of the land area of a province and city is defined and proposed by the Prime Minister and approved by the National Assembly.

Article 12 Creation Criteria

(a) The criteria for the creation of a province are:

> a suitable geographical location for administration and strategic location for national defense and security;
>
> the presence of good conditions for socio-economic development;
>
> the presence of infrastructure like telecommunication, roads, transportation, markets, electricity, water supply, schools, health facilities;
>
> a population of at least 120,000;
>
> a minimum of five (5) districts

In special cases where all of these criteria are not met, the government may still propose to the National Assembly for consideration and approval.

(b) The criteria for the creation a city are:

Except for Vientiane Capital City , other cities will be created if they meet all of the following criteria:

> occupies a large urban area that is the centre of: economy, politics, socio-culture, tourism, services, commerce, industry, transport and foreign affairs;
>
> makes a significant contribution to the socio-economic development of the country;
>
> Has a population of at least 80,000;
>
> Has a developed infrastructure and public facilities.

Chapter III

Roles, Authorities and Duties of the Governor/Mayor

Article 13 Roles of the Governor/Mayor

The Governor/Mayor is the chief of administration and representative of the province/city. S/he is responsible to the government to fulfill their role, authority and duties.

Article 14 Authorities and Duties of the Governor/Mayor

The governor/mayor shall have the following authorities and duties:

To ensure the effective implementation of the Constitution, laws and rules of the State;

To convene and preside over provincial/city administration meetings;

To study and develop strategies for provincial/city socio-economic development and budget plans;

To implement plans for: socio-economic development; the state budget; defense and security of the province/city; prevention of negative phenomena; and monitoring and inspection of central government projects being implemented in the province/city;

To facilitate and manage the organizations concerned to ensure the timely and accurate accounting of local revenue collections;

To motivate, promote and facilitate the participation of the Lao Front for National Construction, mass organizations, civil society organizations and all economic partners and ethnic people in the socio-economic development of the province/city;

To issue decisions, orders, instructions, notifications and other regulations in accordance with the laws;

To implement citizen management at the local level;

To suspend or cancel other legal acts of lower local administrations, or propose to higher level authorities to cancel legal acts of departments that do not support National laws and regulations;

To propose the creation and abolition of districts and municipalities, and any office within the structure of the province and city administration;

To create, abolish, merge, divide and delineate village boundaries;

To propose the appointment, transfer or demotion of the chief of district, chief of municipality. To propose or acknowledge the appointment of directors, deputy-directors of the provincial/city offices of the line ministries, and equivalent organizations, and the head of offices of the line ministries, and equivalent organizations, in the districts;

To appoint, transfer or demote the Chief or Deputy Chief of the Provincial/City Cabinet, the Deputy Chief of District/Municipality, Chief and Deputy Chief of the District/Municipal Cabinet, Deputy Director of field offices of the line ministries, and equivalent organisations at the district/municipal level, and other personnel according to regulations;

To manage the performance of organizations and personnel in accordance with their authority; including the supervision and reporting on performance of civil servants of line ministries,

To consider, advise or resolve complaints, petitions and proposals from within the civil service, relating to inappropriate behavior or unsatisfactory performance of staff or organizations within the scope of their jurisdiction in accordance with the law;

To regularly report the overall situation in the province/city to the Government;

To cooperate with international organizations as directed by the government;

To assume other authorities and duties in accordance with laws.

Article 15 Authorities and Duties of the Vice Governor and Vice Mayor

The Vice Governor/Vice Mayor shall assist the Governor/Mayor and is also in charge of some functions which are given by the Governor/Mayor.

In case the Governor/ Mayor is unable to implement his/her duties for any reason, the Vice Governor/Vice Mayor takes over.

Article 16 Appointment and Term of Office of the Governor/Mayor, Vice Governor, Vice Mayor

The Governor and Mayor are appointed, transferred or demoted by the President of the State based on the proposal of the Prime Minister.

The Governor/Mayor shall have a five-year term of office and can be reappointed for one more term in the same place.

The Vice Governor, Vice Mayor are appointed, transferred or demoted by the Prime Minister based on a proposal by the Governor/Mayor and shall have a five-year office term and may be reappointed.

Chapter IV

Provincial and City Administration Meeting

Article 17 The Provincial and City Administration Meeting

Regular provincial and city administration meetings shall be held once a month and shall be convened and chaired by the Governor/Mayor. The participants of the provincial and city administration meetings include the Vice Governor, Vice Mayor, Chief of Provincial/City Cabinet, Director of the field offices of the line ministries and equivalent organizations. If necessary, the representatives of the Chief of Districts, Chief of Municipality or representatives of concerned parties may be invited to attend.

In cases where an emergency or urgent matter arises, the Governor/Mayor can call a special meeting.

In each meeting, minutes of the meeting shall be recorded. The minutes shall be approved and signed by the Chairman, and then distributed to the participants and concerned parties for implementation. In cases where there is a decision on important issues, a resolution of the meeting shall be prepared.

Article 18 Agenda of the Provincial and City Administration Meeting

The agenda or topics to be considered and agreed upon in the provincial and city administration meeting should include:

Socio-economic strategy and development plans of the province and city;

Province and city budget plans and annual budget amendments or adjustments;

Creation, abolition of districts, municipalities and organizational structure of the province/city for consideration by the Government;

Draft legal acts of the province/city;

Consideration of investment projects in the province/ city ;

Report on the implementation of planned activities of the province/ city;

Annual report to the government;

Local defense and security, and international relations and cooperation;

Personnel management issues.

The provincial and city administration meeting may also discuss other important and necessary issues.

PART III DISTRICT ADMINISTRATION

Chapter I
Location, Role, Functions and Organization Structure

Article 19 District

A district is a level of local administration under the supervision of a Province or Capital City . A district is composed of several villages.

Article 20 Role and Functions of District Administration

The role of district administrations is to manage political, economic, socio-cultural affairs and human resources; protect/preserve and utilize natural resources, the environment and other resources; manage national and local defense and security, and foreign affairs as assigned by the Province/Capital City.

Article 21 The Organization Structure and Personnel of the District Administration

The organization structure of the district administration is comprised of the following:

    the District Cabinet; and

    The field offices of the line ministries and equivalent offices in the district.

The personnel of district administration is comprised of:

    Chief of district;

    Vice Chief of district;

    Chief and Deputy Chief of the District Cabinet;

    Director and Deputy Director of line offices in the district; and

    Permanent staff of the district administration.

Article 22 Location and Role of the Chief of District Cabinet

The district cabinet is part of the organization structure of the district. The role of the district cabinet is to: assist the district chief in their management of tasks; formulate program and project plans; study, finalize, draft, research and edit documents; coordinate with concerned parties; provide information; supervise and support the implementation of legal acts of higher level and the district authorities; and facilitate the operation of the district administration.

Further details of the organization structure, personnel, authority and duties of the District Cabinet are outline by specific regulations.

Article 23 Location, Role and Functions of the Field Offices of the Line Ministries and Equivalent Organizations in the District

The field offices of the line ministries and equivalent organization are part of the organization structure of the district administration. The role of the field offices is to manage their own sector's responsibilities as assigned by the province, capital city and line ministries and equivalent organizations; implement legal acts of higher authorities and socio-economic development plans of the province, capital city and district.

Further details of the organization structure, personnel, authority and duties of field offices of the line ministries and equivalent organizations of the district are outline by specific regulations.

Chapter II

Creation of the District

Article 24 Creation, Abolition, Division, Merger and Land Area Definition

The creation, abolition, division, merger or definition of land area of a district is defined and proposed by the Governor or Mayor and approved by the Government

Article 25 Criteria Creation:

The criteria for the creation of a district are:

A suitable geographic location for administration;

A population of at least 30,000 for districts in the low land and 20,000 for those in the high land. Special cases will be decided by the government;

The presence of infrastructure and conditions for socio-economic development.

Chapter III

Roles, Functions, Authorities and Duties of the District Chief

Article 26 Roles of the District Chief

The District Chief is the chief of administrative and representative of the district. S/he is responsible to the provincial and Capital city to fulfill their role, authority and duties.

Article 27 Authorities and Duties of the District Chief

The District Chief shall have the following authorities and duties:

To ensure the effective implementation of the constitution, laws and rules of the State;

To convene and preside over district administration meetings;

To study, develop strategies for district socio-economic development and budget plans;

To implement plans for: socio-economic development; the state budget; defense and security of the district; prevention of negative phenomena; monitoring and inspection of the central, provincial and Capital City investment projects being implemented in the district;

To facilitate and manage the organizations concerned to ensure the timely and accurate accounting of revenues in the district;

To motivate, promote and facilitate the participation of the Lao Front for National Construction, mass organizations, civil society organizations and all economic parties and ethnic people in the socio-economic development of the district;

To issue decisions, orders, instructions, notification and other regulations in accordance with laws;

To implement citizen management in the district;

To suspend or cancel other legal acts of lower local administration; or propose to higher level authority to cancel legal acts of higher local administration that do not support National Laws and regulations;

To propose the creation and abolition of villages and any offices within the structure of the district administration;

To propose appointment, transfer or demote of deputy districts chief, Chief, deputy Chief of the district Cabinet;
To propose appointment or acknowledge an appointment of deputy directors of field offices of the line ministries and equivalent organizations in the districts;

To appoint, transfer or demote the heads and deputy heads of units of the district administration and other staff in accordance with the regulations; to approve the election or appointment of the villages chiefs;

To manage the performance of the organization and personnel in accordance with their authority, including the supervision and reporting on performance of civil servants of line ministries;

To consider, advise or resolve complaints, petitions and proposals from within the civil service, relating to inappropriate behavior or unsatisfactory performance of staff or organization within the scope of their jurisdiction in accordance with the laws;

To regularly report the overall situation in the district to the Governor or Mayor;

To cooperate with international organization as directed by the province or Capital City ;

To assume other authorities and duties in accordance with the laws.

Article 28 Authorities and Duties of Vice District Chief

The Vice District Chief shall assist the District Chief and is also in charge of some functions which are given by the District Chief.

In the case District Chief is unable to implement her/his duties for any reason, the Vice District Chief takes over.

Article 29 Appointment and Term of Office of the Chief and Vice District Chief

The District Chief is appointed, transferred or demoted by the Prime Minister based on the proposal of the Governor/Mayor.

The District Chief shall have a five - year term of office and can be reappointed for one more term in the same place.

The Vice District Chief is appointed, transferred or demoted by the Governor/Mayor based on a proposal of the District Chief and shall have a five- year office term and may be reappointed.

Chapter IV

District Administration Meeting

Article 30 The District Administration Meeting

Regular district administration meetings shall be held once a month and shall be convened and chaired by the district chief. The participants of the districts administration meeting include the Vice District Chief, Chief of the Districts Cabinet, Directors of field offices of the line ministries and equivalent organizations. If necessary, the representatives of other concerned parties may be invited to attend.

In cases where an emergency or urgent matter arises, the District Chief can call a special meeting.

In each meeting, minutes of the meeting shall be recorded. The minutes shall be approved and signed by the Chairman, and then distributed to the participants and concerned parties for implementation. In cases where there is a decision on important issues, a resolution of the meeting shall be prepared.

Article 31 The Agenda of the District Administration Meeting

The agenda or topics to be considered and agreed upon in the district administration meeting should include:

Socio-economic strategy and development plans of the districts;

District budget plan and annual budget amendments or adjustments;

Create/Abolition of villages and organization structure of district to considerate by higher level authority ;

Draft legal acts of the district;

Consideration of investment projects in the district;

Report on the implementation of planned activities of the district;

Annual report to the Governor, Mayor;

Local defense and security of the district and international relation and cooperation;

Personnel management issues.

The district administration meeting may also discuss other important and necessary issues.

PART IV MUNICIPAL ADMINISTRATION

Chapter I

Location, Role, Functions and Organization Structure

Article 32 The Municipality

A municipality is a level of local administration which is in an urban area. It is the provincial capital where the Provincial/City Administration Offices are located. The urban centers of other districts can be upgraded to a municipality if they meet all of the criteria defined by law such as high population density; and socio-economic, political, cultural and public service development. A municipality is comprised of several villages.

Article 33 Role and Functions of Municipal Administration

The municipal administration is local administration at the district level under the supervision of the Chief of Municipality.

The role and functions of a municipal administration are to manage political, economic, socio-cultural affairs and human resources; protect/preserve and utilize natural resources, the environment and other resources; to plan and implement urban development and public services; to ensure peace and security, and cleanliness of the municipality; to engage in international relation activities assigned by the Province/City.

Article 34 The Organization Structure and Personnel in the Municipality

The organization structure of the municipal administration is comprised of the following:

The municipal administration Cabinet;

Field offices of the line ministries, equivalent organizations, technical and service units.

The personnel of the municipal administration include:

the Mayor and Vice Mayor of the municipality;

Chief and Deputy Chief of the municipal cabinet

Head and Deputy Head of field offices; and staff of the municipal administration.

Article 35 Location, Role and Functions of the Municipal Administration Cabinet

The municipal administration Cabinet is part of the organizational structure of the municipality. Its role is to support the Mayor in managing the municipality's activities; developing and supervising the implementation of plans and programs; drafting, researching and reviewing documents; collaborating and providing information to the relevant parties; monitoring the implementation of legal acts of higher level authorities and the municipality; and facilitating the operation of the municipality.

Further details of the organization structure, personnel, authority and duties of the municipal administration Cabinet is outline by specific regulations.

Article 36 Location, Role and Functions of the Field Offices of the Line Ministries and Equivalent Organizations

The field offices of the line ministries and equivalent organizations are part of the organizational structure of the municipal administration. The role of the field offices is to manage their own sector's responsibilities assigned by the province/city, field offices, equivalent organisation and technical and service units, implement legal acts of higher authorities, and socio-economic development plans of the province/city and municipality.

Further details of the organization structure, personnel, authority and duties of field offices of the line ministries and equivalent organizations of the municipality are outline by specific regulations.

Chapter II

Creation of a Municipality

Article 37 The Creation of a Municipality

The creation, abolition, division, merger or definition of land area of a Municipality is defined and proposed by the Governor or Mayor and approved by the Government.

Article 38 The Criteria for Creation

The Provincial Capital is the municipality where the provincial/City administration offices are located. The urban centers of other districts can be established as a municipality if they meet the following criteria:

Has a population of at least 10,000 people. Exception to this criteria will be decided by the government;

Has a Developed economic, social, cultural area and a developed infrastructure system;

Has an ability to generate revenue to respond to necessary expenditures.

Chapter III

Role, Functions, Authority and Duties of the Municipality Mayor

Article 39 the Role and Functions of the Municipal Mayor

The Mayor of Municipality is the Mayor of the administrative and representative of the municipality. S/he is responsible to the provincial/city to fulfill their role, authority and duties.

Article 40 The Authority and Duties of the Municipality Mayor

The Chief of Municipality shall have following rights and duties:

To ensure the effective implementation of the Constitution, laws, rules of the state;

To convene and preside over municipal administration meetings;

To study, develop strategies, for municipality socio-economic development and budget plans;

To implement plans for: socio-economic development; the state budget; defense and security of the municipality; prevention of negative phenomena; monitoring and inspection of all municipal, provincial, city and central government investment projects being implemented in the municipality;

To facilitate and manage the organizations concerned to ensure the timely and accurate accounting of revenue in the municipality;

To motivate, promote and facilitate the participation of the Lao Front for National Construction, mass organizations, civil society organizations and all economic parties and ethnic people in the socio-economic development of the municipality;

To issue decisions, orders, instructions and notification other regulations in accordance with laws;

To implement citizen management in the municipality;

To suspend or cancel other legal acts of lower local administrations; or propose to higher level authority the cancel legal acts of higher local administration that do not support National laws and regulations;

To propose the creation and abolition of villages and any offices within the structure of the municipal administration;

To propose appointment, transfer or demote of the Vice Municipal Mayor, Chief, Deputy Chief of the Municipality Cabinet; To propose appointment or acknowledge an appointment of the Deputy Directors of the field offices of the line ministries and equivalent organizations in the Municipality.

To appoint, transfer or demote the heads, deputy heads of Units of the Municipality administration and other staff in accordance with the regulations; to approve the election or appointment of the Villages Chiefs;

To formulate, implement and supervise socio-economic, and cultural development plans; and manage security and order,

To develop and implement urban planning, maintain infrastructures, manage socio-cultural, sports and municipal service delivery including roads, electricity, water supply, markets, schools, hospitals, recreation facilities, sewage system, garbage collection, to protect river banks, to manage natural disasters, for instance, fire and flood; to clean and protect the environment, to provide public lights, parks and other amenities and facilities;

To manage and regulate building construction and other proposed developments according to the urban plan of the municipality;

To Manage the performance of the organization and personnel in accordance with their authority, include the supervision and reporting on performance of civil servants of line ministries;

To manage revenues and expenditures, properties, vehicles and other equipment of the municipality in accordance with regulations;

To consider, advise or resolve complaints, petitions and proposals from within civil service, relating to inappropriate behavior or unsatisfactory performance of staff or organization within the scope of their jurisdiction;

To regularly report the overall situation in the municipality to the Governor, Mayor;

To collaborate and cooperate with international organization as directed by province/city;

To assume other authorities and duties in accordance with the laws.

Article 41 Authority and Duties of Vice Municipality Mayor

The Vice Municipality Mayor shall assist the Municipality Mayor and is also in charge of some functions which are given by the Municipality Mayor.

In the case Municipality Mayor is unable to implement her/his duties for any reason, the Vice Municipality Mayor takes over.

Article 42 Appointment and Term of Office of the Chief and Vice Chief of Municipality

The Municipality Mayor is appointed, transferred or demoted by the Prime Minister based on the proposal of the Governor/ City Mayor.

The Municipality Mayor shall have a five - year term of office and can be reappointed for one more term in the same place.

The Vice Municipality Mayor is appointed, transferred or demoted by the Governor/ City Mayor based on a proposal of the Municipality Mayor and shall have a five- year office term and may be reappointed.

Article 43 Revenues of municipality

The revenues of the municipality are derived from the state budget, service charges/fees, local taxes, contributions from people and other revenues specified by regulations.

Chapter IV

Municipal Administration Meeting

Article 44 The Municipal Administration MeetingRegular Municipality administration meeting shall be held once a month and shall be convened and chaired by the Municipality Mayor. The participants of the Municipality administration meeting include the Vice Municipality Mayor, Chief of the Municipality Cabinet, Directors of field offices of the line ministries and equivalent organizations, Heads of technical and service Units. If necessary, the representatives of other concerned parties may be invited to attend.

In cases where an emergency or urgent matter arises, the Municipality Mayor can call a special meeting.

In each meeting, minutes of the meeting shall be recorded. The minutes shall be approved and signed by the Chairperson, and then distributed to the participants and concerned parties for implementation. In cases where there is a decision on important issues, a resolution of the meeting shall be prepared.

Article 45 The Agenda of the Municipality Meeting

The agenda or topics to be considered and agreed upon in the district administration meeting should include:

Socio-economic strategy and development plans of the Municipality;

Municipality budget plan and annual budget amendments or adjustments;

Construction projects, improvement and maintenance of infrastructures and services of the municipality

Create/Abolition of villages and organization structure of Municipality to considerate by higher level authority ;

Consideration of investment projects in the Municipality

Draft legal acts of the Municipality;

Report on the implementation of planned activities of the Municipality;

Annual report to the Governor, City Mayor;

Local defense and security of the Municipality and international relation and cooperation;

Personnel management issues.

The Municipality administration meeting may also discuss other important and necessary issues.

PART V VILLAGE ADMINISTRATION

Chapter I
Location, Role, Functions and Organization Structure

Article 46 The Village

The village is a unit of local administration at the grassroots level. It is under the supervision of the district or municipality. A village is comprised of several households.

Article 47 Role and Functions of Village Administration

The role and functions of the village administration is to implement and manage the socio-economic development plans of the village, to ensure security and order, to protect/preserve natural resources and the environment within the village

Article 48 the Organization Structure of the Village Administration

A village is headed by a Village Chief and assisted by a Deputy Chief and some functional units.

Article 49 the Village Chief Election

The Village Chief is elected by eligible voters in the village and acknowledged by the Chief of District or Mayor of Municipality.
In special circumstances, the Village Chief may be appointed or removed by the Chief of District or Mayor of Municipality.
The Deputy Village Chief can be appointed or removed by the Chief of District/ Mayor of Municipality in accordance with the proposal of the Village Chief.
The term of office of the Village Chief and Deputy Village Chief is three years. They can be re-elected or re-appointed.

Chapter II

Creation of a Village

Article 50 The Creation of a Village

A village is created, merged, divided, abolished or its land area defined by the Governor/Mayor in accordance with the proposal of the District Chief or Mayor of Municipality.

Article 51 The criteria for creation of a Village

The criteria to create a village are the following:

1. A suitable geographical location for administrative services

2. Population:

    The village in urban area should have a population of at least 1,000;

    The village in low land area should have a population of at least 500 ;

    The village in high land area/remote area should have a population of at least 200;

3. Socio-economic development conditions must be sustainable.

Chapter III

Role, Functions, Authority and Duties of the Village Chief

Article 52 The Role and Functions of the Village Chief

The Village Chief, who is the chief executive of the Village administration, represents the Village and is responsible to the District, or Municipality administration and all villagers, in the implementation of his/her role, authority and duties.

Article 53 Authority and Duties of Village Chief

The Chief of Village shall have the following authority and duties:

    To implement the Constitution, laws, resolutions, orders, socio-economic development plans to improve the living conditions of the population; to protect natural resources and the environment; and to maintain peace and security and the orderliness in the village;

    To disseminate the government policies and laws to all people in the village; and educate, mobilize and encourage harmony and solidarity of the people to practice their rights and meet their obligations;

    To motivate, promote and facilitate the participation of the Lao Front for National Construction, mass organizations, civil society organizations and all economic parties and ethnic people in the socio-economic development of the village;

To preserve and promote good national traditions and cultures of the multi-ethnic Lao people; discourage negative phenomena and superstitious beliefs; to promote education within the community and to educate the community to be responsible for hygiene and sanitation;

To manage the people in the village; to support the people to get a more stable employment and sustainable livelihood;

To convene and preside over village administration meetings and attend meetings convened by higher level authority;

To propose to the District Chief /Mayor to appoint or remove the Deputy Chief of village;

To issue rules and notifications in accordance with laws;

To propose to higher level authority to suspend orders or cancel some activities which are against laws, rules and the common interests of the village;

To resolve local conflicts, complaints of the people within the scope of her/his authority;

To regularly report the overall situation in the village to the district Chief/Municipality Mayor;

To receive some allowances in accordance with laws;

To assume other authority and duties in accordance with laws.

Article 54 Rights and Duties of the Deputy Chief of Village.

The Deputy Chief of Village is to assist the Village Chief, and is in charge of some functions assigned by the Chief of Village. In the case when the Chief of Village is unable to implement her/his duties for any reason, the Deputy Chief of Village takes over.

Chapter IV

Village Administration Meeting

Article 55 The Village Administration Meeting

Regular Village administration meeting shall be held once a month and shall be convened and chaired by the Village Chief. The participants of the Village administration meeting include: the Vice Chief of the village, and heads of units. If necessary, the representatives of concerned parties shall be invited to attend.

In cases where an emergency or urgent matter arises, the Village Chief can call a special meeting.

In each meeting, minutes of the meeting shall be recorded. The minutes shall be approved and signed by the Chairperson, and then distributed to the participants and concerned parties for implementation.

Article 56 The Agenda of the Village Meeting

The agenda or topics to be considered and agreed upon in the village meeting are the following:

Village strategy, socio-economic and environmental development plans;

Proposal for the creation/abolition of some offices in the organization structure of the village for consideration of higher level authority;

Considerate investment projects in the village;

Draft rules of the village;

Report on the implementation of planed activities of the village;

Annual report to the chief the district/municipality Mayor;

Local defense and security of the village.

The Village administration meeting may also discuss other important and necessary issues.

Article 57 The Village Meeting

The Chief of village convenes and chairs the village meeting. The participants in the village meeting are comprised of the Chief of village, deputy Chief of village, heads of units, and heads of families. The meeting is organized as required or as advised by higher level authority.

PART VI WORKING METHODS AND LOCAL ADMINISTRATION FINANCE

Article 58 The Working Methods of Local Administration

The local administrations operate in line with the principles of centralized democracy and unified leadership; individuals have responsibility as guided and supervised by leadership;

To do their work following plans, program, project, defined timelines, in accordance with the situation and conditions of each level;

To collaborate with concerned parties in all activities. In case when there is disagreement over some issues, these shall be submitted to higher level authorities for consideration and approval;

To supervise, evaluate and report the activities in the locality and report to higher level;

The local administration at the different levels must have its performance inspected by the people, by its own level and by higher level inspection authority.

Article 59 Local Administration Finance

Local administration finance has two levels of budget: provincial budget unit and district budget unit. The village is a basic unit for revenue collection and it incurs expenditures following rules and laws provided by the district level budget unit.Local administration finance must operate in line with the principles of centralized state budget; also the local budget shall be managed according to rules and laws and implement socio-economic development plans and annual plans which are approved by government for local administration.

The person who has the highest financial decision making function is the Governor/Mayor or a person assigned by the Governor/Mayor of the province/city. At the district administration level, it is the Chief of District/Mayor or a person who is assigned to this role.

PART VII FINAL PROVISIONS

Article 60 Stamp

The local administration at each level shall have its own stamp for official use.

Article 61 Implementation

The government is responsible to implement this law.

Article 62 Dates of Effect

This law is effective from the day the President of Lao PDR issues the decree.

Any regulations, provisions and rules that are inconsistent with this law shall be cancelled.

President of National Assembly

LAW ON THE GOVERNMENT OF THE LAO PDR

CHAPTER I GENERAL PROVISIONS

Article 1. Purpose of the Law on the Government

The purpose of the Law on the Government is to define the principles of the organization, function and working methods of the Government to ensure the efficient management of socio-economic affairs . The Law covers the use of national natural resources and the protection of the environment, ensuring the implementation of the laws of the State for the purpose of making the country strong and prosperous, upgrading the living standards of the people, and ensuring a peaceful and equitable society.

Article 2. Position and role of the Government

The Government of the Lao People's Democratic Republic is the executive organ of the State, approved by the National Assembly and responsible to the National Assembly and the President of the Republic for the execution of management of the state in regard to political, economic, cultural, and social matters, the use of national resources, the protection of environment , national defense and security and foreign affairs.

Article 3. Basic principle of the operation of the Government

The Government operates in line with the principle of centralized democracy in accordance with the Constitution and the laws, with the Lao People's Revolutionary Party as the leading nucleus, and Lao Front for National Construction , the mass organizations and social organizations as its forces. The Government uses educational, economic and administrative means to manage the State economy and society.

Article 4. The term of office of the Government

The term of office of the Government corresponds to the term of office of the National Assembly. Whenever the term of office of the Government comes to an end and the National Assembly has not yet approved a new Government, the incumbent Government will continue to perform its functions.

CHAPTER II THE STRUCTURE, DUTIES AND RESPONSIBILITIES OF THE GOVERNMENT

Article 5. Structure of the machinery of Government

The machinery of the Government of the Lao People's Democratic Republic consists of the Prime Minister's Office, ministries and ministry-equivalent organizations, approved by the National Assembly.
The organization of the machinery of Government should reflect the real needs of the

country at any given time.

Article 6. Structure of the Government

The Government is composed of the Prime Minister, Deputy Prime Ministers, Ministers and Chiefs of the Committees equivalent to the ministry.

Article 7. Rights and duties of the Government

to implement the Constitution, laws and resolutions of the National Assembly, state decrees and acts of the President of the Republic, organize the dissemination of laws, inculcate respect of laws in the public's mind, and define measures to protect the rights and legitimate interests of the people.

to map out strategic plans for socio-economic development and the fiscal year and submit them to the National Assembly for consideration and approval;

to collectively execute the management of infrastructure, the expansion of economic bases, culture and society, science and technology, fiscal and monetary policies, and to manage and ensure the efficient use and protection of the property of the state and collective and individual property, as stipulated in the Constitution and laws;

to report on its own activities to the National Assembly, and the standing committees of the National Assembly, prior to the National Assembly organizing the Congress and reporting to the President.

to study and submit draft laws to the National Assembly for adoption and draft acts to the standing committees of National Assembly for consideration,

to study and submit draft presidential decrees to the President for approval.

to issue decrees and decisions on state management, socio-economic management, science and technology, human resource development, protecting and using the environment and other natural resources; defense and security, and foreign affairs;

to organize, lead, manage, and supervise the work of various sectors and local administrations to ensure efficiency and with regard to the law;

to ensure all people are treated equally by the laws of the country;

to strengthen and supervise national defense, security and public order, build the people's armed forces, implement the decisions on military conscription, and define necessary measures to defend the country;

to suspend or rescind decisions and instructions, suggestions and circulars of the ministries, the ministry - equivalent organizations, and other agencies under direct authority of the government, and local administrations, if they run counter to the laws;

to create or abrogate districts and to define the boundaries of districts and municipalities in accordance with proposals of Governors and City Mayors;

to organize, conduct and monitor state inspections in order to counter the violation of laws and corruption and other weaknesses, and resolve the people's complaints and petitions with regard to illegal activities of civil servants and state management authorities at each level, as stipulated by law;

to cooperate, negotiate, and sign treaties and agreements with foreign countries, manage and supervise foreign affairs and the implementation of the signed treaties and agreements;

to exercise other rights and execute other duties, as stipulated by the Constitution and laws.

CHAPTER III GOVERNMENT MEETINGS

Article 8. Government meetings

The Prime Minister convenes and chairs the Government meeting to be held once a month. The meetings can only be opened if at least two-thirds of the Government's members attend .

The members of Government have the duty to attend each Government meeting. In addition, other persons concerned may be invited to attend the meeting. Those who are not members of the Government are permitted to take part in the discussions but they do not have the power to vote. Decisions at the Government meetings are taken by simple majority. If no majority can be reached, the decision of the Chairman will be final.

In case of emergency, extraordinary meetings can be convened by the Prime Minister or at the proposal of at least one-third of the members of Government.

Regarding the meeting mentioned above, the Government should request the Governors and City Mayors to participate in the meeting twice a year to inspect and supervise the implementation activities of the local authorities.

There will be minutes prepared at each Government meeting, to be certified by the Chairman and distributed to the Government members and the concerned organizations to implement.

Article 9. Matters to be submitted to the Government meetings

Matters to be considered and approved at the Government meetings are the following:

Strategic plans for state socio-economic development;

Annual State budget plans and State budget modifications;

Draft laws, draft decree-laws, and draft decrees;

Creation, abrogation, merger, and separation of ministries, ministry-equivalent organizations, provinces, city and special zones; definition of province, city and special zone boundaries before proposing to the National Assembly for consideration and approval;

Creation, abrogation, merger, and separation of the organizations under direct authority of the Government;

Creation, abrogation, merger, separation or definition of the boundaries of districts and municipalities.

Reports on the activities of Government;

Defense, security and foreign relations;

Negotiation regarding contents of treaties and agreements with foreign countries;

Reports to the National Assembly and President of the Republic;

In addition to these above-mentioned matters, the Government meetings can put forward other matters deemed relevant.

Article 10. Special Meeting of the Government

The special meeting of the Government is a meeting of the Government's members requested and chaired by President, which can be held any time when the country faces an economic crisis, social, cultural or natural disaster, or an emergency regarding defense, security or foreign relations,

CHAPTER IV ROLE, RIGHTS AND DUTIES OF THE PRIME MINISTER

Article 11. Role of the Prime Minister

The Prime Minister is the Head of Government, whose role is to guide the work of the Government and local administration .

Article 12. Rights and duties of the Prime Minister

The Prime Minister has the following rights and duties:

to convene and chair Government meetings;

to monitor and supervise the implementation of Government activities and the implementation of the decisions of the National Assembly and the implementation of the decisions of Government meetings and the activities of the Ministries, Ministry-equivalent organizations, provinces, cities, and other organizations under direct authority of the government ;

to make proposals to the National Assembly for the appointment, transfer or removal of Deputy Prime Ministers, Ministers, Ministers to the Prime Minister's Office and Head of Ministry equivalent organizations for consideration and approval;

to make proposals to the President of the Republic for the appointment or recall of plenipotentiary representatives of the Lao People's Democratic Republic in foreign countries;

to make proposals to the President of the Republic for the appointment, transfer or removal of Governor and City Mayors, and make proposals regarding the promotion to and demotion from the rank of General of the National Defense and Security force;

to appoint, transfer, or remove the following: Vice-Ministers, Vice-Minister to the Prime Minister's Office and Deputy Head of Ministry-equivalent organizations, Head and Deputy Head of Thabouangs, Director Generals, Vice-Governors, Vice-City Mayors, Chiefs of District, Heads of Municipality, Heads of organizational authorities under direct authority of the Government and other equivalent positions;

to promote to or demote from the rank of the Colonel in the National Defense and Security Forces;

to issue decrees, agreements instructions and suggestions related to the implementation of policies, laws and regulations and the Government's plans; to issue Decrees on organization and activities of the Ministries, Ministry-equivalent organizations, Thabouangs and Local Administration authorities;

to present an annual report regarding the execution of Government functions to the National Assembly, or standing committees of the National Assembly, prior to the National Assembly organizing the Congress and reporting to the President of the Republic;

to delegate his/her authority and duties to one of the Deputy Prime Ministers whenever he/she is absent or unable to execute his/her duties;

to resign from his/her position when he/she finds him/herself unable to execute his/her duties for health or other reasons;

to execute other rights and duties, as stipulated by the Constitution and laws.

Article 13. Appointment of the Prime Minister

The Prime Minister is appointed or removed by the President of the Republic after the approval of the National Assembly.

Article 14. The role of Deputy Prime Ministers

Deputy Prime Ministers assist the Prime Minister in leading and supervising the general work of the Government, and are responsible for specific functions allocated by the Prime Minister. When the Prime Minister is absent, the Deputy-Prime Minister who receives delegation of powers acts on his behalf.

Deputy Prime Ministers have the right to resign when they consider themselves unable to execute their duties for health or other reasons.

Article 15. Appointment of Deputy Prime Ministers,

Deputy Prime Ministers are removed by the President of the Republic, after the National Assembly has approved.

CHAPTER V THE PRIME MINISTER'S OFFICE

Article 16. Role of the Prime Minister's Office

The Prime Minister's Office is an organization within the organization of the Government's machinery. It has the role to assist the government, coordinate and summarize all questions related to the work of the Government, study and facilitate the implementation of the work of the Government, Prime Minister and other organizations under direct authority of the Government.

Article 17. Organization of the machinery of the Prime Minister's Office

The Prime Minister's Office consists of the Cabinet of the Prime Minister, the Committee of the Government Secretariat, Thabouangs and organizations under direct authority of the governmen t.

Article 18. Personnel Organization structure of the Prime Minister's Office

The Prime Minister's Office is under the direct responsibility of the Prime Minister. There are Deputy Prime Ministers, Ministers to the Prime Minister's Office, Vice-Ministers to the Prime Minister's office, Chief and Deputy Chiefs of the Cabinet of the Prime Minister, Chief and Deputy Chiefs of the Committee of the Government Secretariat, Chief and Deputy Chiefs of Thabouangs, Chief and Deputy Chiefs of the organizations under direct authority of the Government, Director General and Deputy Director Generals of Departments, Directors and Deputy Director of divisions and technical officers.

Article 19. Rights and duties of the Prime Minister's Office

The Prime Minister's Office has the following rights and duties:

to make preparations, arrange minutes and inform on the results of Government meetings ;

to collect and summarize internal and external information and inform the Government and Prime Minister;

to study and analyze issues and submit reports to the Government and Prime Minister to assist in the development of policy on, strategic development plans, socio-economic and cultural management, defense and security, foreign affairs, protecting national resources and the environment;

to manage the career areas which are not under the Ministries and Ministry-equivalent organizations;

to ensure favorable conditions for the effective functioning of the Government and Prime Minister and other organizations which are under the Prime Minister's Office;

to coordinate with the Office of the Party Central Committee, National Assembly, President of the Republic, Ministries, Ministry-equivalent organizations, Governors, cities, the Lao Front for National Construction and Central Mass Organisations, to ensure a united, consistent approach to the main tasks of Government;

to exercise all other rights and duties assigned by the Prime Minister and as stipulated by the Constitution and laws.

Article 20. The role of the Minister to the Prime Minister's Office

The Minister to the Prime Minister's Office is a Government member who acts as Chief of staff for the Government, responsible for tasks assigned by the Prime Minister.

Article 21. The function and authorities of the Minister to the Prime Minister's Office.

The Minister to the Prime Minister's Office has the following functions and authorities:

to develop and implement the decisions of the Government meetings in the respective sectors;

to monitor, manage and inspect the implementation of Planning under their responsibility;

to issue agreements, instructions and circulars in order to improve the efficiency of areas under their responsibility;

to suspend implementation or abolish agreements, instructions, suggestions, and circulars of lower level organizations which are under his/her authority. They has the right to propose to amendment or cancel juristic acts of other organizations, provinces or cities which are in contradiction of regulations under its own responsibility;

to identify priorities for implemention of the annual plan;

to submit draft laws, presidential decrees and governmental decrees related to their respective sectors, to the government;

to appoint or remove Deputy Director Generals, Directors and Deputy Directors of divisions of the department;

to collaborate and cooperate and sign agreements with foreign countries, in accordance with the official authorization of the Government;

to resign from his/her position when he/she finds him/herself unable to execute his/her duties for health or other reasons;

to exercise all other rights and duties as assigned by the Prime Minister or stipulated by the Constitution and laws.

Article 22. Role of Vice-Ministers to the Prime Minister's Office

The Vice-Ministers to the Prime Minister's Office have the role to assist the Government and are responsible for specific tasks as assigned by the Prime Minister or Minister to the Prime Minister's Office. The term of office of the Vice-Ministers to the Prime Minister's Office are equivalent to the term of office of the Government. Vice-Ministers to the Prime Minister's Office have the right to resign when they consider themselves unable to execute their duties for health or other reasons.

CHAPTER VI MINISTRIES AND MINISTRY-EQUIVALENT ORGANIZATIONS

Article 23. Position and role of Ministries and Ministry-equivalent organizations

Ministries and ministry-equivalent organizations are elements of the Government machinery, which act as Chiefs of staff for the Government and execute macro management in their respective sectors throughout the country.

Article 24. Organization of the machinery of the Ministries and the Ministry-equivalent organizations

Ministries and Ministry-equivalent organizations are composed of the Offices of the Ministries and Ministry-equivalent organizations, departments, divisions, institutes and technical units, which are defined by the Decrees of the Prime Minister.

Article 25. Organization of Ministries and Ministry-equivalent organizations .

Ministries and Ministry-equivalent organizations consist of Ministers or Heads of Ministry-equivalent organizations, Vice-Ministers or Deputy-Heads, Heads of the Minister's Office, Deputy-Heads of the Minister's Office, Heads of Departments and Deputy-Heads of Department, Heads of division and Deputy Heads of division, Heads of Institutes and Deputy-Heads of Institutes, Heads and Deputy-Heads of technical units and technical staff.

Article 26. Rights and duties of Ministries and Ministry-equivalent organizations

Ministries and Ministry-equivalent organizations have the following rights and duties:

to study and draft policies and strategic plans for their respective sectors to be submitted to the Government;

to study and translate policies, plans and decisions of the Government into programmes and detailed projects in the sectors for which they are responsible;

to propose to amend or draft laws, Presidential acts, Presidential decrees, decrees to the Government; to issue agreements, instructions, suggestions and circulars in order to support the execution of macro management in their respective ministries;

to monitor and manage the vertical line activities and personnel of their respective sectors, by collaborating in a unified manner with the local administrations;

to train the personnel in their respective sectors;

to organize and manage foreign relations as authorized by the Government;

to supervise and summarize the implementation of activities in their respective sectors and report to the Government and the Prime Minister;

to exercise all other rights and other duties specifically assigned by the Government and as stipulated by the Constitution and laws.

Article 27. Role of Ministers and Heads of Ministry-equivalent organizations

Ministers and Heads of Ministry-equivalent organizations are members of the Government as Heads of the sector, and assist the Government in the macro-management of their respective sectors.

Article 28. Rights and duties of Ministers, Heads of Ministry-equivalent organizations.

Ministers and Heads of Ministry-equivalent organizations have the following rights and duties:

to develop and implement the decisions of the Government meetings in their respective sectors;

to guide, manage and supervise the implementation of activities in their respective sectors;

to issue agreements, instructions and circulars in order to raise the efficiency of the management in their sectors;

the right to suspend or abolish the implementation of agreements, instructions, suggestions and circulars of the lower level of organizations under their responsibility. They also have the right to propose amendments to, suspend or abolish the implementation by, or juristic acts of, other organizations or local administrations which are in contradiction with the regulations and principles of their respective sectors or in contradiction with the laws;

to decide on the necessary measures to be taken in order to implement the annual plan;

to submit proposals or draft laws and draft Presidential acts, Presidential decrees and decrees related to their respective sectors, to the Government;

to appoint, transfer or remove the Deputy Heads of Minister's offices, Deputy Director General of departments, Heads of divisions and Deputy Heads of divisions, Heads and Deputy Heads of units. Also, to appoint, transfer, or remove the Chief and Deputy Chief of the provincial department and Head of Office at the district level through discussion with local administration authorities;

to assign particular tasks to Vice-Ministers, Deputy-Heads of the Ministry-equivalent organizations; to assign one of the Vice-Ministers or Vice-Presidents of Ministry-equivalent organizations to act as Minister or Head when they are absent or unable to perform their duties;

to cooperate and sign agreements and conventions with foreign countries, as authorized by the Government;

to resign from his/her position when he/she finds him/herself unable to execute his/her duties for health or other reasons;

to exercise all other rights and duties as assigned by the Prime Minister or as stipulated by the Constitution and laws.

Article 29. The roles of Vice-Minister and Deputy Heads of Ministry-equivalent

organizations

The Vice-Minister and Deputy-Heads of Ministry-equivalent organizations have the role to assist the Minister and Head of Ministry-equivalent organizations in monitoring and supervising general work of the Ministry, Ministry-equivalent organizations, and responsiblity for specific tasks assigned by the Minister and Ministry-equivalent organizations.

The term of office of the Vice Minister and Deputy Head of the Ministry-equivalent organizations is equivalent to the term of the Government.

Vice-Ministers and Deputy-Heads of Ministry-equivalent organizations should resign from their position when they find themselves unable to execute their duties for health or other reasons;

CHAPTER VII WORKING METHODS OF THE GOVERNMENT.

Article 30. Working methods of the Government

The Government functions in line with the principles of a centralized democracy, through unified team management responsibilities with increased individual responsibilities. The Government attaches great importance to meetings as a way to improve its functioning.

Article 31. Activities of the Government members

The Government members must respect each other's role and collaborate with each other.

In cases where there is no consensus of opinion among the Government members, the Prime Minister is requested to find solutions to the problems and arbitrate.

Concerning foreign relations, the Government members must solicit authorization from the Prime Minister.

Article 32. Relationship with the National Assembly

The Government has the obligation to report annually to the National Assembly on its activities, and to submit its strategic socio-economic plan and state budget, as well as modifications to the state budget, to the National Assembly for consideration and approval. The Government has the obligation to explain and answer questions relating to the execution of Government duties or the activities of particular Government members, when such questions are raised by the National Assembly or some of its members.

During the recess of the National Assembly, the Government members have the obligation to report to the Standing Committees of the National Assembly on their activities and provide information at the request of the National Assembly standing committees.

Concerning foreign relations or important domestic tasks , the Government must seek agreement from the National Assembly. Foreign relations related to important treaties or ratification agreements must be submitted to the National Assembly for approval by the Government .

Article 33. Relationship with the President of the Republic

The Government reports on its activities to the President of the Republic. When it is deemed necessary, the Government will invite the President of the Republic to preside over the Government meeting.

Article 34. Relationship with the People's Supreme Court and the Public Prosecutor-General

Along with the Supreme Court and the Public Prosecution Institutes, the Government follows up and supervises the enforcement of law and deterrent measures against social weak points.

In cases of necessity , the Government may invite the President of the Supreme Court and the Public Prosecutor-General to attend Government meetings.

Article 35. Relationship with Lao Front for National Construction , Mass Organizations and Social Organizations

In order to ensure the efficiency of its activities, the Government must consult and exchange ideas and opinions with the Lao Front for National Construction, the Lao People's Revolutionary Youth Union, the Lao Federation of Trade Unions, the Lao Women's Union and social organizations, and mobilize the organizations mentioned above to participate in state management and socio-economic management. They should advise on the guidelines and decisions taken at Government meetings as well as on relevant important situations, answer questions and create conditions to enable the Lao Front for National Construction , mass organizations and social organizations to operate in line with their roles.

In cases of necessity, representatives of the Lao Front for National Construction , mass organizations and social organizations may be invited to attend Government meetings.

Article 36. Consideration of and solutions to people's complaints and petitions or people's proposals.

While implementing its activities, the Government and its members must listen to the ideas and opinions of the people.

The government must consider and resolve the complaints, petitions and proposals of the people regarding illegal activities of civil servants and state management authorities at each level as stipulated in the laws

CHAPTER VIII FINAL PROVISIONS

Article 37. Implementation

The Government of the Lao People's Democratic Republic implements this law .

Article 34. Effectiveness

This law replaces the law on the Council of Ministers of the Lao People's Democratic Republic No 01/95, dated 08 March 1995.

This law becomes effective on the day the Resident of State issues the State Decree to promulgate it. All provisions and regulations which run counter to this law are abrogated.

Vientiane ,

PUBLIC SERVICE REGULATIONS OF LAO PDR

After the promulgation of Prime Minister's Decree No.171/PM dated 17 November 1993 concerning the public service regulations on the classification of rank and grade of public service dated 11 November 1993 for the last 10 years, public service has undergone improvements and development by adopting uniform management system throughout the country facilitating the organizations in the planning, employment, transfer, promotion, capacity building and application of policies.

Nevertheless, weaknesses are observed in public service in the past and some issues remain pending which were the main causes of lax application of public service regulations on the one hand and on the other hand the content of the previous public service regulations was not complete and sufficiently strict.

To pursue the strengthening of public service and address the weaknesses and pending issues of the past, Prime Minister issued Decree No. 82/PM concerning the public service regulations of Lao PDR dated 19 May 2003. Basically, the fundamental content of the previous regulations are kept untouched while some provisions, articles are added, improved more clearly and strictly.

Therefore, as a reference for the implementation, Prime Minister Office issues the following instructions:

I. Objectives

- For better understanding of directives, guidelines and policies of the government concerning the public administration in the new era;

- To advise, explain some contents of the Decree more clearly for better understanding and uniform implementation;

II. Additional Instructions to some contents of Decree No.82/PM

1. General Provisions (Chapter I)

1) Public servants of Lao PDR defined in Article 2 include the people employed, appointed in the organization of the Party, Government, Lao National Front for Construction, Mass Organization at central, provincial and district levels and in overseas representative offices of Lao PDR.

2) Government employees without public servant status constitute of employees in administrative positions levels 1,2,3 and 4 as defined in Article 2 of Decree No.173/PM dated November 11, 1993 concerning the definition of civil administrative position of Lao PDR; non-Party member of Parliament, soldiers, police, employees of state-owned enterprises and employees-under-contract;

3) Employees-under-contract are the people employed in the organization of the Party, government, Lao National Front for Construction and Mass Organization at central and local levels based on contracts; the recruitment of employees-under- contract is based on the quota allocated by the government. The duration of the contract is based on the agreement between the parties; the organization responsible for the management of employee-under-contract is the Department of Organization and Personnel of concerned organization; the salary of employees-under-contract is to be applied based on the regulations of Ministry of Finance and each organization has to plan for the need of Employee-under- contract on yearly basis;

4) Public administration principles of Lao PDR as defined in the Article 4 which is to be centralized and uniformly implemented throughout the country means the administration under the same regulations on the basis of division of level of administration i.e. the division of responsibility between the central (Prime Minister's Office), sectoral (Ministries, Ministry-equivalent organizations, Presidential Office, Party organizations, Lao National Front for Construction, People's Court, Supreme Court) and local levels (provincial and districts).

5) The selection, the selection test and the recruitment defined in Article 4 is the selection, selection test and the recruitment of Lao Nationals for public service the process of which has to abide by the equity principles meaning that every Lao citizen has the equal opportunity to apply for the selection; "open" means dissemination of information about different processes; "objectivity" means in conformity with the reality, collegial decision; "fair" means in conformity with the regulations and the principles;

2. Ranks, grades and professional groups of public servants (Chapter 2)

Ranks, grades and professional groups of public servants defined in Article 5 through Article 7 have the following meaning:

1) Public servants classified under rank I and II are called: administrative assistants. Public servants of rank I are the graduates or having certificate of completion of Upper Secondary School downward; public servants of rank II are the ones having certificate of completion of first level of vocational education. Example: typist, driver etc...

2) Public servants of rank III, IV and V are called: technical staff graduated from middle-level technical education upward.

3) Public servants of Lao PDR constitute of many professional sectors; each sector constitutes of many professional groups; for example: agriculture, livestock, veterinary, irrigation etc...

3. Management positions and work positions of public service (Chapter 3)

1) The classification of management positions of public service is defined in Article 2 of Decree No.173/PM, dated November 11, 1993 concerning the definition of management

positions of civil service of Lao PDR for the positions in the category 5 through category 10 until further change.

2) For the work positions of public servants, instructions No.0472/PM dated September 30, 2003 concerning the positions are to be applied.

4. Obligations and duties of public servants (Chapter 4)

Additional instructions to be applied for the obligations and duties of public servant defined in Article 10 through 21 are the following:

1) Obligations and duties of public servants defined in Article 16 are meant for those employed as public servant within the first 5 years before being accepted for a permanent position in the concerned organization. Newly employed public servant has to carry out their duties in the grassroots/district level or village level for at least 2 years to get practical experiences along with the learned theory.

2) Transferring public servants to carry out their duties in the grassroots level should be based on local requirements and adequate needs of relevant sector. To address these issues, relevant ministry, sector should make adequate decisions as to how to carry out those obligations. The implementation should be based on the plan and under detailed collaboration with relevant local authorities; the execution of this obligation could be done anytime within the first 5 years of service.

3) Ministries and sectors are responsible for salary, compensation and other policies while local authorities are responsible for the operations and provision of accommodation for public servants transferred to perform their duties in the localities according to the local capacity.

4) For public servants having received scholarship from the government or from international organizations assisting Lao PDR for in-country or overseas study, following procedures are applied prior and subsequent to the study:

• Before the study, relevant ministry, sector or local authority must advise the candidate to write application form, take an oath and to get endorsement from guarantors. After completion of the study, he/she has to continue the public service and abide strictly by the state regulations.

• After completion of the study, he/she has to continue the public service for at least a period double the duration of the study. In case he/she wishes to resign from public service, the relevant public servant has to pay back to the state the amount double of what he/she has received.

• In case of impossibility of pay back, relevant discipline committee shall invite the public servant and the guarantor(s) for discussion and measures according to the rules of law will be applied; in case a non-governmental organization wishes to employ that person, that organization is accountable to pay back to the government equivalent to the amount of scholarship received without any special policies.

5) Concerning the declaration of assets, liabilities of public servants, their spouse and children as defined in Article 19, it is aimed at public servants in the levels 5 to 10 and all public servants working with the collection of revenue for the national treasury.

The declaration of assets and liabilities are under the direct responsibility of Ministries, organizations and localities and are to be conducted once a year according to the form issued by the Prime Minister's Office.

The inventory of assets and liabilities are to be kept confidential; only relevant organizations and organizations dealing with the investigation are eligible to know and shall not be disclosed to others.

6) Public servants officially transferred to work and receiving regular salary from international organizations or from projects both domestic or overseas are entitled to pay income tax according to the rules of Law by the usual financial body of their organization.

Relevant organization or local authority will inform the Ministry of Finance to cancel the payment of salary of the relevant public servant; while the already budgeted salary transferred to the account of the relevant Ministry, organization or localities has to be returned to the national treasury budget.

5. Rights and benefits of public servants (Chapter 5)

Public servants transferred to work in remote and dangerous areas, working with toxic substances shall be entitled to receive incentives adequately; relevant sectors will study the principles for the implementation of those policies in collaboration with Ministry of Finance and other relevant parties and submit a proposal to the government for consideration and for accurate and uniform implementation.

6. Prohibition (Chapter 6)

1) Public servants are prohibited to run businesses of their own which are related to the works under their responsibility.

2) Public servants are prohibited to run businesses as executives or managers of the business enterprise unless appointed by the state.

If public servants breach the rules stipulated in Chapter 6, discipline commission of different levels are to take adequate disciplinary measures according to Chapter 14 and 16 and report to higher public administration organization.

7. Employment (Chapter 7)

• Recruitment for public service

1) Recruitment of new public servant shall be strictly based on work positions defined in the organization structure and on the quota allocated by the government for each fiscal year.

2) In each fiscal year, ministries, organizations and localities must submit plan for requirement of new public servants to central administration organization; new public servants requirement plan is based on the needs and the available positions.

3) The public servant statistic data and new public servants requirement plan shall be sent to Department of Public Service Administration and Public Service on 31 May no later than 31 May of each year. If ministries, organizations and localities report the statistical data of public service and new public servants beyond the deadline, those plans will not be consolidated in the overall plan for approval:

4) The person to be selected for public service position shall be good student, have clear bio-data, qualifications and be accountable as well as be a graduate from domestic or foreign institutions and shall strictly comply with required conditions as stipulated in Article 39.

5) A test or selection test is part of the recruitment process depending on the case. In case, many candidates are applying for the same position, a test has to be organized to ensure equity principle and to select the best.

In case, only a limited number of candidates apply for a vacant position, a test might not be needed; direct selection is applicable.

6) The candidates for the selection for public service are based on the results of the test or the selection. In case the employees-under-contract are among the candidates, if the results of their test or selection are close to the results of the other candidates, employee-under-contract shall have priority because these people have learned and accumulated some experiences.

The employee-under-contract having worked continuously at the same place for 3 years and having passed the test shall be accepted as permanent status public servant without any training period. The begin date for employment is the date when the employment agreement is signed.

7) After the successful test or selection and the employment agreement is signed, relevant ministry, organization and localities has to prepare documents (based on the form in the annex) and send to Department of Public

Administration and Public Service for control and approval concerning the ranking, seniority, educational qualifications etc...

The recruitment of new employee is to be conducted twice per year in the second and the fourth quarter of fiscal year.

8) The recruitment of police, soldiers and state enterprise for public service in ministries, organizations and localities shall be based on the actual requirements of the work, vacant positions and shall be within the quota allocated by the government;

The ranking for soldiers, police shall follow the Decree of Prime Minister No.31/PM, dated 12 February 1994 pertaining to the equivalence of ranking between the armed force and civil sector or based on educational qualifications and the case of higher benefit is to be applied.

9) To ensure the uniform implementation for policies stipulated in Paragraph 3 of Article 46, the public servant being transferred as defined in Paragraph 1 and 2 shall transfer the money for the social insurance in former organization to the state social insurance fund.

- Ranking and grading of public servants

The ranking and grading of public servant basically is to follow Decree 172/PM as previously, but after the issuance of Decree 82/PM dated 19 September 2003, following points are to be implemented:

1) For public servants of rank IV having Master Degree or equivalent, Phd. Degree or equivalent which were already allocated a rank before Decree 82/PM, 2 additional grades are to be applied.

For example: Mr. A having ranked 4, grade 7 before will now have rank 4, grade 7+2= 9.

For the education level above Bachelor degree specializing in one particular field, one additional grade is to be applied.

2) For public servant having graduated after the issuance of Decree 82/PM, the followings are to be implemented:

o For public servants having a salary equal or more than Grade 5 Master degree or equivalent, Grade 6 above Master degree, Grade 7 Phd. degree of Rank 4, one additional grade for the study and one additional grade for public servant continuing the study are to be applied:

For example: Mr. B is public servant of Rank 4 Grade 8 is sent for a Phd. degree, after the completion, based on previous ranking, he shall be of Rank 4 of Grade 10; based on new ranking system, he shall be of Rank 4 Grade 10+2= Rank 4 Grade 12.

    o For public servant under Rank 5 Master degree or equivalent, 6 above Master degree, 7 Phd. degree of Rank 4, the new ranking rule is to be applied added by one Grade for public servant continuing the study.

For example: Ms. C is public servant of Rank 4 Grade 3 is sent for study Master Degree for 2 years; after completion, based on usual ranking system she shall be of Grade lower than 5 Master degree or equivalent; based on new ranking rule she shall be of Rank 4 Grade 5+1= Rank 4 Grade 6.

    o For public servants of Rank II, III having successfully passed the promotion test, following ranking rules are to be applied:

    - For public servants having lower salary index, following ranking system is to be applied:

For example: Ms. D if of Rank II Grade 8 in the second quarter of year 2003 having passed promotion test, she shall be of Rank III Grade 1 in quarter II of year 2004.

    - For public servants having equal or higher salary index, following ranking system is to be applied.

For example: Mr. E if of Rank II Grade 13. The new rank shall be Rank III Grade 5.

    o For public servant of rank I, II and III having completed higher level vocational education, the ranking is to be applied as the following:

    - For public servants having lower salary index, usual ranking is applied added by one grade (for study duration of one year and above).

Example: Ms. F if of rank III grade 5 after bachelor degree completion, she shall be of rank IV grade 2+1

    - For public servant having salary equal or higher, following ranking rule is applied.

For example: Mr. G is of rank III grade 14. The new index shall be Rank IV grade 6+1

3) Ministry of Education shall issue instructions pertaining to the equivalence of certificates of graduates from different institution systems both domestic and international.

8. Training (Chapter 8)

Public servants undergoing training have the rights for compensation similar to permanent status public servants as stipulated in the Decree 82/PM with exception for some policies as the following:

    o Compensation policies for the spouse and children;

    o Transferring to other places, unless there is urgent requirement or being removed from public service following disciplinary measures;

    o Annual leave

    o Special leave to stay with the spouse being transferred or studying abroad;

After completion of the training, subject to compliance to all required conditions, the trained public service shall be employed as permanent status public servant receiving full salary and the date of the service starts from the date of becoming permanent status public servant.

9. Status of public servants (Chapter 9)

1) All work leaves of public servants have to be officially authorized by relevant organization.

2) Work leaves for medical treatment shall not take more than 12 months from the date of permission; Beyond that limit, relevant organization shall consider implementing one-time compensation policy or compensation for the loss of workforce as stipulated in the Instructions No.2282 dated 12 October 1994 pertaining to the implementation of Decree concerning the social insurance for government staff-public servants.

3) Public servants are authorized to take a work leave to stay with the spouse being transferred or conducting research abroad for 1 yea and over, but relevant public servant must have served in public service for at least 3 years and has to submit a written request to concerned organization for consideration. During the leave, the relevant public servant shall not receive salary and compensations; this period shall not be counted as period of public service. Upon the return, he/she has to report to concerned organization and submit a request for re-employment to concerned organization for consideration. After that, Department of Public Administration and Public Service has to be informed for follow-up.

10. Transfer of public servants (Chapter 10)

Transferring of public servants is based on actual requirements and is the mandate of minister, chief of central organization, provincial governor, municipality mayor, district governor and chief of municipality according to the rules of Law.

Transferring public servants to localities has to abide strictly by the Decree 21 dated May 8, 1993 in which it is stipulated that transferring shall be related to evaluation of the performance.

Transferring of public servants should be in line with the expertise; transferring public servants subjectively, not in line with the expertise, without coordination are to be avoided.

Transferring of public servants shall be adequately supported by relevant documents, correct procedures and methods as stipulated in the Notice No. 08 dated January 4, 2001 pertaining to the implementation of public administration and reduction of staff.

11. Promotion of ranks, grades (Chapter 12)

1) Rank promotion

Rank promotion is achieved by 4 different ways: promotion based on the certificate(s), promotion based on seniority, promotion based on the test and promotion based on administrative positions; details are stipulated in Article 66; special notice is disseminated for the promotion based on the test;

2) Grade promotion

Regular promotion of grade of public servant is based on the results of the performance evaluation of previous year.

One-year early promotion is the promotion for public servant whose performance is outstanding in 5 consecutive years. The promotion shall take place in quarter II or quarter IV of year 5 after the evaluation of the performance of quarter I of that year.

Promotion based on seniority has to be conducted strictly in sequence and based on ranking number in the list of the candidates for promotion which takes place in quarter II and quarter IV of each fiscal year.

Public servant the evaluation of whom is weak 2 years consecutively shall be excluded from regular promotion.

3) Adjustment of grades

For Public servant having graduated Bachelor degree in a particular field, Master degree or equivalent, above Master degree, Phd. degree or equivalent and staff of state enterprises appointed to the Deputy-Director of department or above before the promulgation of Decree No. 82/PM dated May 17, 2003 pertaining to the regulations of Public Service of Lao PDR, the salary has to be adjusted. For staff from state enterprises transferred to public service under different forms, the Instructions

No.01/DPA dated November 26, 1993 concerning the ranking and grading of public servants are to be applied.

All previous and future rank, grade adjustments shall be submitted by ministries, organizations and localities to Department of Public Administration and Public Service within Prime Minister' Office for control and approval.

12. Compensation and remuneration (Chapter 13)

For public servants who are sent to Vietnam for study or research for more one year or above, the Notice No.240 dated June 9, 1997 is to be applied; implementation of 100% salary policy for married and 90% for single public servant.

13. Sanctions methods (Chapter 16)

> 1) Mistakes of public servants should be considered strictly following the procedures starting from the investigation, mutual critics within the working unit first. If no change is observed, the relevant organization shall conduct a second round of investigation under the presence of mass organization followed by a written record and pledges.
>
> 2) If after the investigation and the pledge, the relevant public servant keeps commit mistakes more seriously, the relevant organization shall prepare documents to submit to disciplinary committee to take measures;
>
> 3) By considering disciplinary measures, the committee shall invite the relevant public servant in written form to protect him/herself and to explain the reasons and show evidences.

Taking decisions on disciplinary measures in the absence of relevant public servant is to be avoided unless he/she refuses to join.

Following the decision on disciplinary measures, the committee shall submit the case to relevant Minister, President of equal ranking organization, provincial governor, mayor, Chief of Special Zone, district governor and chief of municipalities for consideration.

The period of the decision process as stipulated in the Article 80 starts from the day when the committee receives the document from relevant organization until the day of the decision of Minister, President of equal ranking organization, provincial governor, mayor, chief of Special Zone, district governor and chief of municipality.

In case the public servant are found at fault and the Court has ordered punishment according to the Law, the committee shall consider and propose to higher authority to decide about the status of the relevant public servant such as to remove from public service or to let continue to serve in public service after having served the sentence. In case of sentence of 6 months and over, the disciplinary measures applied to public servant of rank 3 defined in Article 76 is to be applied.

14. Training and capacity building (Chapter 17)

Training of public servants constitutes of 3 categories:

1) Basic training means explaining to new public servants to understand about:

- Regulations for public servants of Lao PDR;

- Rules of the management within the organization;

- Positions, roles, duties and organization structure of the concerned organization

- Coordination regime

- Other issues relating to roles and duties of concerned organization.

2) Regular in-service training means training, capacity building in political theory, technical field especially for public servants based on the annual evaluation of performance and training plan.

3) Training prior to assuming new duty and position means training, capacity building in political theory and technical field and other required basic knowledge to prepare for a new and more complicated duty or to assume a new administrative position of higher level.

The selection of public servants for training or capacity building shall be based on the following conditions:

- Results of the evaluation of past performance;
- Requirements of the organization and the works;
- Target for assuming the vacant position or an management position.

The candidates for further study period of 3 years and over shall have motivation for self-development, good health and be aged less than 45 years.

15. Termination of public service (Chapter 18)

1) All public servants reaching the age of retirement and having fulfilled the period of public service shall receive pension as defined by the regulations. Department of organization and personnel of ministry, organization and organization committee of province, municipality, Special Zone after having considered who shall retire and who

are still needed to continue working shall submit a proposal to Department of Public Administration and Public Service to issue an official notice one year in advance and the relevant public servant does not need to submit application.

After one year, at scheduled time period, the relevant organization shall submit the list of public servants complied with all conditions for retirement to the leading body of Ministry, organization, province, Vientiane municipality, Special Zone to consider who shall retire and who is needed to work further then submit to Department of Public Administration and Public Service for official approval which shall occur in quarter II and IV of each fiscal year.

2) Public servants willing to have early retirement shall receive a bonus compensation called: one-time compensation. The early retirement is implemented and valid only after the written request is approved by the organization. Public servants willing to have early retirement who ceases to work before the approval are considered irresponsible and policies shall not be implemented. Public servants serving in public service for less than 5 years desiring to resign from public service shall not receive any compensation policy.

3) Leaving the duty means cease to serve in public service without authorization from the organization. Public servants leaving the duty consecutively for one month and over without reason are considered desertion and are to be wiped out from the list of public servants.

16. Public administration (Chapter 19)

Public administration in Lao PDR is based on centralized democracy implemented uniformly throughout the country with division of level of administration between the central, ministry, equal ranking organization, province and district.

Each level of public administration is an organization implementing its mandate as secretariat to each level of authority in public administration with the following duties:

- Central public administration organization has the role of macro-level public administration throughout the country and has the following duties:

1) Study, develop the directives, plan and policies of the Party concerning public service into strategic plan, public administration development plan in each period;

2) Study, consolidate training plan, capacity building throughout the country in each period; coordinate with ministries, organizations and institutions for training and capacity building of public servants according to the plan;

3) Study, draft the Law and regulations pertaining to the public administration and submit to competent authority for consideration and promulgation;

4) Support, monitor and supervise the implementation of Law and regulations pertaining to public administration in ministries, provinces and districts;

5) Manage centrally and uniformly the number of public servants throughout the country in each period;

6) Study, define the quota of new public servants to propose to the government for approval; after the government's approval, allocate the quota to different targets according to plan and monitor the implementation every fiscal year;

7) Consider, solve or propose to higher competent authority the complaints of public servants within the limit of rights defined by the rules of Law.

8) Contact, cooperate with foreign countries and international organizations for assistance in funding and expertise aiming at gradually developing public administration;

9) Others as assigned by the government.

• Ministry or equal ranking organization level public administration organization has the following duties:

1) Study and develop strategic plan for public servants development within the organization based on strategic plan and general plan of central public administration organization;

2) Study public servants allocation plan, arrangement and training or capacity building of public servants within the sector;

3) Manage public servants within the sector quantitatively and qualitatively and implement policies according to public administration regulations;

4) Control, support the implementation of directives, plan and policies, regulations pertaining to public administration within the sector;

5) Strengthen the organization system, and improve the efficiency public administration apparatus in the sector;

6) Manage, collect statistical data and information pertaining to public administration and report to central public administration organization;

7) Consolidate and report the implementation of policies pertaining to public administration in the sector to central public administration organization according to the regulations.

• Provincial level public administration organization has the following duties:

1) Assist central public administration organization in the study and development of strategic plan to develop public administration within the organization apparatus;

2) Study the allocation plan, arrangement and training/capacity building of public servants within the organization;

3) Manage public servants quantitatively and qualitatively and implement policies according to the regulations of public administration;

4) Control, support the organization in the implementation of directives, plan and policies, regulations pertaining to public service administration in the sector;

5) Improve the organization system, public service apparatus for better efficiency;

6) Manage, collect statistical data and information pertaining to public service administration and report to central public service administration organization;

7) Assist ministries, equal ranking organizations in public administration of vertical line sector based in the localities;

8) Consolidate and report the implementation of policies pertaining to provincial and district public administration to central public administration organization according to the regulations.

• District level public administration has the following duties:

1) Assist provincial public administration organization in the study and development of strategic plan to develop public administration within the organization apparatus;

2) Study the allocation plan, arrangement and training/capacity building of public servants within the organization;

3) Control, support the organization in the implementation of directives, plan and policies, regulations pertaining to public administration in the sector;

4) Improve the organization system, public service apparatus for better efficiency;

5) Manage, collect statistical data and information pertaining to public administration and report to provincial public administration organization;

6) Assist ministries, equal ranking organizations in public administration of vertical line sector based in the district;

TRAVELING TO LAOS

US STATE DEPARTMENT SUGGESTIONS

COUNTRY DESCRIPTION: Laos is a developing country with a socialist government that is pursuing economic reform. Outside of Vientiane, the capital, and Luang Prabang, tourist services and facilities are relatively undeveloped.

ENTRY REQUIREMENTS: A passport and visa are required. Visas are issued upon arrival in Laos to foreign tourists and business persons, subject to certain conditions, at the following points of entry: Wattay Airport, Vientiane; Luang Prabang Airport; Friendship Bridge, Vientiane; Ban Huay Xai, Bokeo Province; and Vantao, Champasak Province. In the United States, U.S citizens may apply for visas and obtain further information about entry requirements directly from the Embassy of the Lao People's Democratic Republic, 2222 S St. N.W., Washington, D.C. 20008, tel. 202-332-6416, fax 202-332-4923, Internet home page: http://www.laoembassy.com. U.S. citizens should not attempt to enter Laos without valid travel documents or outside official ports of entry. Unscrupulous travel agents have sold U.S.-citizen travelers false Lao visas, which have resulted in those travelers being denied entry into Laos.

SAFETY AND SECURITY: The security situation in Laos can change quickly. Please refer to any Department of State Public Announcements for Laos for additional information.

Since the Spring of 2000, a number of bombings have occurred in public places frequented by foreign travelers in Vientiane, and there have been credible reports of other explosive devices found in Savannakhet and Pakse cities. While there is no evidence that this violence is directed against American citizens or institutions, American citizens should be aware that more such incidents could occur in the future. American citizens traveling to or residing anywhere in Laos are advised to exercise caution and to be alert to their surroundings.

Persons traveling overland in some areas, particularly Route 13 north between Kasi and Luang Prabang; Saisombun Special Zone; Xieng Khouang Province, including the Plain of Jars; and Route 7 east from the Route 13 junction, run the risk of ambush by insurgents or bandits. There have been violent incidents in these areas in the past year. Some groups have warned of impending insurgent attacks in these areas. Americans considering travel outside urban centers by road or river are advised to contact relevant Lao government offices and the U.S. Embassy for the most current security information.

American citizens should also avoid traveling on or across the Mekong River at night along the Thai border. In some areas, Lao militia forces have been known to shoot at boats on the river after dark.

INFORMATION ON CRIME: While Laos generally has a low rate of crime, visitors should exercise appropriate security precautions and remain aware of their surroundings. Street crime has been on the increase, particularly motorcycle drive-by theft of handbags and backpacks. The loss or theft abroad of a U.S. passport should be reported immediately to the local police and the U.S. Embassy. Useful information on safeguarding valuables and protecting personal security while traveling abroad is provided in the Department of State pamphlet, *A Safe Trip Abroad*, available from the Superintendent of Documents, U.S. Government Printing Office, Washington, D.C. 20402, via the Internet at http://www.access.gpo.gov/su_docs, on the Bureau of Consular Affairs home page at http://travel.state.gov and autofax service at 202-647-3000, or at the U.S. Embassy in Vientiane.

MEDICAL FACILITIES: Medical facilities and services are severely limited and do not meet Western standards. The blood supply is not screened for HIV or AIDS.

MEDICAL INSURANCE: U.S. medical insurance is not always valid outside the United States. U.S. Medicare and Medicaid programs do not provide payment for medical services outside the United States. Doctors and hospitals often expect immediate cash payment for health services. Uninsured travelers who require medical care overseas may face extreme difficulties.

Please check with your own insurance company to confirm whether your policy applies overseas, including provision for medical evacuation, and for adequacy of coverage. Serious medical problems requiring hospitalization and/or medical evacuation to the United States can cost tens of thousands of dollars. Please ascertain whether payment will be made to the overseas hospital or doctor or whether you will be reimbursed later for expenses that you incur. Some insurance policies also include coverage for psychiatric treatment and for disposition of remains in the event of death.

Useful information on medical emergencies abroad, including overseas insurance programs, is provided in the Department of State, Bureau of Consular Affairs brochure, *Medical Information for Americans Traveling Abroad*, available via the Bureau of Consular Affairs home page at http://travel.state.gov and autofax service at 202-647-3000.

OTHER HEALTH INFORMATION: Vaccination recommendations and prevention information for traveling abroad may be obtained through the Centers for Disease Control and Prevention's international travelers hotline from the United States at 1-877-FYI-TRIP (1-877-394-8747), via its toll-free autofax service at 1-888-CDC-FAXX (1-888-232-3299), or via their Internet site at http://www.cdc.gov.

ROAD SAFETY: While in a foreign country, U.S. citizens may encounter road conditions that differ significantly from those in the United States. The information below concerning Laos is provided for general reference only, and may not be totally accurate in a particular location or circumstance:
Safety of Public Transportation: Poor
Urban Road Conditions/Maintenance: Poor

For additional analytical, business and investment opportunities information,
please contact Global Investment & Business Center, USA
at (703) 370-8082. Fax: (703) 370-8083. E-mail: ibpusa3@gmail.com
Global Business and Investment Info Databank - www.ibpus.com

Rural Road Conditions/Maintenance: Poor
Availability of Roadside Assistance: Poor

Roads are mostly unpaved, pot-holed and poorly maintained in most parts of the country, although there has been a successful effort to improve roads and drainage in the capital in recent years. There are no railroads. Public transportation in Vientiane is generally poor and unreliable, and it is very limited after sunset. Taxis are available. Drivers speak little or no English. Most taxis are old and poorly maintained. Traffic is increasing, and local drivers remain undisciplined. Pedestrians and drivers should exercise great caution at all times. Theoretically, traffic moves on the right, but most cars, like pedestrians and bicycles, use all parts of the street. Cyclists pay little or no heed to cars on the road, and bicycles are rarely equipped with functioning lights or reflectors. This makes driving especially dangerous at dusk and at night. Defensive driving is necessary. The U.S. Embassy in Vientiane advises its personnel to wear helmets, gloves, and sturdy shoes while operating motorcycles.

AVIATION OVERSIGHT: Serious concerns about the operation of Lao Aviation, particularly regarding its safety standards and maintenance regime, have caused the U.S. Embassy to advise its personnel to limit domestic travel on Lao Aviation to essential travel only. Americans who are required to travel by air within Laos may wish to defer their travel or consider alternate means of transportation.

Also, since there is no direct commercial air service at present, nor economic authority to operate such service between the U.S. and Laos, the U.S. Federal Aviation Administration (FAA) has not assessed Laos' Civil Aviation Authority for compliance with international aviation safety standards for oversight of Laos' air carrier operations. For further information, travelers may contact the Department of Transportation within the U.S. at tel. 1-800-322-7873, or visit the FAA Internet home page at http://www.faa.gov/avr/iasa/iasa.pdf. The U.S. Department of Defense (DOD) separately assesses some foreign air carriers for suitability as official providers of air services. For information regarding the DOD policy on specific carriers, travelers may contact the DOD at tel. 1-618-229-4801.

RELIGIOUS WORKERS: Religious proselytizing or distributing religious material is strictly prohibited. Foreigners caught distributing religious material may be arrested or deported. The Government of Laos restricts the import of religious texts and artifacts. While Lao law allows freedom of religion, the government registers and controls all associations, including religious groups. Meetings, even in private homes, must be registered, and those held outside established locations may be broken up and the participants arrested.

MARRIAGE TO A LAO CITIZEN: The Lao Government imposes requirements on foreigners intending to marry Lao citizens. U.S. citizens may obtain information about these requirements at the U.S. Embassy in Vientiane. A marriage certificate is not issued by the Lao Government unless the correct procedures are followed. Any attempt to circumvent Lao law governing the marriage of Lao citizens to foreigners may result in deportation of the foreigner and denial of permission to re-enter Laos. Similar restrictions exist prohibiting the cohabitation of Lao nationals with nationals of other countries.

PHOTOGRAPHY AND OTHER RESTRICTIONS: Police and military may arrest persons taking photographs of military installations or vehicles, bridges, airfields and government buildings, and confiscate their cameras. Confiscated cameras are seldom returned to the owners. The photographers may be arrested. Export of antiques, such as Buddha images and other old cultural artifacts, is restricted by Laotian law.

CRIMINAL PENALTIES: While in a foreign country, a U.S. citizen is subject to that country's laws and regulations, which sometimes differ significantly from those in the United States and do not afford the protections available to the individual under U.S. law. Penalties for breaking the law can be more severe than in the United States for similar offenses. Persons violating the law, even unknowingly, may be expelled, arrested or imprisoned. Penalties for possession, use or trafficking in illegal drugs in Laos are strict, and convicted offenders can expect jail sentences and fines. Local police and immigration authorities sometimes confiscate passports when outstanding business disputes and visa matters remain unsettled.

CONSULAR ACCESS: The United States and Laos are parties to the Vienna Convention on Consular Relations (VCCR). Article 36 of the VCCR provides that if an arrestee requests it, foreign authorities shall, without delay, inform the U.S. Embassy. U.S. consular officers have the right to be notified of a U.S. citizen's detention and to visit the arrestee. Lao authorities do not always notify the U.S. Embassy or grant U.S. consular officers access to incarcerated U.S. citizens in a timely manner. Nevertheless, American citizens who are arrested or detained in Laos should always request contact with the U.S. Embassy.

CUSTOMS REGULATIONS: Lao customs authorities may enforce strict regulations concerning temporary importation into or export from Laos of items such as religious materials and artifacts, and antiquities. It is advisable to contact the Embassy of the Lao People's Democratic Republic in Washington for specific information regarding customs requirements. (Please see sections on "Religious Workers" and "Photography and Other Restrictions" above.)

CHILDREN'S ISSUES: For information on international adoption of children and international parental child abduction, please refer to our Internet site at http://travel.state.gov/children's_issues.html or telephone (202) 736-7000.

REGISTRATION/EMBASSY LOCATION: U.S. citizens living in or visiting Laos are encouraged to register at the U.S. Embassy where they may obtain updated information on travel and security within the country. The U.S. Embassy is located at Rue Bartholonie (near Tat Dam), B.P. 114, in Vientiane; mail can be addressed to American Embassy Vientiane, Box V, APO AP 96546; telephone (856-21) 212-581, 212-582, 212-585; duty officer's emergency cellular telephone (856-020) 511-740; Embassy-wide fax number (856-020) 518-597; Embassy-wide fax number (856-21) 212-584; Internet home page: http://usembassy.state.gov/laos/.

PRACTIVCAL INFORMATION FOR TRAVELERS

The Lao People's Democratic Republic, strategically located at the hub of Indochina- sharing borders with China, Vietnam, Cambodia, Thailand and Myanma ☐ is emerging as the region's newest fledgling economy.

After a lengthy period of political instability, the Lao People's Democratic Republic was established in 1975. As a result of the government's New Economic Mechanism launched in 1986, and with Lao PDR's imminent entry into ASEAN, the past decade has been marked by unprecedented growth. Signs of new prosperity are especially visible in the capital of Vientiane, where advancements in infrastructure and services have been occurring rapidly.

Parallel to this recent economic development is the opening of Lao PDR as a tourist destination. With its rich culture, traditional lifestyle, expanding economy and unspoil natural beauty, the Lao PDR welcomes adventurers and business visitors alike.

Step in and experience the great diversity of cultural sights and attractions, restaurants, leisure activities and shopping areas. The Lao PDR is yours to discover.

CULTURAL FESTIVALS

Colorful religious and cultural festivals involve the whole community ☐ come and celebrate in distinctive Lao style. Some of the major festivals are featured on these two pages. If you are fortunate enough to be here for one of our holidays, we hope you will join in the festivities with us.

Pi Mai ☐ Mid-April

From the washing of religious icons to the drenching of friends and strangers, water is central to *Pi Mai* or Lao New Year celebrations. Wander through temple compounds as worshippers pour perfumed water over Buddha images ☐ and each other. Even if you miss the significance of cleansing and renewal, you won't escape the traditional water throwing. Expect to be ambushed by celebrants with buckets of water. No one stays dry - or really wants to - during *Pi Mai*.

Three days in mid-April are official public holidays. Exact dates are announced by the government.

Boun Bang Fai - May

On the verge of planting season, the Rocket Festival or *Boun Bang Fai* is held to coax rain and fertility back to the earth. Bamboo rockets adorned with brightly colored decorations are carried to the launch in rowdy procession. Some celebrants paint their faces or wear wild masks and outlandish costumes. All come to enjoy Lao music, dance, and drama – especially the bawdy *maw lam* – at its most playful.

Join Boun Bang Fai celebrations on weekends in May at varying locations.

Boun Khao Phansa – July to October

Boun Khao Phansa is the first day of the Buddhist Lent, which is held from full moon in July to full moon in October. During this time of austerity, monks fast and people make offerings to gain merit. Traditionally, no weddings or celebrations are scheduled during these three months.

Early in the morning on the first day of Lent, people flock to temples carrying silver bowls full of gifts to offer the monks. For a breathtaking sight, go to one of the larger temples, like *That Luang*, where hundreds of worshippers – mostly women in vividly-colored silks – kneel row upon row.

Boun Ok Phansa – October/November

Boun Ok Phansa – the final and most important day of Lent – also features an early morning temple ceremony. After dusk, candlelit processions grace temple grounds and buildings glow with candles burning in honor of Buddha.

Also after dusk is *Lai Heua Fai*, a river ceremony during which small hand-made boats is floated down-river by people praying and making vows. The candlelit rafts hob away into darkness, symbolically dismissing bad luck, disease, and sin. This festival is similar to Thailand's *Loy Krathong* festival, which is held in December.

Boun Souang Heua – October

Held the day after *Ok Phansa*, *Boun Souang Heua* or the Boat race Festival draws crowds of excited spectators to the Mekong River. Fifty-member teams in wooden longboats row to the rhythm of drums as they compete for the coveted trophy. The races are held close to Vientiane. A carnival provides additional entertainment along the riverbank.

Boun That Luang – November

Held during the time of the full moon in November, the *That Luang* Festival is celebrated in honor of Lao PDR's national shrine. The festival begins with a Morning Prayer and alms giving ceremony on the first day of the three-day festival.

Masses of faithful worshippers come to pay homage to the hundreds of monks gathered at *That Luang*. This ceremony, like *Khao Phansa*, is solemn yet colorful.

A carnival held during these three days offers food and handicraft stalls, bumper cars, a shooting gallery, curiosity booths, pinball, games of chance, and musical entertainment. For sports fans, the highlight of *Boun That Luang* is *tee khee*, or field hockey.

In 1995, two weeks before the actual festival, an international trade fair was held for the first time. Many large local and international companies were present at this important event.

Lao National Day December 2

On this important public holiday, parades and speeches commemorate the 1975 Lao People's Revolutionary Victory over the monarchy.

Vietnamese & Chinese New Year January/February

Firecrackers explode all through this holiday, and mouth-watering sweetmeats and other delicacies are made especially for the occasion. Celebrations are held in January or February, with many business and market stalls closing for three days.

OFFICIAL HOLIDAYS

The following official public holidays for 1996 have been announced by the Prime Minister's Office:

1-3 January International New Year's Day

20 January Military Day (Military only)

8 March Lao Women's Day (Women only)

13-15 April Lao New Year

1 May Labor Day

7 October Teacher's Day (Teachers only)

2 December Lao National Day

VIENTIANE

Vientiane's small size allows easy travel around the city. Most tourist attractions and shopping areas are within walking distance of major hotels. If preferred, most tour operators can organize a one-day tour to these attractions. For day excursions outside Vientiane, it is best to consult a travel agent.

That Luang

The national shrine of the country, *That Luang*, or Great Sacred Stupa, stands 45 meters tall and is believed to contain a relic of the Lord Buddha. The original structure was built by King Setthathirath in 1566, and the present structure was restored in 1953. The gold-colored central structure of this stupa echoes the curving lines of an elongated lotus bud, and the gold is a symbol of the country's wealth. This shrine is the center of the *That Luang* festival held in November.

Revolutionary Monument

Located close to That Luang, this monument stands as a memorial to those who died in the Revolutionary War.

Patuxai

Built in 1962, *Patuxai*, or the Victory Monument, is a memorial to those who died in wars before the Revolution. Known to some as *Anousavali*, or "the monument," the arch and the surrounding park area attract those who wish to relax with friends and watch Vientiane's traffic speed by. For 200 kip, energetic visitors can climb to the top of the monument for a view of the city. The *Patuxai* itself is open from 08:00 to 17:00, but people continue to enjoy the park into the evening.

That Dam

An old legend tells of a seven-headed dragon that protected the people of Vientiane from Siamese invaders during the 1828 war. This dragon is said to be hidden under *That Dam*, or the Black Stupa, and continues to protect the city to this day.

Revolutionary Museum

This impressive example of French colonial architecture houses a collection of artifacts weapons paintings and photographs depicting the history of the Lao People's Revolution. Most captions are written in Lao and English.

Wat Sisaket

Wat Sisaket is the oldest temple in Vientiane-only one to survive the Siamese invasion in 1828. All other temples have since undergone extensive restoration.

The *wat* features a library, which was ransacked during the invasion, as well as unique frescoes and a grand total of 6,840 Buddha images, hundreds of which are framed in small wall niches.

Wat Phra Keo

Once the royal temple of the Lao monarchy, *Wat Phra Keo* was built in 1566. After being destroyed by the Siamese invaders in 1828 it was rebuilt between 1936 and 1942, and has been used as a museum since the 1970s. The main building-which originally housed the *Phra Keo*, or Emerald Buddha-now contains fine examples of Buddhist sculpture and artifacts including antique drums and palm leaf manuscripts. A short description of each exhibit is given in French.

Wat Simuang

Wat Simuang was built when King Setthathirath established Vientiane as the nation's capital in 1563. This temple enshrines the foundation pillar of Vientiane, and is home to the city's guardian spirit.

Local folklore surrounding the temple's construction tells of a pregnant girl who, for the good of the city, sacrificed herself to the spirit by jumping into the hole before the foundation pillar was lowered.

This temple is one of Vientiane's most popular centers of worship, largely because it houses a Buddha image believed to answer the questions of worshippers who lift it three times, repeating the same question each time. The oddly shaped image is always surrounded by fruit and flowers-offerings of thanks from those who have received its answers.

Wat Ong Teu

Wat Ong Teu, or the Temple of the Heavy Buddha, is the residence of the Deputy Patriarch of the Lao monastic order. The Deputy Patriarch directs Vientiane's Buddhist Institute where monks from all over Laos come to study. The temple also houses a 16th century Buddha weighing several tones.

Suan Vathanatham

Located near the Lao-Thai Friendship Bridge, *Suan Vathanatham* (National Ethnic Cultural Park) offers the visitor a taste of Lao PDR's cultural and natural heritage. Shady paths wind past traditional Lao architecture, an small zoo (featuring alligators, bears, monkey, snakes, hawks, civets, and jungle cats), textile and handicraft shops, food and drink stands, towering dinosaurs, and sculptures of Lao literacy characters including *Sinxai* and the Four Eared Elephant.

Wat Xieng Khouan (Buddha Park)

Situated by the Mekong River about 21 kilometers out of Vientiane municipality, *Wat Xieng Khouan*, despite its name, is not a temple but a sculpture park. Created in 1958, the park captivates visitors with unusual and somewhat disturbing Buddhist and Hindu imagery. For a bizarre experience, climb into the three level model of hell. *Wat Xieng Khouan* offers food and drinks stalls, and is a popular spot for picnics and recreation.

SPORT AND LEISURE ACTIVITIES

Golf

Santisouk Lane Xang Golf and Resort

Located on Thadeua Road, out toward the Friendship Bridge, this gold course claims an international standard. Along with a nine-hole course, the Santisouk Lane Xang offers a driving range, gold shoes and club rental, shower room, and restaurant.

Vientiane Golf Course

The first golf course in Lao PDR, the nine-hole Vientiane golf course is located at Km 6 on Route 13 South.

Night Life

Vientiane offers a wide range of nightclubs and bars with an unique blend of Eastern and Western music. The city's dance floors cater to different tastes from the traditional Lao lamvong to rap. Many establishments offer entertaining light and sound shows and feature popular local bands.

Dokmaideng Fun Park

The Dokmaideng Fun Park is Vientiane's choice destination for children of all ages for an afternoon or evening of bumper cars, swing rides, miniature trains, and video games. Plans are underway to expand the park, adding a waterslide and more.

Thoulakhom Zoo

Another place that is worth visiting is Vientiane province's Thoulakhom Zoo. Located fifty kilometers north of Vientiane municipality, this zoo features many exotic and rare animals from Lao PDR's jungles, from magnificent tigers to mouse deer, elephants, monkeys, parrots, and the newly arrived kangaroos.

SHOPPER'S HEAVEN

Lao PDR is treasure trove of exquisite handicrafts and antiques. Silk and cotton textiles, hand-woven baskets, fine silver-work, detailed woodcarvings, traditional musical instruments and pottery are the pride of the Lao artisan tradition. Art galleries in town feature a wide selection of drawings, watercolors, and oil paintings by local artists.

Many small jewelry and handicraft shops dot the city, and the main shopping center, the *Talat Sao*, houses a head-spinning array of woven textiles, antiques, silver items, and gold jewelry.

Talat Sao

The *Talat Sao* (Morning Market) is comprised of three large pavilions, each with its own Lao style green-tiled roof. The *Talat Sao* offers the shopper everything from silk and fine jewelry to toiletries, electronic equipment and hardware.

The second level of this market is crammed with silver and gold smiths, and there is a good selection of handicrafts and antiques both upstairs and downstairs. The Morning Market also has conveniently-located licensed moneychangers.

Credit Cards

Credit cards are becoming more widely used in Laos, with the most common being VisaCard, MasterCard and American Express. Most major hotels, restaurants and some shops will accept credit cards, but many of the smaller shops, even in the Morning Market, only accept cash.

Nongbouathong Village Weavers

Traditional Lao textile weaving is proudly upheld in this village, and the exquisite results are displayed at the local Pheng Mai Gallery. Nongbouathong village is just a ten-minute drive out of town, and lovers of weaving should not miss this opportunity to watch the weavers at their looms.

The Art of Silk

This silk museum is run by the Lao Women's Union and features a variety of traditional silk pieces created by skillful weavers from different provinces. The items on display are also for sale.

Culinary Treats

Visitors are pleasantly surprised by the many excellent eating establishments in Vientiane. From fabulous Lao, French, Italian, Chinese, Indian, Japanese, and Thai restaurants to mouth-watering chicken roasted over open grills in street stalls, even the most choosy eater will find something to satisfy the plate.

Noodle Houses and Street Stalls

Vientiane abounds with noodle houses-just ask a local to point out the most popular places in town. Different restaurants specialize in different types of noodle dishes, so be adventurous and savour the variety.

Street stalls add undeniable character to the city, and most of them start bustling at sunset. For a Lao food extravaganza, visit Khounboulom Road in the heart of town and try sweet sticky rice with cononut, rich Lao cakes, and loti, the egg pastry roll-ups drizzled with sweetened condensed milk... The list goes on and on and you will not be disappointed.

TRAVELLING OUTSIDE VIENTIANE

Major provincial capitals are serviced by regular Lao Aviation domestic flights. Although internal travel permits are no longer required by foreigners travelling to these areas, it is advisable that travel outside Vientiane is organized through one of the major travel agencies listed in the Gold Pages.

Luang Prabang

This lovely town nestled in the mountains was once capital of Laos. A short forty-minute flight from Vientiane, Luang Prabang is a step back to a time when tradition, culture and religion motivated most activities in Lao society.

Visit the Royal Palace Museum for a fascinating glimpse into the past. Personal artifacts of the Royal Family and gifts from foreign governments are especially interesting. Take a boat trip to *Tham Ting* Caves to see the hundreds of Buddha images enshrined there years ago to protect them from invaders.

Xieng Khouang & Plain of Jars

Xieng Khouang province is home to the Plain of Jars. Scattered across a grassy slope 12 kilometers outside of the provincial capital, are more than 300 ancient stone jars weighing up to six tonnes each. Xieng Khouang was one of Lao PDR's most heavily bombed provinces between 1964 and 1973.

Tham Piu care is a sobering historical sight. *Tham Piu* was used as a bomb shelter by Lao villagers until 1969 when a single rocket fired into the cave killed about 400 people - mostly women and children. Rock debris and human bones from the explosion still litter the cave.

Travelling through the Region

Vientiane is a convenient point from which to travel to other parts of Indochina. The capital is serviced by the national flag carrier, Lao Aviation, and a growing number of foreign airlines, including Air Cambodia, Air Vietnam, Southern China Airlines, Silk Air and Thai International Airways.

Travel from Vientiane to Thailand is convenient with the recent opening of the Australian-built Friendship Bridge, the first bridge across the Mekong River. From the border town of *Nongkhai*, the nearest Thai airport is 60 kilometers away in *Udon Thani*.

BUSINESS INFORMATION

Hotels in Vientiane

There are several excellent hotels and guest-houses in Vientiane offering clean, air-conditioned comfort and genuine Lao hospitality. Most hotels have restaurants, and some of the larger ones have business facilities with facsimile and word processing services. A wide range of prices and features serves the needs of every traveler.

Transport within Vientiane

Vientiane is a small city and easy to move around in. Travelling by jumbo or tuk-tuk is inexpensive and convenient. These vehicles can be hailed from the side of a street or found waiting for customers near markets, restaurants, and hotels. It is wise to know the Lao name of your destination. For most destinations in the city, you should pay no more than 500 kip per passenger. Negotiate the fare before starting on your journey. Taxis are available for hire. Most taxis congregate around the Morning Market and the newer ones have meters. Bicycles and motorcyles can also be hired for a nominal fee.

Clothing and Climate

The climate is tropical, with the monsoons from June until October and the dry season from November to May. The winter months, December to February, can be quite cool and light jackets and sweaters are recommended. If you travel in the provinces during winter months warmer clothing is required as it gets very cold in the mountain areas.

In Vientiane, keep your clothing light, simple and modest. Natural fibers such as silk and cotton are recommended.

Water

Tap water is unsafe for drinking, but purified bottled water is available everywhere. It is not advisable to ear food that has just been rinsed under the tap. Avoid unpeeled fruit and uncooked vegetables.

Electricity

The Lao PDR uses 220 volt power at 50 HZ. Power pints will accept a plug with two flat pins or two round pins. Various adaptors can be purchased at the Morning Market.

For additional analytical, business and investment opportunities information,
please contact Global Investment & Business Center, USA
at (703) 370-8082. Fax: (703) 370-8083. E-mail: ibpusa3@gmail.com
Global Business and Investment Info Databank - www.ibpus.com

SUPPLEMENTS

IMPORTANT WEBSITES

National Assembly of Laos
- http://www.na.gov.la/

Official Gazette
- http://www.laoofficialgazette.gov.la
Ministry of Information and Culture
- http://www.mic.gov.la/

The domestic statistics sector
http://moha-statistic.net23.net

Ministry of Commerce
- http://www1.mot.gov.vn/laowebsite/lao/index.asp

Ministry of Finance
- http://www.mof.gov.la/

Ministry of Foreign Affairs
- http://www.mofa.gov.la/

National Statistical Center
- http://www.maf.gov.la/index.html

Lao Trade Promotion Center
- http://www.laotrade.gov.la/

Organization for Science and Environment
- http://www.stea.gov.la/

Internal and External Investors Department
- http://invest.laopdr.org/

Tax Department
- http://laocustoms.laopdr.net/

Office of the Lao PDR Representative
- http://www.un.int/lao/

National Institute of Agriculture and Forestry Research
- http://www.nafri.org.la/

The Renewable Energy Association for Sustainable Development
- http://www.resdalao.org.la/

**For additional analytical, business and investment opportunities information,
please contact Global Investment & Business Center, USA
at (703) 370-8082. Fax: (703) 370-8083. E-mail: ibpusa3@gmail.com
Global Business and Investment Info Databank - www.ibpus.com**

National Chamber of Commerce and Industry
- http://www.lncci.laotel.com/

The National Mekong River Commission
- http://www.lnmcmekong.org/

Lao National Internet Exchange Point (Laonix)
- http://www.laonix.net.la/

Water Authority of Lao PDR
- http://www.wasa.gov.la/

Luang Prabang Provincial Office
- http://www.luangprabang.gov.la

WEB SITES OF ORGANIZATIONS IN LAOS

United Nations - APCICT
Homepage - http://www.unapcict.org
APCICT Virtual Academy - http://e-learning.unapcict.org
E-Co Hub - http://www.unapcict.org/ecohub

United Nations Development for Democracy
- http://www.undplao.org/

UXO Clearance Unit of Lao PDR
- http://www.uxolao.org/

Jica
- http://www.jica.laopdr.org/

UNFPA
- http://lao.unfpa.org/

SNV
- http://www.snv.org.la/

Poverty Reduction Index
- http://www.prflaos.org/

The Child
Support Agency - http: //www.scn.laopdr.org

Micro-Project Development
- http://www.microprojects-lao.org/

Lao Rehabilitation Foundation
- http://www.laofoundation.com/

IMPORTANT CONTACTS

MINISTRIES

1. Presidential Office
Mr. Banhsa Detvongsone............21 4209

2. National Assembly
Mr. Outhay Phatthana............ 41 3543

3. Prime Minister's Office
Mr. Seng Chantho.................. 21 3656

4. *National Sports Committee*
Mr. Phaiboon Chantamaly...................... 21 6009

5. National Geographic Department
Reception................................... 21 4917

6. *Office of the Party Central Committee*
Mr. Phouthone..4 1 3921

7. Party Central Committee Organization Board
Mr. Kham Ouan..41 2076

8. Central Control Committee
Central Control Committee Office.....................................41 2869, 41 4090

9. Propaganda & Training Committee of Central Committee
Mr. Bounsaveng Hongsavanh....................41 3037

10. Lao Front for National Construction
Mr. Chanthi Sitthibandith..........................21 3756

11. Commission for External Relations of Central Committee of LPDR
Mr. Thongtham Latanasouk....................41 4046

12. Kaysone Phomvihane Museum
Mr. Singthong Singhapanya........................ 41 3167

13. State Planing Committee
Mr. Khamphong Pholsena........................21 6562

14. People's Supreme Court
Ms. Kaisy Vikaiyalai.................................41 2172

15. Public Prosecutor General's Office
Mr. Oukham Sysounon.............................25 2670

16. The Lao Federation of Trade Union
Mr. Solasack Phetpalignavanh...................22 2473

17. Lao Women's Union
Ms. Houmphone Duangdavong..................21 4310

18. Lao Youth Union
Ms. Sonepheng Phamisay..........................41 6627

19. Lao Red Cross Society
Mr. Khonsavanh Chanthakham.................21 4504

20. Ministry of Agriculture & Forestry
Mr. Sompong
Souvannamethy.....................41 5361

21. Ministry of Commerce
Mr. Thongsi
Bounmatham....................020 503 090

22. Ministry of Financial
Mr.
Kongmoun...
41 2406

23. Ministry of Foreign Affaire
Mr.
Somvang...
41 4047

24. Ministry of CTPC
Mr. Math
Sounmala.......................41
2093

25. Ministry of Public Health
Mr.
Maiphone...............................
22 2630

26. Ministry of Education
Mr.
Phay.......................................
21 6004

27. Ministry of Justice
Mr. Somphone
Boupphaphan.......................22 2779

28. Ministry of Information & Culture
Mr. Vayolin
Phasavath...............................21 2413

29. Ministry of National Defense
Mr.
Leumxay...
41 4854

30. Ministry of Interior
Communication
Dept......................................21 2508

31. Ministry of Industry & Handicraft
Mr.
Chanthavisith...
41 5805

32. Ministry of Labor & Social Welfare
Mr. Somphone
Boupphapha.........................22 2779

33. Bank of Lao PDR
Reception...
......21 3109

34. Lao Telecommunications
Autocom Office..............................21
6465, 21 6466

35. ETL
Reception...
......21 5153

36. EPL
Mr. Someboune
Nouhouang.........................21 4843

37. EDL
Mr.
Somsanith...
21 2800

38. Lao Water supply Enterprise
Ms.
Noy...
41 2882

39. Department of Civil Aviation
Department
Office..51 2163

40. Lao Buddhist Fellowship Organization
Ven.

Bounthavy..............................4 5 1608

41. NOSPA
Ms. Khampanh.............................. 75 2180

42. National University of Laos
Mr. Khamtoun..............................4 1 6071

BANKS

Banks in Lao

Agricultural Promotion Bank
58 Hengboun St Ban Haysok
Tel. (021) 21 2024   Fax. (021) 21 3957
E-mail: apblao@laotel.com

Banque pour le Commerce Exterieur Lao
1 Pangkham St Ban Xiang nyeun
Tel. (021) 22 3190
Fax. (021) 21 3202, (021) 22 3012
E-mail: bcelhovt@laotel.com

Lao Development Bank
19 Pangkham Rd
P.O BOX 2700
Tel. (021) 21 3300, (021) 21 3302
Fax. (021) 21 3304, (021) 22 2506
E-mail: lmbltdho@laotel.com

Lao-Viet Bank
05 LaneXang Ave Unit 03 Ban Hatsadi Neua
Tel. (021) 25 1422   Fax. (021) 21 2197
Website: www.laovietbank.com

Vientiane Commercial Bank Ltd
1st Floor VTCB Building 33 LaneXang Ave Ban Hatsadi
Tel. (021) 22 2727   Fax. (021) 22 2715

Bangkok Bank
Ban Hatsadi
Tel. (021) 21 3560   Fax. (021) 21 3561

Joint Development Bank
75/1-5 LaneXang Ave Ban Hatsadi
Tel. (021) 21 3536   Fax. (021) 21 3534, (021) 21 3530
Website: www.jdbbank.com

Public Bank Berhad
100/1-4 Taladsao St Ban Hadsadi
Tel. (021) 22 3394   Fax. (021) 22 2743
E-mail: pbbvte@laotel.com

Siam Commercial Bank Public Corporation
117 LaneXang Ave Ban Sisaket
Tel. (021) 21 3501

Standard Chartered
08/3 Lane Xang Avenue
P.O. Box 6895 Vientiane Lao PDR
Tel. (021) 22 2251
Fax. (021) 21 7254

Thai Military Bank Public Co Ltd
69 Khounboulom St Ban Sihom
Tel. (021) 21 7174, (021) 21 6486
Fax. (021) 21 6486

CONSULTANTS

BCS Ltd
40 Unit 2 Ban Oupmoung Luang Prabang Rd
Tel: (021) 21 7541

BDG Consultants
B. Watchan Tha, M. Chanthaboury
P.O.Box 7426
Tel. (021) 25 0250
Fax. (021) 21 8494
E-mail: peterevans@laopdr.com
Website: http://www.bluegrass.laopdr.com

Bureau d'Etudes Lao
205 Setthathirath B. Mixay
Tel: (021) 21 5806
Fax: (021) 21 5802
E-mail: bel@pan-laos.net.la

Franklin Advisory Services
2nd Floor VTCB Building Lane Xang
Ave Ban Hatsadi
Tel: (021) 21 7604
Fax: (021) 21 7604

KPMG
Km. 2, B. Khunta, Luang Prabang Rd.
P.O. Box 6978
Vientiane, Lao PDR
Tel: (856 21) 219 491-3
Fax: (856 21) 219 490
Email: kpmglaom@loxinfo.co.th

Lao C.B.S Co Ltd
50 Luang Prabang Rd Ban Oupmoung
Tel: (021) 21 9841, (021) 22 3125
Fax: (021) 22 3125, (021) 21 8600

Lao Inter Mix
66 Luang Prabang Rd Ban Sithan Neua
Tel: (021) 21 2957
Fax: (021) 22 3545

Manley Enterprise Co Ltd
66 Nokeokoummane St Ban Mixay
Tel: (021) 21 4403

Marubeni
43/8 Thadeua Rd Ban Thatkhao
Tel: (021) 21 3539
Fax: (021) 21 5657

Mekoxab
111 Thadeua Rd B. Phaxay
P.O.Box 8695, Sisatanak
Tel/Fax. (021) 35 1963
E-mail: mekoxab@laotel.com
Website: www.businessinlao.com

Midas Economic
Luang Prabang Rd Ban Sihom
Tel: (021) 22 2450

PriceWaterhouseCoopers
Unit 1, Fourth Floor
Vientiane Commercial Building
33 Lane Xang Ave.
P.O. Box 7003
Vientiane
Tel: (856 21) 222 718
Fax: (856 21) 222 723
e-mail: pwc-laos@loxinfo.co.th

Santi Phatthana Services
50 Phanyasi St Unit 5 Ban Sithan Neua
Tel: (021) 21 6640
Fax: (021) 21 5973

SavAngh Advisors & Services Ltd
37/10 Unit 9 Ban Hatsadi
PO Box 7331
Tel. (856 21) 214 173 / 250 945
Fax (856 21) 219 243
E-mail: savandara@savangh-advisors.com
Website: http://www.savangh-advisors.com

SK Consultants
Phonthan Rd Ban Phonthan Neua
Tel: (021) 41 6015
Fax: (021) 41 4568

MULTILATERAL AID AGENCIES

World Bank
B. Phonsay, M. Saysettha, Vientiane Municipality
Tel. 41 4209

Asian Development Bank
Lane Xang Ave, Vientiane Municipality
Tel. 25 0444

International Monetary Fund
B. Xiangngeun, M. Chanthaboury,

Vientiane Municipality　　　　　　　　　Tel/Fax. 21 3206

CUSTOMS OFFICE CODES

VIENTIANE	10
1. Banvang	10.1
2. Salakham	10.2
PHONGSALY	02
3. Mouangkhoa	02.1
4. Pakha	02.2
LUANGNAMTHA	03
5. Nateuay	03.1
6. Botenh	03.2
OUDOMXAY	04
BOKEO	05
7. Houaysai	05.1
8. Muongmone	05.2
LUANGPRABANG	06
HOUAPHANH	07
9. Nameo	07.1
10. Pahang	07.2
11. Xiengkheuang	07.3
SAYABOURY	08
12. Kenethao	08.1
XIENGKHOUANG	09
13. Namkan	09.1
VIENTIANE MUNICIPALITY	01
14. Thanaleng	01.1
15. Wattay Airport	01.2
16. Post	01.3
17. Fuel	01.4
18. Thadeua	01.5
19. Friendship Bridge	01.6
BOLIKHAMXAY	11
20. Khamkeuth	11.1
	11.2

21. Paksan	11.3
22. Namkading	
	12
KHAMMOUANE	12.1
23. Thakhek	12.2
24. Paksebangfai	12.3
25. Hineboune	12.4
26. Chilo	
	13
SAVANNAKHET	13.1
27. Denesavanh	13.2
28. Khanthaboury	13.3
29. Thapasoom	13.4
30. Kengkabao	
	14
SALAVANE	14.1
31. Paktaphane	
	15
SEKONG	
	16
CHAMPASACK	16.1
32. Vangtao	16.2
33. Vennekhame	
	17
ATTAPEU	17.1
34. Phouyang	
	18
Special Zone	
	99
Headquarters	

Annex II

COUNTRY AND CURRENCY CODES

Country Name	Country Code	Currency Code
AFGHANISTAN	AF	AFA
ALBANIA	AL	ALL
ALGERIA	DZ	DZD
AMERICAN SAMOA	AS	USD
ANDORRA	AD	ESP/FRF
ANGOLA	AO	AOK
ANGUILLA	AI	XCD
ANTIGUA AND BARBUDA	AG	XCD

ARGENTINA	AR	ARP
ARMENIA	AM	RUR
ARUBA	AW	AWG
AUSTRALIA	AU	AUD
AUSTRIA	AT	ATS
AZERBAIJAN	AZ	RUR
BAHAMAS	BS	BSD
BAHRAIN	BH	BHD
BANGLADESH	BD	BDT
BARBADOS	BB	BBD
BELARUS	BY	RUR
BELGUIM	BE	BEF
BELIZE	BZ	BZD
BENIN	BJ	XOF
BERMUDA	BM	BMD
BHUTAN	BT	INR/BTN
BOLIVIA	BO	BOB
BOSNIA-HERZEGOVINA	BA	
BOTSWANA	BW	BWP
BOUVET ISLAND	BV	NOK
BRAZIL	BR	BRC
BRITISH INDIAN OCEAN TERRITORY	IO	USD
BRITISH VIRGINIS	VG	USD
BRUNEI DARUSSALAM	BN	BND
BULGARIA	BG	BGL
BURKINA FASO	BF	XOF
BURUNDI	BI	BIF
Entity Name		
CAMEROON	CM	XAF
CANADA	CA	CAD

CAPE VERDE	CV	CVE
CAYMAN IS	KY	KYD
CENTRAL AFRICAN REPUBLIC	CF	XAF
CHAD	TD	XAF
CHILE	CL	CLP
CHINA	CN	CNY
CHRISTMAS IS	CX	AUD
COCOS (KEELING) ISLANDS	CC	AUD
COLOMBIA	CO	COP
COMOROS IS	KM	KMF
CONGO	CG	XAF
COOK IS	CK	NZD
COSTA RICA	CR	CRC
COTE D'IVOIRE	CI	XOF
CROATIA	HR	
CUBA	CU	CUP
CYPRUS	CY	CYP
CZECH REPUBLIC	CZ	CZK
DENMARK	DK	DKK
DJIBOUTI	DJ	DJF
DOMINICA	DM	XCD
DOMINICAN REPUBLIC	DO	DOP
EAST TIMOR	TP	TPE
ECUADOR	EC	ECS
EGYPT ARAB REP OF	EG	EGP
EL SALVADOR	SV	SVC
EQUATORIAL GUINEA	GQ	GOE
ESTONIA	EE	
ETHIOPIA	ET	ETB

FAEROE IS	FO	DKK
FALKLAND ISLANDS (MALVINAS)	FK	FKP
FIJI	FJ	FJD
FINLAND	FI	FIM
FRANCE	FR	FRF
FRENCH GUIANA	GF	FRF
Entity Name		
FRENCH POLYNESIA	PF	XPF
FRENCH SOUTHERN TERRITORIES	TF	FRF
GABON	GA	XAF
GAMBIA	GM	GMD
GEORGIA	GG	RUR
GERMANY, FEDERAL REPUBLIC OF	DE	DEM
GHANA	GH	GHC
GIBRALTAR	GI	GIP
GREECE	GR	GRD
GREENLAND	GL	DKK
GRENADA	GD	XCD
GUADELOUPE	GP	FRF
GUAM	GU	USD
GUATEMALA	GT	GTQ
GUINEA	GN	GNS
GUINEA-BISSAU	GW	GWP
GUYANA	GY	GYD
HAITI	HT	HTG
HEARD AND MCDONALD ISLANDS	HM	USD
HONDURAS	HN	HNL
HONGKONG	HK	HKD
HUNGARY	HU	HUF

ICELAND	IS	ISK
INDIA	IN	INR
INDONASIA REP OF	ID	IDR
IRAN, ISLAMIC REPUBLIC OF	IR	IRR
IRAQ	IQ	IQD
IRELAND	IE	IEP
ISRAEL	IL	ILS
ITALY	IT	ITL
JAMAICA	JM	JMD
JAPAN	JP	JPY
JORDAN	JO	JOD
KAMPUCHEA, DEMOCRATIC	KH	KHR
KAZAKHSTAN	KK	RUR
Entity Name		
KENYA	KE	KES
KIRIBATI	KI	AUD
KOREA, DEM PEOPLE'S REPUBLIC OF	KP	KPW
KOREA, REPUBLIC OF	KR	KRW
KUWAIT	KW	KWD
KYRGYZSTAN	KG	RUR
LAOS PEOPLE DEMOCRATIC REPUBLIC	LA	LAK
LATVIA		
LEBANON	LV	
LESOTHO	LB	LBP
LIBERIA	LS	ZAR/LS
LIBYA	LR	LRD
LIECHSTENSTEIN	LY	LYD

LITHUANIA	LI	CHF
LUXEMBOURG	LT	
	LU	LUF
MACAU	MO	MOP
MALAGASY REPUBLIC	MG	MGF
MALAWI	MW	MWK
MALAYSIA	MY	MYR
MALDIVES REP OF	MV	MVR
MALI	ML	MLF
MALTA	MT	MTL
MARSHALL IS	MH	USD
MARTINIQUE	MQ	FRF
MAURITANIA	MR	MRO
MAURITIUS	MU	MUR
MEXICO	MX	MXP
MICRONESIA	FM	USD
MOLDOVA	MD	RUR
MONACO	MC	FRF
MONGOLIAN PEO REP	MN	MNT
MONTSERRAT	MS	XCD
MOROCCO	MA	MAD
MOZAMBIQUE	MZ	MZM
MYANMAR	BU	BUK
Entity Name		
NAMIBIA	NA	ZAR
NAURU	NR	AUD
NEPAL	NP	NPR
NETHERLANDS	NL	NLG
NETHERLANDS ANTILLES	AN	ANG
NEW ZEALAND	NZ	NZD

NEW CALEDONIA	NC	XPF
NICARAGUA	NI	NIC
NIGER	NE	XOF
NIGERIA	NG	NGN
NIUE	NU	NZD
NORFOLK ISLAND	NF	AUD
NORTHERN MARIANA IS	MP	USD
NORWAY	NO	NOK
OMAN	OM	OMR
PAKISTAN	PK	PKR
PALAU	PW	USD
PANAMA	PA	PAB/USD
PAPUA NEW GUINEA	PG	PGK
PARAGUAY	PY	PYG
PERU	PE	PES
PHILIPPINES	PH	PHP
PITCAIRN	PN	NZD
POLAND	PL	PLZ
PORTUGAL	PT	PTE
PUERTO RICO	PR	USD
QATAR	QA	QAR
REUNION	RE	FRF
ROMANIA	RO	ROL
RUSSIA	RU	RUR
RWANDA	RW	RWF
SAINT KITTS-NEVIS	KN	XCD
SAINT LUCIA	LC	XCD
SAINT VINCENT AND THE GRENADINES		

Entity Name	VC	XCD
SAN MARINO	SM	ITL
SAO TOME AND PRINCIPE	ST	STD
SAUDI ARABIA	SA	SAR
SENEGAL	SN	XOP
SEYCHELLES	SC	SCR
SIERRA LEONE	SL	SLL
SINGAPORE	SG	SGD
SLOVAK REPUBLIC	SK	SKK
SLOVENIA	SI	
SOLOMAN IS	SB	SBD
SOMALI	SO	SOS
SOUTH AFRICA	ZA	ZAR
SPAIN	ES	ESP
SRI LANKA	LK	LKR
ST HELENA	SH	SHP
ST PIERRE ET MIQUELON	PM	FRF
SUDAN	SD	SDP
SURINAM	SR	SRG
SVALBARD AND JAN MAYEN IS	SJ	NOK
SWAZILAND	SZ	SZL
SWEDEN	SE	SEK
SWITZERLAND	CH	CHP
SYRIAN ARAB REPUBLIC	SY	SYP
TAIWAN	TW	TWD
TAJIKISTAN	TJ	RUR
TANZANIA	TZ	TZS
THAILAND	TH	THB
TOGOLESE	TG	XOF
TOKELAU	TK	NZD

TONGA	TO	TOP
TRAINIDAD AND TOBAGO	TT	TTD
TUNISIA	TN	TND
TURKEY	TR	TRL
TURKMENISTAN	TM	RUR
TURKS AND CAICOS IS	TC	USD
TUVALU	TV	AUD
Entity Name		
UGANDA	UG	UGS
UKRAINE	UA	RUR
UNITED ARAB EMIRATES	AE	AED
UNITED KINGDOM	GB	GBP
UNITED STATES	US	USD
UNITED SATES MINOR OUTLYING ISLANDS	UM	USD
URUGUAY	UY	UYP
UZBEKISTAN	UZ	RUR
VANUATU	VU	VUV
VATICAN CITY STATE	VA	ITL
VENEZUELA	VE	VEB
VIETNAM SOC REP OF	VN	VND
VIRGIN ISLANDS (US)	VI	USD
WALLIS AND FUTUNA	WF	XPF
WESTERN SAHARA	EH	ESP/MAD
WESTERN SAMOA	WS	WST
YEMEN ARAB REPUBLIC OF	YE	YER
YEMEN PEOPLE'S DEMOCRATIC REPUBLIC	YD	YDD

YUGOSLAVIA	YU	YUD
ZAIRE	ZR	ZRZ
ZAMBIA	ZM	ZMK
ZIMBABWE	ZW	ZWD

THE DECLARATION FORM

The declaration form or single administrative document is used for all customs transactions; import, export or transit. It must be complete to be acceptable in customs.

The declaration form has three segments.

1. In the first section(Boxes No.1-23) enter general information on importer, exporter and declarant as well as transport and transaction details.

2. In the second section (Boxes No.24-42) enter details on the item declared, including amount of duties and taxes payable or exempted.

3. Summary of Payment and Responsibility of Declaration Section.

It is presented in the form of (i.) a header sheet, which is used to declare importation, exportation or in transit information for each commodity item (ii.) continuation sheets to declare other commodity items and (iii.) section sheet for official use.
Note. Declaration forms are on sale at all Regional Customs offices.
Instructions to fill each box of the form.

Box No.1   Declaration Regime

Inscribe one of the following codes to identify the type of transaction the declaration is for:

Regime Code	Description
10	Exportation of domestic Goods
14	Exportation under a drawback regime
20	Temporary Exportation
35	Re-Exportation
40	Importation of goods for Home consumption.

4A	Importation of goods for diplomatic use, returning residents, and humanitarian assistance; samples, educational materials and certain religious articles.
4B	Goods ex-warehoused to duty free shops
4C	Goods ex-warehoused for exportation out of Lao PDR
45	Home Consumption of Goods after temporary admission
47	Home Consumption of Goods entered under a warehousing regime
50	Temporary Importation
62	Re-Importation of Goods Exported temporarily
70	Warehousing of Goods
80	Transit

Office Codes.

Enter the code of the office where the declaration is presented. See Annex I for a list of all customs offices and their codes.

Manifest /Airway bill number.

Enter the cargo control number from the air waybill if the goods arrive or leave by air or from the manifest if goods arrive or leave by any other mode of transport.
Declaration Number and Date.

Customs will assign the declaration number and the date when the declaration is presented and registered with customs.

Box No.2   Exporter and Address

If you enter goods for exportation, indicate your name and address as well as the taxpayer identification number (TIN) issued by the Tax Department. If you have not yet been issued a TIN please obtain a number from the nearest tax office and use it on all subsequent customs declarations. Also include your office telephone number. For diplomatic and personal exportations, leave the number field blank.

Box No.3   Gross Mass Kg.

Indicate the gross weight in kilograms of the entire consignment of goods as declared on the manifest or air waybill.

Box No.4   Items

Indicate the total number of items as shown on the invoice.

Box No.5   Total Packages.

Indicate the total number of packages as declared on the manifest or airway bill. In case of bulk cargo, indicate BULK only.

Box No. 6   Importer and Address

If you enter goods for importation, indicate your name and address as well as the taxpayer identification number (TIN) issued by the Tax Department. If you have not been issued a TIN please obtain a number from the nearest tax office and use it on all subsequent customs declarations. Also include your office telephone number. For diplomatic and personal importations, leave the number field blank.

Box No.7   Consignee.

If you are importing goods on behalf of another person, or the other party holds title to the good at time of importation indicate the name and address of the consignee as well as the TIN issued by the Tax Department. Please contact the nearest tax office for a number and use on all subsequent declarations, or obtain the TIN number from the consignee if one has been issued to the consignee by the tax department. For diplomatic importations, leave the number field blank.

Box No.8   Declarant.

If you are a licensed agent authorized to transact business in customs, enter the TIN issued by the Tax Department. If you do not have a TIN, contact the nearest tax office.

Box No.9   Country of Consignment/Destination.

For importation, indicate the country and the code from where the goods have been consigned.
For exportation, indicate the country and the code to where the goods are exported or re-exported.

See Annex II: List of Country and Currency Codes.

Box No.10   Type of License.

Indicate the type of trade or industry license held by you.

Box. No.11   Delivery Terms.

Indicate the terms of delivery of goods either CIF for importation, or FOB for exportation.

Box No.12   Total Invoice in Foreign Currency.

For importation, indicate the total amount of the invoice in foreign currency. See list of Country and Currency Codes in Annex II.

Box No.13   Total Invoice in Local Currency.

Enter here the total value of the invoice in Kip by converting the value declared in box No. 12 with the rate of exchange indicated in box No.16. If there is only one item, this value should correspond to the value declared in box no.38. If there are many items, the total value should correspond to the total of values declared in all the boxes no.38 on the Continuation sheets.

Box No.14   Total FOB (Exports)

Indicate the FOB value of the goods in foreign currency.
(if known)
Box No. 14   Total FOB (Imports)

Enter the FOB value in foreign currency. (if known)

Box No.15   Total FOB Ncy (Import/Export)

For import, leave blank.
For export, indicate the FOB value of the goods in Kip.

Box No.16   Rate of Exchange.

Indicate the rate of exchange of the foreign currency to the Kip and the code of the foreign currency. (The exchange rate shall be that which is in force at time of importation, unless otherwise advised).

Box No.17   Mode of Transport.

Indicate the mode of transport, the voyage number. Also the country code of the nationality of the aircraft, truck or ship.
(if known)

The codes for mode of transport are:

SEA	1
RAIL	2
ROAD	3
AIR	4

Box No.18   Port of Loading/Unloading.

For imports indicate the name and the code of the foreign country where goods are loaded,

For exports, indicate the name and the code of the foreign country where goods are destined.

See Annex II for a list of Country Codes.

Box No.19   Place of Shipping/ Landing.

For imports, indicate the place in Lao PDR where goods have arrived. At export, or re-export, indicate the place in Lao PDR from where the goods are exported or re-exported.

Box No.20   Entry/Exit Office.

Indicate the code of the Lao customs office where the declaration is presented for clearance.

In a transit operation, indicate the code of the customs office where the transit operation commences. Also indicate the code of the exit customs office where the transit operations is to be terminated.

Box No.21   Identification Warehouse (Leave blank until bonded warehouses are established)

Indicate the code of the bonded warehouse where goods are to be warehoused or ex-warehoused.

Box No.22   Financial and Banking Data.

Indicate the terms of payment of the transaction, as well as the name of the bank and the branch where payment for the commercial transaction is made.

Box No.23   Attached Documents.

Indicate the codes of attached documents, which support your declaration. (Documents must be originals or certified as true copies).

1	Invoice
2	Manifest
3	Airway bill
4	Packing List
5	Certificate of Origin (If required)
6	Phytosanitary Certificate (If required)
7	Import Permit from Ministry of Trade (If required)
8	Import permit from Ministry of Agriculture (If required)
9	Import Permit from Ministry of Heath (If required)
10	Authorization from Department of Transport (If required)
11	If claiming duty and tax exemptions, documents authorizing such exemptions must be presented with the declaration.

Box No.24   Marks, Numbers and Description of Goods

Indicate the marks and numbers of the packages as shown on the manifest or airway bill.

If goods arrive or leave by containers, indicate the container number as shown on the manifest.

The total number of packages should correspond to the total number of packages indicated in box No.5.

Give a detailed description of the goods. Avoid, as far as possible, trade names. Except in the case of vehicles and electronic devices, provide make and model.

Box No.25   No. of Items.

Indicate the number of items on the invoice.

Box No.26   Tariff Code

Indicate the classification code of the commodity imported. This classification code in based on the AHTN and must be eight digits.

Box No.27   Customs Procedure Codes.
(Leave blank at this time)

Box No.28   Country of Origin/Destination

For imports, indicate the code of the country of origin of the goods imported, if the country of origin of the goods is different from the country where the goods have been consigned.

Box No.29   Zone.
It the goods originate from ASEAN member countries and are supported by a certificate of origin enter ASEAN. For other countries enter GEN. At export enter XPT.

Box No.30   Valuation Code

Indicate the code of the valuation method used to determine the customs value for duty.

There are six valuation methods and coded as follows:

	VALUATION METHOD	Code	
	Transaction Method	1	
	Identical Goods Method	2	

	Similar Goods Method	3	
	Deductive Method	4	
	Computed Method	5	
	Flexible Method	6	

Note: The transaction valuation method must be used as the primary method for valuation if possible.

Box No.31   Gross Mass.

Enter the gross weight in kilograms for the item on the first page only. The total weight of all items on the continuation sheets in the declaration should be equal to the weight declared in box no.3 of the general segment.

Box No.32   Net Mass.

Enter the net weight of the goods in kilograms for each item declared. If a continuation sheet is used a net mass must be inscribed for each item.

Box No.33   FOB Foreign Currency.

Enter the FOB value of the item in foreign currency (if known).

Box No.34   FOB Local Currency, only if transport and insurance are not prepaid by exporter. If prepaid, enter the value that includes transportation and insurance.

Enter the FOB value of the item in Kips, only if transport and insurance are not prepaid by exporter. If prepaid, enter the value that includes transportation and insurance.

Box No. 35   Freight.

Enter the amount of freight paid or payable for the item in Kip. For a shipment of various items, the freight charges are apportioned according to freight paid or payable and by weight. If freight is prepaid by exporter and included in the value, mark the box "Prepaid".

Box No.36   Insurance.

Enter the amount of insurance in Kip for the item.

For a shipment of various items, the insurance paid or payable is to be apportioned.

If the insurance is prepaid by the exporter and included in the value, mark the box "prepaid"

Box No.37   Other Costs.

Enter other costs and expenses incurred for the import of goods and paid to the exporter for the imported goods.

Box No.38   Customs Value in Local Currency.

Enter the customs value for the item, which is the total of values of boxes 33, 34, 35 and 36.

Box No. 39   Supplementary Unit/Quantity.

Some of the most common international units of quantity are as follows:

	Unit	Code	
	Cubic Metre	MTQ	
	Gigawatt-hour	GWH	
	Hundred	CEN	
	Kilogram	KGM	
	Litre	LTR	
	Metre	MTR	
	Number	NMB	
	Number of packs	NMP	
	Square Metre	MTK	
	Ten	TEN	
	Ten Pairs	TPR	
	Thousand	MIL	
	Tonne	TNE	

Enter any of the code, which describes the unit quantity of goods imported/exported. If the units of imports or exports are not included in this list, consult a customs officer for more detailed lists.

Box No.40   Duty Payable.

Enter the amount of duties and taxes payable for the item declared per category of duty, tax and excise.

Enter also the taxable base for each category of duty, tax and excise. Duty rate is calculated on the Customs value. The tax is calculated on the customs value plus the duty payable. The excise tax is calculated on the customs value plus duty payable plus tax payable.

For other items of the declaration, on the continuation sheets enter the duty, tax and excise payable.

Box No.41   Permit Numbers.

Enter permit number and date of issue for the shipment, if required.

Box No.42   Previous Declaration.

If the declaration refers to a previous declaration, the registration number and date of the previous declaration is entered here.

Present a copy of the previous declaration with the declaration you have just prepared.

Responsibility of Declaration

You must enter your full name, indicate the capacity in which you are acting. And sign the declaration.

You must also indicate the mode of payment by which duty and taxes are to be paid.

After you have completed your declaration, you can now lodge it at the designated customs office where your goods are held.

After customs review and approval of the declaration, please make the payment of all applicable duties and taxes, and present a copy of the payment receipt to the customs office where the declaration was presented.

On receipt of the customs release note, present the release note to the warehouse keeper for delivery of the imported goods and sign for receipt of the goods or have the carrier sign for receipt.

STRATEGIC STATISTICS

BASIC DATA

LAND AREA   236,800 km2

POPULATION   4,474,000 persons

No.	Provinces	Population	No.	Provinces	Population
1	Attopeu	84,000	10	Phongsaly	152,000
2	Bokeo	106,000	11	Savannakhet	692,000
3	Bolikhamsay	155,000	12	Saravane	243,000

4	Champasack	490,000	13	Sayaboury	200,000
5	Houaphanh	238,000	14	Sekong	60,000
6	Khammouane	265,000	15	Vientiane Prefecture	503,000
7	Luang Namtha	128,000	16	Vientiane Province	330,000
8	Luang Praba	365,000	17	Xieng Khouang	196,000
9	Oudomsay	193,000	18	Special Region	74,000

LAOS GLOSSARY

Asian Development Bank
Established in 1967, the bank assists in economic development and promotes growth and cooperation in developing member countries. The bank is owned by its forty-seven member governments, which include both developed and developing countries in Asia and developed countries in the West.

Association of Southeast Asian Nations (ASEAN)
Founded in 1967 primarily for economic cooperation and consisting of Brunei (since 1984), Indonesia, Malaysia, the Philippines, Singapore, and Thailand. Laos has had observer status since 1992 and applied for membership in July 1994.

ban
Village; grouped administratively into *tasseng* (q.v.) and *muang* (q.v.).

dharma
Buddhist teaching or moral law; laws of nature, all that exists, real or imaginary.

fiscal year (FY)
October 1 to September 30.

gross domestic product (GDP)
A value measure of the flow of domestic goods and services produced by an economy over a period of time, such as a year. Only output values of goods for final consumption and intermediate production are assumed to be included in the final prices. GDP is sometimes aggregated and shown at market prices, meaning that indirect taxes and subsidies are included; when these indirect taxes and subsidies have been eliminated, the result is GDP at factor cost. The word *gross* indicates that deductions for depreciation of physical assets have not been made. Income arising from investments and possessions owned abroad is not included, only domestic production. Hence, the use of the word *domestic* to distinguish GDP from gross national product (q.v.).

gross national product (GNP)
The gross domestic product (GDP--q.v.) plus net income or loss stemming from transactions with foreign countries, including income received from abroad by residents and subtracting payments remitted abroad to nonresidents. GNP is the

broadest measurement of the output of goods and services by an economy. It can be calculated at market prices, which include indirect taxes and subsidies. Because indirect taxes and subsidies are only transfer payments, GNP is often calculated at factor cost by removing indirect taxes and subsidies.

Hmong
Largest Lao Sung (*q.v.*) ethnic group of northern Laos. This tribal group dwells at higher elevations than other ethnic groups. During the period of the Royal Lao Government (RLG) (*q.v.*), the Hmong were referred to as Meo.

International Monetary Fund (IMF)
Established on July 22, 1944, the IMF began operating along with the World Bank (*q.v.*) on December 27, 1945. The IMF is a specialized agency affiliated with the United Nations that takes responsibility for stabilizing international exchange rates and payments. The IMF's main business is the provision of loans to its members when they experience balance of payments difficulties. These loans often carry conditions that require substantial internal economic adjustments by the recipients. In 1994 the IMF had 179 members.

karma
Buddhist concept of the sum of one's past actions, which affect one's current life and future reincarnations.

khoueng
Province; first order administrative division.

kip(k)
Lao currency. In June 1994, US$1=R721.

Lao Issara
Free Laos. Movement formed in 1945 to resist any attempt to return to French colonial status.

Lao Loum
Literally translated as the valley Laotian. Inclusive term for people of Tai stock living in Laos, including lowland Lao and upland Tai. Group of lowland peoples comprising the majority population of Laos; generally used to refer to ethnic Lao, the country's dominant ethnic group (approximately 66 percent of the population according to the 1985 census), and speaking Tai-Kadai languages, including Lao, Lue, Tai Dam (Black Tai), and Tai Deng (Red Tai).

Lao Patrocitic Front (LPF) (Neo Lao Hak Xat)
Sucessor to Neo Lao Issara (*q.v.*), the political arm of the Pathrt Liberation Army (*q.v.*)--formerly known as the Pathet Lao (q.v.)--is its milituary arm.

Lao People's Army
Formed in 1976 when the Lao People's Liberation Army (LPLA-- *q.v.*) was restructured after the establishment of the Lao People's Democratic Republic in December 1975.

Lao People's Liberation Army (LPLA)
Official title of Pathet Lao armed forces, more commonly known as the communist revolutionaries, or guerrilla forces. The LPLA originated with the Latsavong detachment, formed in January 1949 by Kaysone Phomvihan, and steadily increased in number to an estimated 8,000 guerrillas in 1960 and an estimated 48,000 troops between 1962 and 1970.

Lao People's Revolutionary Party (LPRP) (Phak Pasason Pativat Lao)
Founded secretly in 1955 as the Phak Pasason Lao (Lao People's Party--LPP); name changed in 1972. Seized full power and became the ruling (communist) party of Laos in 1975. The LPRP Central Committee formulates party policy; it is dominated by the Political Bureau (Politburo) and the Secretariat and maintains control by placing its members in key institutions throughout the government and the army.

Lao Sung
Literally translated as the Laotian of the mountain top--those who traditionally live in the high altitudes in northern Laos. In official use, term denotes a category of ethnic groups that speak Tibeto-Burmese, Miao-Yao languages; chiefly the Hmong (*q.v.*) (Meo) group of highland or upland minorities but also the Mien (Yao) and Akha. According to the 1985 census, these groups make up approximately 10 percent of the population.

Lao Theung
Literally, Laotian of the mountain slopes; group--including Kammu, Loven, and Lamet--that traditionally lives in medium altitudes, practices swidden, or slash-and-burn-agriculture, and speaks Mon-Khmer languages and dialects. According to the 1985 census, approximately 24 percent of the population. Regarded as original inhabitants of Laos, formally referred to by ethnic Lao as *kha*, or slave.

mandala
Indian geopolitical term referring to a variable circle of power centered on a ruler, his palace, and the religious center from which he drew his legitimization.

muang (*muong*)
Administrative district; also an independent principality; comprises several *tasseng* (*q.v.*), second order administrative divisions.

Lao Patriotic Front (LPF) (Neo Lao Hak Xat)
Successor to Neo Lao Issara (*q.v.*), the political arm of the Pathet Lao (*q.v.*) during the Indochina Wars (1946- 75). The Lao People's Liberation Army (*q.v.*)--formerly known as the Pathet Lao (*q.v.*)--is its military arm.

Neo Lao Issara
 Free Laos Front--organization established by former Lao Issara (Free Laos) (*q.v.*) to continue anti-French resistance movement with the Viet Minh (*q.v.*); succeeded by Neo Lao Hak Xat (Lao Patriotic Front--LPF) (*q.v.*) in 1956.

net material product
 Gross material output minus depreciation on capital and excluding "unproductive services." According to the World Bank (*q.v.*), net material product is "a socialist concept of national accounts."

Nonaligned Movement
 Established in September 1961 with the aim of promoting political and military cooperation apart from the traditional East and West blocs. As of 1994, there were 107 members (plus the Palestine Liberation Organization), twenty-one observers, and twenty-one "guests."

Pathet Lao (Lao Nation)
 Literally, land of the Lao. Until October 1965, the name for the Lao People's Liberation Army (*q.v.*), the military arm of the Lao Patriotic Front (*q.v.*).

Royal Lao Government (RLG)
 The ruling authority in Laos from 1947 until the communist seizure of power in December 1975 and the proclamation of the Lao People's Democratic Republic.

Sipsong Panna
 Region in southern Yunnan Province, China, from which migrated many groups that now inhabit Laos.

Southeast Asia Treaty Organization (SEATO)
 Established in September 1954 as a result of the 1954 Geneva Agreements to stop the spread of communism in Southeast Asia. SEATO never had an active military role and was ultimately disbanded in June 1977 following the success of the communist movements in Cambodia, Laos, and Vietnam in 1975. Original signatories to SEATO were Australia, Britain, France, New Zealand, Pakistan, the Philippines, Thailand, and the United States.

tasseng
 Administrative unit; territorial subdivision of *muang* (*q.v.*), subdistrict grouping of ten to twenty villages.

That Luang
 Most sacred Buddhist stupa in Vientiane and site of annual festival on the full moon of the twelfth month.

Theravada Buddhism
 Predominant branch of Buddhism practiced in Laos, Cambodia, Sri Lanka, and Thailand.

United Nations Children's Fund (UNICEF)
Acronym retained from predecessor organization, United Nations International Children's Emergency Fund, established in December 1946. Provides funds for establishing child health and welfare services.

United Nations Development Programme (UNDP)
Created by the United Nations in 1965, the UNDP is the world's largest channel for multilateral technical and preinvestment assistance to low-income countries. It functions as an overall programming, financing, and monitoring agency. The actual fieldwork is done by other UN agencies.

United Nations High Commissioner for Refugees (UNHCR)
Established by the United Nations in 1949, it did not become effective until 1951. The first world institution to aid refugees, the UNHCR seeks to ensure the humanitarian treatment of refugees and find a permanent solution to refugee problems. The agency deals with the international protection of refugees and problems arising from mass movements of people forced to seek refuge.

Viet Minh
Coalition of Vietnamese national elements formed in May 1941 and dominated by the communists in their movement calling for an uprising against the French colonial government.

World Bank
Informal name used to designate a group of four affiliated international institutions: the International Bank for Reconstruction and Development (IBRD), the International Development Association (IDA), the International Finance Corporation (IFC), and the Multilateral Investment Guarantee Agency (MIGA). The IBRD, established in 1945, has as its primary purpose the provision of loans at market-related rates of interest to developing countries at more advanced stages of development. The IDA, a legally separate loan fund but administered by the staff of the IBRD, was set up in 1960 to furnish credits to the poorest developing countries on much easier terms than those of conventional IBRD loans. The IFC, founded in 1956, supplements the activities of the IBRD through loans and assistance designed specifically to encourage the growth of productive private enterprises in the less developed countries. The MIGA, founded in 1988, insures private foreign investment in developing countries against various noncommercial risk. The president and certain senior officers of the IBRD hold the same positions in the IFC. The four institutions are owned by the governments of the countries that subscribe their capital. To participate in the World Bank group, member states must first belong to the Intentional Monetary Fund (IMF--*q.v.*).

SELECTED TOUR OPERATORS IN LAOS

The following list is issued by the National Tourism Authority of Lao PDR. This is not an exhaustive list of travel companies. You are advised to contact the travel company directly for their up-to-date itineraries and prices.

Dafi Travel Co., Ltd
093/4 Samsenthai St,
P.O. Box 5351,
Vientiane

Lao Tourism Co., Ltd
08/02 Lane Xang Ave,
P.O. Box 2511,
Vientiane

Luang Prabang Tourism Co., Ltd
P.O. Box 356,
Sisavangvong Rd,
Luang Prabang.

Phathanakhet Phoudoi Travel Co., Ltd
Phonxay Rd,
P.O. Box 5796,
Vientiane

Phathana Saysomboune Travel & Tour Co., Ltd
Km 5, 13 South Rd,
12/G Chommanytai Xaysetha DTR,
P.O. Box 7117,
Vientiane

Chackavane Travel & Tour
92 Thongkankham Rd,
P.O. Box 590,
Vientiane

Raja Tour
03 Heng boon St,
P.O. Box 3655,
Vientiane

Sode Tour
114 Quai Fa Ngum,
P.O. Box 70,
Vientiane

LAO PDR EMBASSIES AND CONSULTATE-GENERAL

Country	Address
Brunei Darussalam	Embassy of the Lao PDR Tel : 673-2-345 666 Fax : 456-888
Cambodia	Embassy of the Lao PDR 15-17 Mao Tse Tung Boulvard P.O. Box 19 Phnom Penh Tel : 855-23-982 632 Fax : 720 907
Indonesia	Embassy of the Lao PDR Jl. Patra Kuningan XIV No.1.A Kuningan Jakarta Selatan - 12950 Tel : 62-21-522 9602, 522 7862 Fax : 522 9601
Malaysia	Embassy of the Lao PDR I Lorong Damai Tiga Kuala Lumpur 55000 Tel : 60-3-248 3895, Residence: 245 6023 HP : 60-012 218 0075 Fax : 60-3- 242 0344
Myanmar	Embassy of the Lao PDR NA I Diplomatic Quarters Franser Road Yangon Tel : 95-1-222 482, 227 445 Fax : 227 446
The Philippines	Embassy of the Lao PDR N. 34 Lapu-Lapu Street Magallences Village Makati City, Manila Tel & Fax : 63-2-833 5759
Singapore	Embassy of the Lao PDR 179-B Gold Hill Centre Thomson Road Tel : 65-250 6044 Fax : 65-250 6214

For additional analytical, business and investment opportunities information, please contact Global Investment & Business Center, USA at (703) 370-8082. Fax: (703) 370-8083. E-mail: ibpusa3@gmail.com
Global Business and Investment Info Databank - www.ibpus.com

Thailand	Embassy of the Lao PDR 520-502/ 1-3 Soi Ramkhamheng 39 Bangkapi Bangkok 10310 Tel : 539 6667 Fax : 66-2-539 6678 Consulate General of the Lao PDR Khonkaen Tel : 66-43-223 698, 223 473, 221 961 Fax : 223 849
Vietnam	Embassy of the Lao PDR 22 Rue Tran Bing Trong Hanoi Tel : 84-4-8- 25 4576, 29 6746 Fax : 22 8414 Consulate General of the LAO PDR 93 Larteur ST, District 1 Ho Chi Minh City Tel : 84-8-8- 29 7667, 29 9275 Fax : 29 9272 Consulate General of the LAO PDR 12 Tran Quy-Cap Danang Tel : 84-51-8- 21 208, 24 101 Fax : 22 628
Australia	Embassy of the Lao PDR I Dalman Crescent O' Malley Canberra ACT 2606 Tel : 61-2- 6286 4595, 6286 6933 Fax : 6290 1910
China	Embassy of the Lao PDR 11 Salitun Dongsie Jie Bejing 100 600 IfsTel : 86-1- 6532 1224 Fax : 6532 6748 Consulate General of the Lao PDR Room 3226 Camellia Hotel 154 East Dong Feng Road Kunming 650041 Tel : 86-871- 317 6623, 317 6624

	Fax : 317 8556
France	Embassy of the Lao PDR 74 Ave Raymond Poincare 75116 Paris Tel : 33-1- 4553 0298, 4553 7047 Fax : 4727 5789
Germany	Embassy of the Lao PDR Am Lessing 6 53639 Koeningswinter Tel : 49- 2223 21501 Fax : 2223 3065
India	Embassy of the Lao PDR E53 Panchsheel Park New Delhi-17 Tel : 91-11-642 7447 Fax : 642 8588
Japan	Embassy of the Lao PDR 3-3-22 Nishi-Azabu Minato-Ku Tokyo 106 Tel : 81-3-5411 2291, 5411 2292 Fax : 5411 2293
Russia	Embassy of the Lao PDR Ul Katchalova 18 Moscow 121 069 Tel : 7-095-203 1454, 291 8966 Fax : 290 4246, 291 7218
Sweden	Embassy of the Lao PDR Badstrandvagen 11 11265 Stockholm Tel : 46-8-618 2010, 695 0160 Fax : 618 2001
United States of America	Embassy of the Lao PDR 2222 S Street NW Washington DC 10022 Tel : 1-202- 332 6416, 332 6417 Fax : 332 4923 Permanent Mission of the Lao PDR 317 East 51st Street

| | New York, NY 10022

Tel : 1-212- 832 2734
Fax : 750 0039 |

BASIC TITLE FOR LAOS

TITLE	ISBN
Lao People's Democratic Republic Traders and Investors Handbook	1438728093
Lao People's Democratic Republic Traders and Investors Handbook	1433028778
Laos A "Spy" Guide - Strategic Information and Developments	1433028786
Laos A Spy" Guide"	1438728107
Laos Business and Investment Opportunities Yearbook	1433028794
Laos Business and Investment Opportunities Yearbook	1438728115
Laos Business and Investment Opportunities Yearbook Volume 1 Strategic Information and Opportunities	1438777132
Laos Business Intelligence Report - Practical Information, Opportunities, Contacts	1433028808
Laos Business Intelligence Report - Practical Information, Opportunities, Contacts	1438728123
Laos Business Law Handbook - Strategic Information and Basic Laws	143877026X
Laos Business Law Handbook - Strategic Information and Basic Laws	143877026X
Laos Business Law Handbook - Strategic Information and Basic Laws	1433028816
Laos Business Law Handbook - Strategic Information and Basic Laws	1438728131
Laos Clothing & Textile Industry Handbook	143872814X
Laos Clothing & Textile Industry Handbook	1433028824
Laos Company Laws and Regulations Handbook	1433070154
Laos Country Study Guide - Strategic Information and Developments	1433028832
Laos Country Study Guide - Strategic Information and Developments	1438728158
Laos Country Study Guide - Strategic Information and Developments Volume 1 Strategic Information and Developments	143877480X
Laos Customs, Trade Regulations and Procedures Handbook	1433028840
Laos Customs, Trade Regulations and Procedures Handbook	1438728166
Laos Diplomatic Handbook - Strategic Information and Developments	1433028859
Laos Diplomatic Handbook - Strategic Information and Developments	1438728174
Laos Ecology & Nature Protection Handbook	1433028867
Laos Ecology & Nature Protection Handbook	1438728182
Laos Ecology & Nature Protection Laws and Regulation Handbook	1433074176
Laos Economic & Development Strategy Handbook	1433028875
Laos Economic & Development Strategy Handbook	1438728190
Laos Education System and Policy Handbook	1433066785
Laos Energy Policy, Laws and Regulation Handbook	1433071932
Laos Export-Import Trade and Business Directory	1433028883
Laos Export-Import Trade and Business Directory	1438728204
Laos Foreign Policy and Government Guide	1433028891
Laos Foreign Policy and Government Guide	1438728212
Laos Industrial and Business Directory	1433028905
Laos Industrial and Business Directory	1438728220
Laos Internet and E-Commerce Investment and Business Guide - Strategic and Practical Information: Regulations and Opportunities	1433028913

For additional analytical, business and investment opportunities information,
please contact Global Investment & Business Center, USA
at (703) 370-8082. Fax: (703) 370-8083. E-mail: ibpusa3@gmail.com
Global Business and Investment Info Databank - www.ibpus.com

TITLE	ISBN
Laos Internet and E-Commerce Investment and Business Guide - Strategic and Practical Information: Regulations and Opportunities	1438728239
Laos Investment and Business Guide - Strategic and Practical Information	1438767986
Laos Investment and Business Guide - Strategic and Practical Information	1438767986
Laos Investment and Business Guide - Strategic and Practical Information	1433028921
Laos Investment and Business Guide - Strategic and Practical Information	1438728247
Laos Investment and Trade Laws and Regulations Handbook	1433076160
Laos Justice System and National Police Handbook	143302893X
Laos Justice System and National Police Handbook	1438728255
Laos Medical & Pharmaceutical Industry Handbook	1433028948
Laos Medical & Pharmaceutical Industry Handbook	1438728263
Laos Mineral & Mining Sector Investment and Business Guide - Strategic and Practical Information	1438728271
Laos Mineral, Mining Sector Investment and Business Guide - Strategic and Practical Information	1433028956
Laos Mining Laws and Regulations Handbook	1433077728
Laos Recent Economic and Political Developments Yearbook	1433063336
Laos Recent Economic and Political Developments Yearbook	1433063336
Laos Recent Economic and Political Developments Yearbook	1433063336
Laos Research & Development Policy Handbook	1433063220
Laos Research & Development Policy Handbook	1433063220
Laos Research & Development Policy Handbook	1433063220
Laos Starting Business (Incorporating) in....Guide	1433066793
Laos Taxation Laws and Regulations Handbook	1433080214
Laos Telecom Laws and Regulations Handbook	1433082063
Laos Telecommunication Industry Business Opportunities Handbook	1433028964
Laos Telecommunication Industry Business Opportunities Handbook	143872828X
Laos Traders Manual: Export-Import, Trade, Investment	1433066807
Laos Transportation Policy and Regulations Handbook	1433066815
Laos: How to Invest, Start and Run Profitable Business in Laos Guide - Practical Information, Opportunities, Contacts	9781433083785

For additional analytical, business and investment opportunities information, please contact Global Investment & Business Center, USA at (703) 370-8082. Fax: (703) 370-8083. E-mail: ibpusa3@gmail.com Global Business and Investment Info Databank - www.ibpus.com

INTERNATIONAL BUSINESS PUBLICATIONS, USA
ibpusa@comcast.net. http://www.ibpus.com

WORLD ISLAMIC BUSINESS LIBRARY
Price: $149.95 Each

Islamic Banking and Financial Law Handbook
Islamic Banking Law Handbook
Islamic Business Organization Law Handbook
Islamic Commerce and Trade Law Handbook
Islamic Company Law Handbook
Islamic Constitutional and Administrative Law Handbook
Islamic Copyright Law Handbook
Islamic Customs Law and Regulations Handbook
Islamic Design Law Handbook
Islamic Development Bank Group Handbook
Islamic Economic & Business Laws and Regulations Handbook
Islamic Environmental Law Handbook
Islamic Financial and Banking System Handbook vol 1
Islamic Financial and Banking System Handbook Vol. 2
Islamic Financial Institutions (Banks and Financial Companies) Handbook
Islamic Foreign Investment and Privatization Law Handbook
Islamic Free Trade & Economic Zones Law and Regulations Handbook
Islamic International Law and Jihad (War(Law Handbook
Islamic Labor Law Handbook
Islamic Legal System (Sharia) Handbook Vol. 1 Basic Laws and Regulations
Islamic Legal System (Sharia) Handbook Vol. 2 Laws and Regulations in Selected Countries
Islamic Mining Law Handbook
Islamic Patent & Trademark Law Handbook
Islamic Taxation Law Handbook
Islamic Trade & Export-Import Laws and Regulations Handbook

For additional analytical, business and investment opportunities information,
please contact Global Investment & Business Center, USA
at (202) 546-2103. Fax: (202) 546-3275. E-mail: rusric@erols.com

LAO PEOPLE'S DEMOCRATIC REPUBLIC

Public Administration
Country Profile

Division for Public Administration and Development Management (DPADM)
Department of Economic and Social Affairs (DESA)
United Nations

January 2005

All papers, statistics and materials contained in the Country Profiles express entirely the opinion of the mentioned authors. They should not, unless otherwise mentioned, be attributed to the Secretariat of the United Nations.

The designations employed and the presentation of material on maps in the Country Profiles do not imply the expression of any opinion whatsoever on the part of the Secretariat of the United Nations concerning the legal status of any country, territory, city or area or of its authorities, or concerning the delimitation of its frontiers or boundaries.

Table of Contents 1

Lao PDR 2

1. General Information 3
   1.1 People 3
   1.2 Economy 3
   1.3 Public Spending 4
   1.4 Public Sector Employment and Wages 4

2. Legal Structure 6
   2.1 Legislative Branch 6
   2.2 Executive Branch 7
   2.3 Judiciary Branch 7
   2.4 Local Government 8

3. The State and Civil Society 11
   3.1 Ombudsperson 11
   3.2 NGOs 11
   3.3 LPRP and mass organizations 11

4. Civil Service 13
   4.1 Legal basis 13
   4.2 Recruitment 13
   4.3 Promotion 13
   4.4 Remuneration 14
   4.5 Training 14
   4.6 Gender 15

5. Ethics and Civil Service 16
   5.1 Corruption 16
   5.2 Ethics 16

6. e-Government 18
   6.1 e-Government Readiness 18
   6.2 e-Participation 19

7. Links 20
   7.1 National sites 20
   7.2 Miscellaneous sites 20

LAO PDR

Click here for detailed map

Source: The World Factbook - Lao PDR

Government type
People's Republic

Independence
19 July 1949 (from France)

Constitution
Promulgated 14 August 1991

Legal system
Based on traditional customs, French legal norms and procedures, and socialist practice

Administrative divisions
16 provinces ('khoueng'), 1 municipality (Vientiane), and 1 special zone (Saysomboune)

Source: The World Factbook - Lao PDR

During the first Indochina war between France and the communist movement in Vietnam, the Pathet Lao (Land of Lao) resistance organization was formed, committed to the communist struggle against colonialism. Laos was not granted full sovereignty until the French defeat by the Vietnamese and the subsequent Geneva peace conference in 1954.

A year later, elections were held in Laos. The resulting Government of National Union collapsed in 1958 and was replaced by a right-wing government. A second Geneva conference, held in 1961-62, provided for the independence and neutrality of Laos. Meanwhile, a growing American and North Vietnamese military presence in the country increasingly drew Laos into the second Indochina war (1954-75).

On December 2, 1975, the king abdicated his throne, and the communist Lao People's Democratic Republic (LPDR) was established. With the abrogation of the 1947 constitution, Lao PDR was governed by Part Resolutions between 1975 and 1991. In 1991, the Supreme People's Council voted in favour of a new Constitution, which provides the official framework for governance in Lao PDR.

The following year, elections were held for a new 85-seat National Assembly. The most recent elections took place in February 2002, when the National Assembly was expanded to 109 members.

Source: UN Capital Development Fund (Lao PDR) - Lao PDR - Fact Finding Mission Report (March 2002) (edited)
U.S. Department of State (Background Notes) - Lao PDR (edited)

1. General Information

1.1 People	Lao PDR	Cambodia	Vietnam	[1]
Population				[a]
Total estimated population (,000), 2003	5,657	14,143	81,377	
Female estimated population (,000), 2003	2,829	7,257	40,827	
Male estimated population (,000), 2003	2,828	6,886	40,550	
Sex ratio (males per 100 females), 2003	100	95	99	
Average annual rate of change of pop. (%), 2000-2005	2.29	2.4	1.35	
Youth and Elderly Population				[b]
Total population under age 15 (%), 2003	42	41	31	
Female population aged 60+ (%), 2003	6	6	8	
Male population aged 60+ (%), 2003	5	3	7	
Human Settlements				[c]
Urban population (%), 2001	20	18	25	
Rural population (%), 2001	80	82	75	
Urban average annual rate of change in pop. (%), '00-'05	4.59	5.54	3.06	
Rural average annual rate of change in pop/ (%), '00-'05	1.71	1.74	0.71	
Education				[d]
Total school life expectancy, 2000/2001	8.3	7	10.4	[1]
Female school life expectancy, 2000/2001	7.4	7	..	[1]
Male school life expectancy, 2000/2001	9.2	8.2	..	[1]
Female estimated adult (15+) illiteracy rate (%), 1999	46.6[i]	42.8[ii]	9.3	[2]
Male estimated adult (15+) illiteracy rate (%), 1999	23.8[i]	19.8[ii]	5.5	[2]
Employment				[e]
Unemployment rate (15+) (%), 2000	..	..	..	[1]
Female adult (+15) economic activity rate (%), 1999	..	74	74[iii]	[2]
Male adult (+15) economic activity rate (%), 1999	..	81	82[iii]	[2]

Notes: [i] 1995; [ii] 1998; [iii] 1989

1.2 Economy	Lao PDR	Cambodia	Vietnam	[2]
GDP				[a]
GDP total (millions US$), 2002	1,680	3,677	35,110	
GDP per capita (US$), 2002	304	294	436	
PPP GDP total (millions int. US$), 2002	9,280[i]	20,585	180,344	
PPP GDP per capita(int. US$), 2002	1,678[i]	1,649	2,240	
Sectors				[b]
Value added in agriculture (% of GDP), 2002	53.5[ii]	35.6	23.0	
Value added in industry (% of GDP), 2002	22.5[ii]	28.0	38.5	
Value added in services (% of GDP), 2002	24.0[ii]	36.4	38.5	
Miscellaneous				[c]
GDP implicit price deflator (annual % growth), 2003	12.6	7.4	5.4	
Private consumption (% of GDP), 2003	..	80.1[iii]	66.0	
Government consumption (% of GDP), 2003	..	5.8[iii]	6.9	

Notes: [i] Estimate is based on regression; other PPP figures are extrapolated from the latest International Comparison Programme benchmark estimates; [ii] 1999; [iii] 2002

---

[1] United Nations Statistics Division:
  [a] Statistics Division and Population Division of the UN Secretariat; [b] Statistics Division and Population Division of the UN Secretariat; [c] Population Division of the UN Secretariat; [d1] UNESCO ; [d2] UNESCO; [e1] ILO; [e2] ILO/OECD
[2] World Bank - Data and Statistics:
  [a] Quick Reference Tables; [b] Data Profile Tables ; [c] Country at a Glance

1.3 Public Spending	Lao PDR	Cambodia	Vietnam	
Public expenditures				3
Education (% of GNP), 1985-1987	0.5	..	..	a
Education (% of GNP), 1995-1997	2.1	2.9	3	a
Health (% of GDP), 1990	0	..	0.9	
Health (% of GDP), 1998	1.2	0.6	0.8	
Military (% of GDP), 1990	..	2.4	7.9	b
Military (% of GDP), 2000	..	2.4	..	b
Total debt service (% of GDP), 1990	1.1	2.7	2.7	
Total debt service (% of GDP), 2000	2.5	1	4.2	

Notes:

1.4 Public Sector Employment and Wages		Lao PDR 1991-1995	Lao PDR 1996-2000	East Asia & Pacific average[4] 1996-2000	.. average[4] 1996-2000	Low income group average[4] 1996-2000
Employment						
Civilian Central Government[5]	(,000)	4.0	..			
	(% pop.)	0.09	..	0.63	..	0.46
Sub-national Government[5]	(,000)	20.0	..			
	(% pop.)	0.46	..	0.63	..	0.46
Education employees	(,000)	38.0	26.4			
	(% pop.)	0.87	0.54	0.76	..	0.91
Health employees	(,000)	7.0	..			
	(% pop.)	0.16	..	0.16	..	0.62
Police	(,000)	..	..			
	(% pop.)	..	..	0.26	..	0.30
Armed forces	(,000)	37.0	29.1			
	(% pop.)	0.85	0.59	0.53	..	0.33
SOE Employees	(,000)	3.0	11.9			
	(% pop.)	0.07	0.25	1.18	..	2.27
Total Public Employment	(,000)	109.0	..			
	(% pop.)	2.5	..	..	..	..
Wages						
Total Central gov't wage bill	(% of GDP)	5.2	..	9.4	..	5.4
Total Central gov't wage bill	(% of exp)	..	..	24.4	..	24.7
Average gov't wage	(,000 LCU)	503	..			
Real ave. gov't wage ('97 price)	(,000 LCU)	867	..			
Average gov't wage to per capita GDP ratio		2.0	..	2.9	..	4.4

Source: World Bank - Public Sector Employment and Wages

---

[3] UNDP - Human Development Report 2002
[a] Data refer to total public expenditure on education, including current and capital expenditures.
[b] As a result of a number of limitations in the data, comparisons of military expenditure data over time and across countries should be made with caution. For detailed notes on the data see SIPRI (2001).
[4] Averages for regions and sub regions are only generated if data is available for at least 35% of the countries in that region or sub region.
[5] Excluding education, health and police – if available (view Country Sources for further explanations).

Overview of government employment (2002-2003):

Item	Qty	Female	(%)	Male	(%)
Civil servants					
Lao Loum	80,532	31,517	39	49,015	61
Lao Theung	5,359	1,907	36	3,452	64
Lao Sung	5,439	1,811	33	3,628	67
Total	91,330	35,235	39	56,095	61
Central gov't					
Lao Loum	74,443	29,788	40	44,655	60
Lao Theung	4,131	1,648	40	2,483	60
Lao Sung	5,105	1,749	34	3,356	66
Total	83,679	33,185	40	50,494	60
Provinces					
Lao Loum	6,089	1,729	28	4,360	72
Lao Theung	1,228	259	21	969	79
Lao Sung	334	62	19	272	81
Total	7,651	2,050	27	5,601	73

Source: UN OHCHR - State Party Report (31 March 2004)

2. Legal Structure

The Lao People's Democratic Republic is a unitary State. Under the Constitution, the country is a people's democratic State. The right of the multi-ethnic people to be master of the country is exercised and guaranteed through the functioning of the political system, with the Lao People's Revolutionary Party as the lead component.

The National Assembly and all other state organizations are established and function in accordance with the principle of democratic centralism.[6]

Source: UN OHCHR - State Party Report (31 March 2004)

2.1 Legislative Branch

Unicameral National Assembly (109 seats; members elected by popular vote to serve five-year terms.[7] *women in parliament*: 25 out of 109 seats: (23%).[8]

The National Assembly consists of a single chamber of 109 representatives, elected for 5 years by direct and secret universal suffrage.

Candidates for National Assembly membership must be screened and approved by the Lao Front for National Construction (see 3.3). In the recent elections, one out of the 166 candidates was not a Party member.

Fact box:
elections: last held 24 February 2002 (next to be held in 2007)
election results: seats by party - LPRP or LPRP-approved (independent, non-party members) 109

National Assembly constituencies are provincial. Each province is represented by at least 3 National Assembly members, but with total provincial representation being thereafter a function of the provincial population size. On Election Day, provincial electors are asked to "eliminate" the candidates that they do not want to represent them.

The National Assembly maintains offices in each province which are intended to facilitate contact between provincial parliamentarians and their constituencies.

Source: UN Capital Development Fund (Lao PDR) - Lao PDR - Fact Finding Mission Report (March 2002) (edited)

The Constitution identifies the National Assembly as the organization of the people's representatives. It is the legislative organ, which has the right to decide the fundamental issues of the nation. It also supervises and oversees the function of the executive and judicial branches of government.

The National Assembly exercises its legislative, representative and oversight functions through the Standing Committee, six parliamentary commissions, a number of internal offices and departments and 18 Provincial Offices.

Only the National Assembly of the Lao People's Democratic Republic has the right to amend the Constitution. The amendment to the Constitution requires the votes of approval cast by at least two-thirds of the total number of the National Assembly members.[9]

Source: UNDP (Lao PDR) - Decentralization Report (Updated 7 March 2004)

---

[6] Constitution of Lao PDR
[7] Source of fact boxes if nothing else stated: The World Factbook - Lao PDR
[8] Inter-Parliamentary Union - Women in National Parliaments
[9] Constitution of Lao PDR

2.2 Executive Branch

> *cabinet:* Council of Ministers appointed by the president, approved by the National Assembly.
> *elections:* president elected by the National Assembly for a five-year term; election last held 24 February 2002 (next to be held in 2007); prime minister appointed by the president with the approval of the National Assembly for a five-year term

The President of the Republic and Head of State is elected by the National Assembly with two-thirds of the votes of all members of the National Assembly attending the session. The term of office of the President of state is five years.

The President, inter alia, promulgate laws approved by the National Assembly, appoints or removes the Prime Minister (with the approval of the National Assembly) and members of the Government, and appoint provincial Governors and municipal Mayors on the recommendation of the Prime Minister.

The government consists of the Prime Minister, Deputy Prime Ministers, ministers and chairmen of the ministry-equivalent committees. The term of office of the government is five years. The Prime Minister appoints deputy ministers and deputy chairmen of ministry-equivalent committees, as well as deputy Governors, deputy Mayors and district Chiefs.

> **Fact box:**
> *chief of state:* President Gen. KHAMTAI Siphadon (since 26 February 1998) and Vice President Lt. Gen. CHOUMMALI Saignason (since 27 March 2001)
> *head of government:* Prime Minister BOUNGNANG Volachit (since 27 March 2001); First Deputy Prime Minister Maj. Gen. ASANG Laoli (since May 2002), Deputy Prime Minister THONGLOUN Sisolit (since 27 March 2001), and Deputy Prime Minister SOMSAVAT Lengsavat (since 26 February 1998)

The Civil Service Decree [Article 9] provides for the various civil servants appointed by the President, the Prime Minister, the ministers, the governor of provinces or prefectures, and district governors.

Source: Constitution of Lao PDR & Civil Service Decree, no. 171 (2003)

2.3 Judiciary Branch

> People's Supreme Court (the president of the People's Supreme Court is elected by the National Assembly on the recommendation of the National Assembly Standing Committee; the vice president of the People's Supreme Court and the judges are appointed by the National Assembly Standing Committee).

The People's Courts are the judiciary organizations of the state comprising the People's Supreme Court, People's Provincial and Municipal Courts, People's District Courts and Military Courts.

The People's Supreme Court is the highest judiciary organization of the state. The People's Supreme Court scrutinizes the sentences reached by the people's local courts and the military courts.

The Vice-President of the People's Supreme Court and the judges of the people's courts at all levels are appointed or removed by the National Assembly Standing Committee.

The Public Prosecution Institutes, which control the appropriate observance of laws by all ministries, organizations attached to the government, social organizations, local administrative organizations, enterprises, state employees and all citizens, consist of the Public Prosecutor-General Institute, the Public Prosecution Institutes of provinces, municipalities, and districts, and the military prosecution institutes.

Source: Constitution of Lao PDR

State structure in LAO PDR

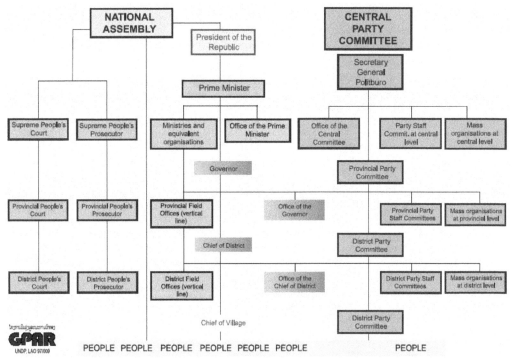

Source: UNDP (Lao PDR) - National Human Development Report (2001)

2.4 Local Government

Prime Ministerial Instruction 01/PM (dated 11 March 2000) and supporting Recommendation 128/SPC (same date) were issued as a first step in reversing the "re-centralization" trend of the 1990s. This policy guidance defined a new planning and budgeting framework, seeking to increase the responsibilities of the provinces, districts and villages. Provinces were to become "Strategic Planning Units", Districts "planning and budgeting units", and villages "implementation units". The intention of this guideline was to devolve planning and budgeting responsibilities to lower levels of public administration.

In order to give stronger backing to the policy shift towards decentralization the Law on Local Administration was approved by the National Assembly in October 2003. It outlines the basic principles concerning the organization, working methods and functions of the local administration at provincial, city, district, municipal and village level. After nearly 10 years of experimenting with the implementation of Resolution nr. 21 (May 1993) and revising and adapting operational procedures accordingly, the law consolidates the principles of a deconcentrated system (upgrading Party Resolution 21 into a state-sanctioned legal framework). Two innovations are significant:

The Law offers opportunities to incrementally establish elected local government bodies ("municipalities") – at least in the more "urban" areas - and to adjust the organizational structures of the local administrations (in particular the districts and municipalities) as part of the process of empowering local authorities and field offices;

The Law also allows for the creation of embryonic consultative bodies at Village and District level (regular Village and District "meetings"), as a first step to opening up the local service delivery, planning and public expenditure management process to people other than local officials.

Additional legislation include Recommendation 475/MF, which is almost entirely devoted to allocating revenue collection and expenditure management responsibilities for the provinces, districts and villages.[10]

Lao PDR is divided into 16 provinces, Vientiane Municipality and Saysomboune Special Zone (administered directly by the armed forces for security reasons). Provinces are, in turn, divided up into a varying number of districts (with a total of 141 districts for the country as a whole), which are themselves made up of villages (between 11,000 and 12,000). In theory, there are no formal administrative level between districts and their constituent villages; in practice, however, district administrations usually tend to group villages into zones or *khet*, made up of several villages. Official government documents frequently refer to three regions – northern, central, and southern – but these are geographical and not administrative units.

Source: UN Capital Development Fund (Lao PDR) - Lao PDR - Fact Finding Mission Report (March 2002) (edited)

Overview of central-local party-state institutional framework

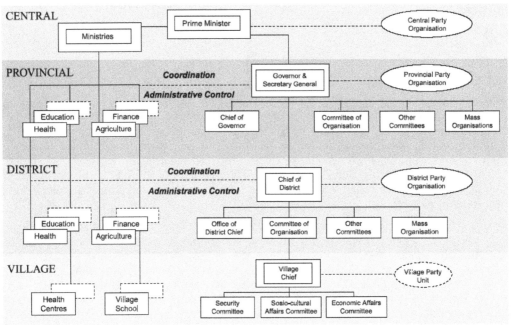

Source: UNDP (Lao PDR) - National Human Development Report (2001)

---

[10] UN Capital Development Fund (Lao PDR) - Lao PDR - Fact Finding Mission Report (March 2002)

The prefecture of Vientiane, the provinces and the special zone are administered by the prefect, the provincial governors and the chief of the special zone, respectively; all of these have the same rank. The districts have district chiefs and the villages have village heads.

The Prefect of Vientiane, the provincial governors, the chief of the special zone, the district chiefs and the village heads have deputies to assist them. The prefect, the governors, the chief of the special zone and the district chiefs are appointed by the Government, while the village heads are directly elected by the villagers themselves.

Source: UN OHCHR - State Party Report (31 March 2004)

Click here for Decentralization Report (updated 7 March 2004)

3. The State and Civil Society

3.1 Ombudsperson

Source: Institution - Title

3.2 NGOs

Click here for Directory of International Non-government Organizations (INGOs) in the Lao PDR

Source: Institution - Title

3.3 LPRP and mass organizations

Since 1975, Lao PDR has been ruled by one party, the Lao People's Revolutionary Party (LPRP). Total Party membership of the LPRP is estimated to be around 100,000 – which is approximately 2% of the total population. Despite this relatively small membership, the Party appears to be present at all levels in Lao PDR – from Vientiane to the villages. Within each line ministry, and at national, provincial and district levels, Party members are organized into committees. There are also "consolidated" Party committees for the overall district and provincial levels.

At the national level, the Party Central Committee (with a current membership of 53) provides the LPRP with a form of national assembly. The Political Bureau (usually referred to as the Politburo) – with a current membership of 11 – operates as the Party's executive body; the Politburo is, by all accounts, the most politically powerful body in Lao PDR. Both the Politburo and the Central Committee are "elected" during the Party's Congresses every five years. Party Congresses are major political events, not only because they choose the LPRP leadership, but also because they determine policy goals and orientations.

- LPRP's representation in the state apparatus includes:
- the President of the Republic and Head of State (the General Secretary of the Party and head of the Politburo);
- the Prime Minister (traditionally a key member of the Politburo);
- all provincial Governors (both members of the Party Central Committee and the General Secretaries of their respective Provincial Party Committees);
- all district Governors (General Secretaries of their respective District Party Committees);
- Ministers (frequently also members of the Politburo or the Central Committee); and
- Ministers (usually Party members).

There are four mass organizations in Lao PDR – the Lao Front for National Construction (commonly referred to as the Lao Front), the Lao Federation of Trades Unions, the Lao Youth Organization, and the Lao Women's Union. They are constitutionally mandated to ".. unite and mobilize all strata of all ethnic groups in order to take part in the tasks of national defense and development..".

These mass organizations are present at all levels – national, provincial, district and village. At district and provincial levels, they report to the Governors in their capacity as General Secretaries of the local Party Committee.

Of the mass organizations, it is the Lao Front which appears to be the most highly regarded at the local level and in rural areas. The Lao Front is responsible for building national solidarity and for ensuring that the interests of ethnic minority groups are taken into account and upheld. It is often considered to be one of the more liberal elements in the country's political system. The Lao Women's Union is also fairly active in rural areas, and is often involved in health programmes and income generating activities.

Although the Constitution explicitly recognizes the freedom of Lao citizens to assembly, no further regulatory framework defines how this constitutional right can be exercised in practice. As a result, civil society organizations (CSOs), as known elsewhere, are not legally recognized in Lao PDR.

Source: UN Capital Development Fund (Lao PDR) - Lao PDR - Fact Finding Mission Report (March 2002)

According to the Constitution, the State shall ensure that the mass media are made capable of contributing to the protection and development of the country. Any use of the mass media to harm the national interest or undermine the Lao people's finest traditions or dignity is prohibited.

All the media in the Lao People's Democratic Republic - press, radio and television - belong to or are controlled by the State.

Source: UN OHCHR - State Party Report (31 March 2004)

4. Civil Service

Overall civil service management is placed under the responsibility of the Department of Public Administration and Civil Service (DPACS) in the Prime Minister's Office, while issues related to the financial management of civil servants are the responsibility of the Department of the Budget in the Ministry of Finance.

Until recently, all personnel management affairs were closely monitored by the Central Committee of Organization and Personnel (CCOP). Since 2001, DPACS is responsible for supervising the management of civil servants in technical positions (Decree No.124/PM, 4/7/2001), while the CCOP manages positions of high leadership.

Source: UNDP (Lao PDR) - Priority areas for Governance Reform (March 2003)

4.1 Legal basis

The new civil service statute was approved in May 2003 (Decree no. 171/PM dated 23 May 2003) identifies civil servants as those who are recruited and appointed to work permanently in the party, state and mass organizations at the central and local levels. The military and the police force are not considered the civil service, and special regulations apply to these sectors.[11]

In contrast with previous regulations, the high-ranking officials (vice-minister level and above) are no longer considered civil servants. The new statute aims to introduce a more performance-oriented and accountable civil service, including provisions to curb nepotism and corrupt practices and output-based performance evaluations. According to the statute newly recruited civil servants are obliged to work at least 2 years at village or district level.

Source: UN Capital Development Fund (Lao PDR) - Lao PDR - Fact Finding Mission Report (March 2002) (edited)

4.2 Recruitment

According to the Civil Service Decree, the recruitment of civil servants must be carried out through selections and entry examinations. Individuals who pass the selective examination must be submitted to a probationary period ranging from 3-18 months depending on qualifications before becoming a civil servant.

Civil servants are classified into six ranks, with 'rank 6' being rank of the high leadership. Each rank between one and five comprises 15 indices however the rank of the high leadership comprises only 4 indexes.

Civil servants are furthermore categorized according to revolutionary activities before 1954, between 1954 and 1975, and according to participation in administrative services from 1975 and onwards.

Source: Civil Service Decree, no. 171 (2003)

4.3 Promotion

Historically, there is a lack of standardized performance management in the Civil Service. The foundations of the current personnel management policies and practices were strongly influenced by the underlying principles of a centrally planned economy.

---

[11] Click here for a comprehensive paper on the Civil Service System of Laos in the late 90's (February 1997)

In general, all civil servants followed a similar career progression, and were promoted one step every two years, unless they showed particularly low moral qualities or required disciplinary action. Consequently, almost all civil servants received their promotion.

Group evaluations have also been a part of the civil service culture in Lao PDR. These have traditionally taken place on a monthly basis within respective work units. The meetings have given employees the opportunity to evaluate themselves, to evaluate each other and even to evaluate their superiors. Practices in some ministries have been different from those observed in others. Even within ministries, practices may have differed from one province to another. The effectiveness of this methodology has increasingly been called into question. Self-criticism and peer-rating are strong devices in flexible and flat structures, but the bureaucratic nature of the Lao civil service obstructs the efficient use of outcomes from group evaluations.

In the new Decree on Civil Servants, heads of organizational units have been encouraged to give selective recognition for good performance which can result in accelerated progression in the salary. Similarly, managers have been encouraged to stigmatize unsatisfactory performance.

The new Civil Service decree legislates for selective recognition of superior performance through accelerated promotion, but as of early 2004 the revised performance appraisal system had not yet introduced. Similarly, the job descriptions upon which appraisal must be placed had not yet been developed in a consistent fashion across the country.

Source: Reforming Performance Management Procedures in the Civil Service in Lao PDR (2004)

4.4 Remuneration

In 1993, a system of pay and allowances for civil servants was developed in order to move away from the previous system of benefits in kind. As part of the comprehensive public service reform strategy, the pay scale for civil servants has been revised and the government is looking into the option of designing a separate pay scale for the positions of high leadership.

Apart from low salary levels the current pay scale is also severely compressed (compression ratio of 2.4) and not competitive with those offered by the private sector.

The Government recognizes that these new salary levels still fall short of the levels needed to encourage a high level of performance from public servants, and will continue to raise salaries as the financial situation of the country permits.

Source: UNDP (Lao PDR) - Priority areas for Governance Reform (March 2003)

4.5 Training

The Government has been steadily upgrading the qualifications of civil servants and orienting recruitment towards candidates with higher technical/specialized (rather than general) qualifications. The number of civil servants with postgraduate qualifications has more than doubled since 1998.

As part of the HRD policies, the Government created the National Organisation for the Study of Politics and Administration (NOSPA) in 1995, resulting from the merger of the National School of Administration and Management (NSAM) and the School for Higher Studies in Political Theory.

NOSPA organizes workshops as well as short and long-term training courses to upgrade the qualifications of senior Government managers so that they are better able to lead the people under their jurisdiction, to motivate, innovate and communicate. Women from the local level are given priority placement in these courses.

In the past, number of four to ten month courses, particularly for local officials, has been organized. Since 1992, four-year Bachelor-level degree courses covering subjects such as public administration, management and political theory (presently about 250 students) have been organized.

Ministries also have their own technical level schools in order to teach public servants the technical skills required for their particular sector.

In 1998, as a result of a two-year nation-wide process, the Government prepared a comprehensive HRD Programme[12], which is still in effect.

At the moment, training activities still happen partially on an ad hoc basis, and not yet sufficiently job-oriented. Other problems that still persist are the lack of proper training manuals or guidelines, lack of co-ordination, duplication of training efforts and insufficient on-the-job training.

Source: UNDP (Lao PDR) - Priority areas for Governance Reform (March 2003) (edited)

4.6 Gender

Source: Institution - Title

---

[12] Capacity Building for Public Management and Community Development (Follow-up Roundtable Meeting, May 12, 1998)

5. Ethics and Civil Service

5.1 Corruption

2003 CPI Score relates to perceptions of the degree of corruption as seen by business people and country analysts and ranges between 10 (highly clean) and 0 (highly corrupt).

Corruption Perceptions Index							
		2003 CPI Score	Surveys Used	Standard Deviation	High-Low Range	Number Inst.	90 percent confidence range
Rank	**Country**						
1	Highly clean	9.7	8	0.3	9.2 - 10.0	4	9.5 - 9.9
..	Lao PDR	..	..	..	..	..	..
133	Highly corrupt	1.3	8	0.7	0.3 - 2.2	6	0.9 - 1.7

Source: Transparency International - Corruption Perceptions Index 2003

Surveys Used: Refers to the number of surveys that were used to assess a country's performance. 17 surveys were used and at least 3 surveys were required for a country to be included in the CPI.
Standard Deviation: Indicates differences in the values of the sources. Values below 0.5 indicate agreement, values between 0.5 and c. 0.9 indicate some agreement, while values equal or larger than 1 indicate disagreement.
High-Low Range: Provides the highest and lowest values of the sources.
Number Institutions: Refers to the number of independent institutions that assessed a country's performance. Since some institutions provided more than one survey.
90 percent confidence range: Provides a range of possible values of the CPI score. With 5 percent probability the score is above this range and with another 5 percent it is below.

In November 1999, the Government adopted an "Anti-Corruption Decree" (Decree No.193/PM, 2/11/1999).

Further to the Anti-corruption decree, the Government has recently decided to extend inspections and audits regarding financial issues to cover all employees in the public service. Consequently, in 2001, a new anti-corruption body (the State Inspection Authority - SIA) was established, reporting directly to the Prime Minister3.

More recently still, the VIIth Party Congress (2001) adopted new directives to combat corruption at all levels and to secure transparency and accountability in Government, by identifying and ensuring that wrong-doings are punished.

Source: UNDP (Lao PDR) - Priority areas for Governance Reform (March 2003)

5.2 Ethics

It has been common practice for several years for Government staff to take other paid work in the evenings and at weekends to improve their income. A World Bank team found that technical staff take time off for parallel employment during regular working hours, often with consultants or contractors engaged on Government projects and sometimes on the same project that they supervise in their Government job.

Source: World Bank (Lao PDR) - Country Procurement Assessment Report (January 10, 2002)

The Government stresses the importance of all civil servants maintaining high ethical standards. It is the aim that new decree on the civil service statute will reinforce these standards, emphasize rewards for integrity and performance, and curtail all activities that entail a possible conflict of interest or an abuse of office. The new decree also includes a provision on whistleblower protection.

Source: UNDP (Lao PDR) - Priority areas for Governance Reform (March 2003) (edited)

6. e-Government

e-Government Readiness Index:

The index refers to the generic capacity or aptitude of the public sector to use ICT for encapsulating in public services and deploying to the public, high quality information (explicit knowledge) and effective communication tools that support human development.

The index is comprised of three sub-indexes: Web Measure Index, Telecommunications Infrastructure Index and Human Capital Index.

Web Measure Index:

A scale based on progressively sophisticated web services present. Coverage and sophistication of state-provided e-service and e-product availability correspond to a numerical classification.

Telecommunications Infrastructure Index:

A composite, weighted average index of six primary indices, based on basic infrastructural indicators that define a country's ICT infra-structure capacity.

Primary indicators are: PC's, Internet users, online population and Mobile phones. Secondary indicators are TVs and telephone lines.

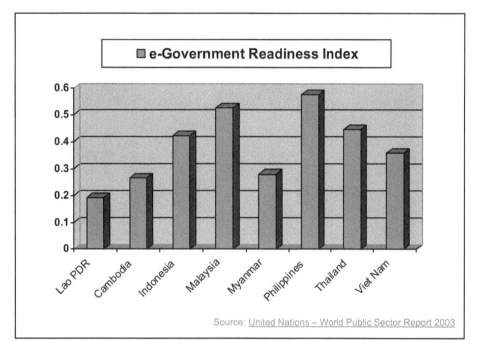

Source: United Nations – World Public Sector Report 2003

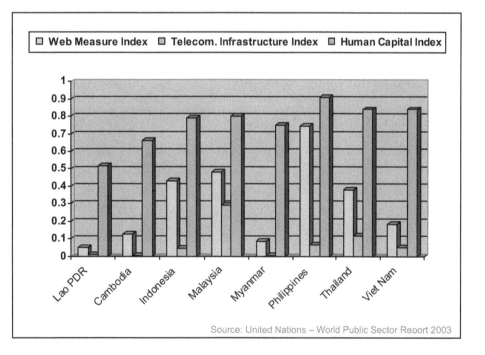

Source: United Nations – World Public Sector Report 2003

Human Capital Index:
A composite of the adult literacy rate and the combined primary, secondary and tertiary gross enrolment ratio, with two thirds of the weight given to adult literacy and one third to the gross enrolment ratio.

e-Participation Index:
Refers to the willingness, on the part of the government, to use ICT to provide high quality information (explicit knowledge) and effective communication tools for the specific purpose of empowerring people for able participation in consultations and decision-making both in their capacity as consumers of public services and as citizens.

e-information:
The government websites offer information on policies and programs, budgets, laws and regulations, and other briefs of key public interest. Tools for disseminating of information exist for timely access and use of public information, including web forums, e-mail lists, newsgroups and chat rooms.

e-decision making:
The government indicates that it will take citizens input into account in decision making and provides actual feedback on the outcome of specific issues.

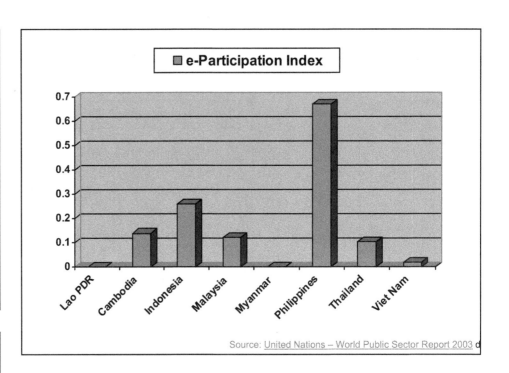

Source: United Nations – World Public Sector Report 2003

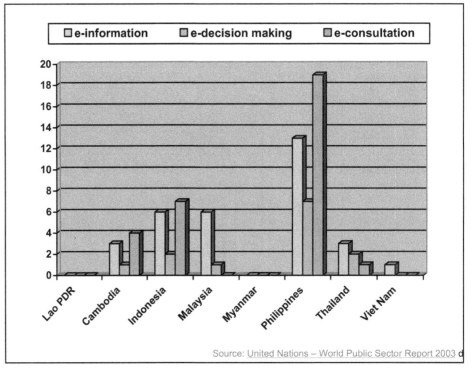

Source: United Nations – World Public Sector Report 2003

e-consultation:
The government website explains e-consultation mechanisms and tools. It offers a choice of public policy topics online for discussion with real time and archived access to audios and videos of public meetings. The government encourages citizens to participate in discussions.

7. Links

7.1 National sites

Authority	Topic
National Assembly	http://www.national-assembly.la/
Ministry of Foreign Affairs	http://www.mofa.gov.la/

7.2 Miscellaneous sites

Institution	Topic
Asian Development Bank (ADB)	http://www.adb.org
Development Gateway	http://www.developmentgateway.org/countryprofile/...
European Union (EU)	http://europa.eu.int/comm/external_relations/lao/intro/index.htm
United Nations in Lao PDR	http://www.unlao.org/
United Nations Capital Development Fund (UNCDF)	http://www.uncdf.org/english/countries/laos
United Nations Development Programme (UNDP)	http://www.undplao.org/
UNDP (Public Administration Reform and Decentralization)	http://www.undplao.org/gpar2.htm
UNPAN	http://www.unpan.org/virtual_library-byregion.asp
World Bank (WB)	http://www.worldbank.org/la

ELECTORAL, POLITICAL PARTIES LAWS AND REGULATIONS HANDBOOK LIBRARY
(PRICE $99.95)

Ultimate handbooks on electoral and political system laws and regulation in selected countries

TITLE
Afghanistan Electoral, Political Parties Laws and Regulations Handbook - Strategic Information, Regulations, Procedures
Albania Electoral, Political Parties Laws and Regulations Handbook - Strategic Information, Regulations, Procedures
Algeria Electoral, Political Parties Laws and Regulations Handbook - Strategic Information, Regulations, Procedures
Angola Electoral, Political Parties Laws and Regulations Handbook - Strategic Information, Regulations, Procedures
Argentina Electoral, Political Parties Laws and Regulations Handbook - Strategic Information, Regulations, Procedures
Armenia Electoral, Political Parties Laws and Regulations Handbook - Strategic Information, Regulations, Procedures
Aruba Electoral, Political Parties Laws and Regulations Handbook - Strategic Information, Regulations, Procedures
Australia Electoral, Political Parties Laws and Regulations Handbook - Strategic Information, Regulations, Procedures
Austria Electoral, Political Parties Laws and Regulations Handbook - Strategic Information, Regulations, Procedures
Azerbaijan Electoral, Political Parties Laws and Regulations Handbook - Strategic Information, Regulations, Procedures
Bahamas Electoral, Political Parties Laws and Regulations Handbook - Strategic Information, Regulations, Procedures
Bahrain Electoral, Political Parties Laws and Regulations Handbook - Strategic Information, Regulations, Procedures
Bangladesh Electoral, Political Parties Laws and Regulations Handbook - Strategic Information, Regulations, Procedures
Barbados Electoral, Political Parties Laws and Regulations Handbook - Strategic Information, Regulations, Procedures
Belarus Electoral, Political Parties Laws and Regulations Handbook - Strategic Information, Regulations, Procedures
Belgium Electoral, Political Parties Laws and Regulations Handbook - Strategic Information, Regulations, Procedures
Belize Electoral, Political Parties Laws and Regulations Handbook - Strategic Information, Regulations, Procedures
Benin Electoral, Political Parties Laws and Regulations Handbook - Strategic Information, Regulations, Procedures
Bermuda Electoral, Political Parties Laws and Regulations Handbook - Strategic Information, Regulations, Procedures
Bhutan Electoral, Political Parties Laws and Regulations Handbook - Strategic Information, Regulations, Procedures
Bolivia Electoral, Political Parties Laws and Regulations Handbook - Strategic Information, Regulations, Procedures
Bosnia and Herzegovina Electoral, Political Parties Laws and Regulations Handbook - Strategic Information, Regulations, Procedures
Botswana Electoral, Political Parties Laws and Regulations Handbook - Strategic Information, Regulations, Procedures
Brazil Electoral, Political Parties Laws and Regulations Handbook - Strategic Information, Regulations, Procedures
Brunei Electoral, Political Parties Laws and Regulations Handbook - Strategic Information, Regulations, Procedures
Bulgaria Electoral, Political Parties Laws and Regulations Handbook - Strategic Information, Regulations, Procedures
Burkina Faso Electoral, Political Parties Laws and Regulations Handbook - Strategic Information, Regulations, Procedures
Burundi Electoral, Political Parties Laws and Regulations Handbook - Strategic Information, Regulations, Procedures
Cambodia Electoral, Political Parties Laws and Regulations Handbook - Strategic Information, Regulations, Procedures
Cameroon Electoral, Political Parties Laws and Regulations Handbook - Strategic Information, Regulations, Procedures
Canada Electoral, Political Parties Laws and Regulations Handbook - Strategic Information, Regulations, Procedures
Cape Verde Electoral, Political Parties Laws and Regulations Handbook - Strategic Information, Regulations, Procedures
Cayman Islands Electoral, Political Parties Laws and Regulations Handbook - Strategic Information, Regulations, Procedures
Central African Republic Electoral, Political Parties Laws and Regulations Handbook - Strategic Information, Regulations, Procedures
Chad Electoral, Political Parties Laws and Regulations Handbook - Strategic Information, Regulations, Procedures
Chile Electoral, Political Parties Laws and Regulations Handbook - Strategic Information, Regulations, Procedures
China Electoral, Political Parties Laws and Regulations Handbook - Strategic Information, Regulations, Procedures
Colombia Electoral, Political Parties Laws and Regulations Handbook - Strategic Information, Regulations, Procedures

TITLE
Comoros Electoral, Political Parties Laws and Regulations Handbook - Strategic Information, Regulations, Procedures
Congo Electoral, Political Parties Laws and Regulations Handbook - Strategic Information, Regulations, Procedures
Congo, Democratic Republic Electoral, Political Parties Laws and Regulations Handbook - Strategic Information, Regulations, Procedures
Cook Islands Electoral, Political Parties Laws and Regulations Handbook - Strategic Information, Regulations, Procedures
Costa Rica Electoral, Political Parties Laws and Regulations Handbook - Strategic Information, Regulations, Procedures
Cote d'Ivoire Electoral, Political Parties Laws and Regulations Handbook - Strategic Information, Regulations, Procedures
Croatia Electoral, Political Parties Laws and Regulations Handbook - Strategic Information, Regulations, Procedures
Cuba Electoral, Political Parties Laws and Regulations Handbook - Strategic Information, Regulations, Procedures
Cyprus Electoral, Political Parties Laws and Regulations Handbook - Strategic Information, Regulations, Procedures
Czech Republic Electoral, Political Parties Laws and Regulations Handbook - Strategic Information, Regulations, Procedures
Denmark Electoral, Political Parties Laws and Regulations Handbook - Strategic Information, Regulations, Procedures
Djibouti Electoral, Political Parties Laws and Regulations Handbook - Strategic Information, Regulations, Procedures
Dominica Electoral, Political Parties Laws and Regulations Handbook - Strategic Information, Regulations, Procedures
Dominican Republic Electoral, Political Parties Laws and Regulations Handbook - Strategic Information, Regulations, Procedures
Ecuador Electoral, Political Parties Laws and Regulations Handbook - Strategic Information, Regulations, Procedures
Egypt Electoral, Political Parties Laws and Regulations Handbook - Strategic Information, Regulations, Procedures
El Salvador Electoral, Political Parties Laws and Regulations Handbook - Strategic Information, Regulations, Procedures
Equatorial Guinea Electoral, Political Parties Laws and Regulations Handbook - Strategic Information, Regulations, Procedures
Eritrea Electoral, Political Parties Laws and Regulations Handbook - Strategic Information, Regulations, Procedures
Estonia Electoral, Political Parties Laws and Regulations Handbook - Strategic Information, Regulations, Procedures
Ethiopia Electoral, Political Parties Laws and Regulations Handbook - Strategic Information, Regulations, Procedures
Fiji Electoral, Political Parties Laws and Regulations Handbook - Strategic Information, Regulations, Procedures
Finland Electoral, Political Parties Laws and Regulations Handbook - Strategic Information, Regulations, Procedures
France Electoral, Political Parties Laws and Regulations Handbook - Strategic Information, Regulations, Procedures
Gabon Electoral, Political Parties Laws and Regulations Handbook - Strategic Information, Regulations, Procedures
Gambia Electoral, Political Parties Laws and Regulations Handbook - Strategic Information, Regulations, Procedures
Georgia Electoral, Political Parties Laws and Regulations Handbook - Strategic Information, Regulations, Procedures
Germany Electoral, Political Parties Laws and Regulations Handbook - Strategic Information, Regulations, Procedures
Ghana Electoral, Political Parties Laws and Regulations Handbook - Strategic Information, Regulations, Procedures
Greece Electoral, Political Parties Laws and Regulations Handbook - Strategic Information, Regulations, Procedures
Guatemala Electoral, Political Parties Laws and Regulations Handbook - Strategic Information, Regulations, Procedures
Guinea Electoral, Political Parties Laws and Regulations Handbook - Strategic Information, Regulations, Procedures
Guinea-Bissau Electoral, Political Parties Laws and Regulations Handbook - Strategic Information, Regulations, Procedures
Guyana Electoral, Political Parties Laws and Regulations Handbook - Strategic Information, Regulations, Procedures
Haiti Electoral, Political Parties Laws and Regulations Handbook - Strategic Information, Regulations, Procedures
Honduras Electoral, Political Parties Laws and Regulations Handbook - Strategic Information, Regulations, Procedures
Hungary Electoral, Political Parties Laws and Regulations Handbook - Strategic Information, Regulations, Procedures
Iceland Electoral, Political Parties Laws and Regulations Handbook - Strategic Information, Regulations, Procedures
India Electoral, Political Parties Laws and Regulations Handbook - Strategic Information, Regulations, Procedures
Indonesia Electoral, Political Parties Laws and Regulations Handbook - Strategic Information, Regulations, Procedures
Iran Electoral, Political Parties Laws and Regulations Handbook - Strategic Information, Regulations, Procedures
Iraq Electoral, Political Parties Laws and Regulations Handbook - Strategic Information, Regulations, Procedures
Ireland Electoral, Political Parties Laws and Regulations Handbook - Strategic Information, Regulations, Procedures
Israel Electoral, Political Parties Laws and Regulations Handbook - Strategic Information, Regulations, Procedures
Italy Electoral, Political Parties Laws and Regulations Handbook - Strategic Information, Regulations, Procedures
Jamaica Electoral, Political Parties Laws and Regulations Handbook - Strategic Information, Regulations, Procedures
Japan Electoral, Political Parties Laws and Regulations Handbook - Strategic Information, Regulations, Procedures
Jordan Electoral, Political Parties Laws and Regulations Handbook - Strategic Information, Regulations, Procedures
Kazakhstan Electoral, Political Parties Laws and Regulations Handbook - Strategic Information, Regulations, Procedures
Kenya Electoral, Political Parties Laws and Regulations Handbook - Strategic Information, Regulations, Procedures
Korea, North Electoral, Political Parties Laws and Regulations Handbook - Strategic Information, Regulations, Procedures

TITLE
Korea, South Electoral, Political Parties Laws and Regulations Handbook - Strategic Information, Regulations, Procedures
Kosovo Electoral, Political Parties Laws and Regulations Handbook - Strategic Information, Regulations, Procedures
Kurdistan Electoral, Political Parties Laws and Regulations Handbook - Strategic Information, Regulations, Procedures
Kuwait Electoral, Political Parties Laws and Regulations Handbook - Strategic Information, Regulations, Procedures
Kyrgyzstan Electoral, Political Parties Laws and Regulations Handbook - Strategic Information, Regulations, Procedures
Laos Electoral, Political Parties Laws and Regulations Handbook - Strategic Information, Regulations, Procedures
Latvia Electoral, Political Parties Laws and Regulations Handbook - Strategic Information, Regulations, Procedures
Lebanon Electoral, Political Parties Laws and Regulations Handbook - Strategic Information, Regulations, Procedures
Lesotho Electoral, Political Parties Laws and Regulations Handbook - Strategic Information, Regulations, Procedures
Liberia Electoral, Political Parties Laws and Regulations Handbook - Strategic Information, Regulations, Procedures
Libya Electoral, Political Parties Laws and Regulations Handbook - Strategic Information, Regulations, Procedures
Liechtenstein Electoral, Political Parties Laws and Regulations Handbook - Strategic Information, Regulations, Procedures
Lithuania Electoral, Political Parties Laws and Regulations Handbook - Strategic Information, Regulations, Procedures
Luxembourg Electoral, Political Parties Laws and Regulations Handbook - Strategic Information, Regulations, Procedures
Macao Electoral, Political Parties Laws and Regulations Handbook - Strategic Information, Regulations, Procedures
Macedonia, Electoral, Political Parties Laws and Regulations Handbook - Strategic Information, Regulations, Procedures
Madagascar Electoral, Political Parties Laws and Regulations Handbook - Strategic Information, Regulations, Procedures
Madeira Electoral, Political Parties Laws and Regulations Handbook - Strategic Information, Regulations, Procedures
Malawi Electoral, Political Parties Laws and Regulations Handbook - Strategic Information, Regulations, Procedures
Malaysia Electoral, Political Parties Laws and Regulations Handbook - Strategic Information, Regulations, Procedures
Maldives Electoral, Political Parties Laws and Regulations Handbook - Strategic Information, Regulations, Procedures
Mali Electoral, Political Parties Laws and Regulations Handbook - Strategic Information, Regulations, Procedures
Malta Electoral, Political Parties Laws and Regulations Handbook - Strategic Information, Regulations, Procedures
Marshall Islands Electoral, Political Parties Laws and Regulations Handbook - Strategic Information, Regulations, Procedures
Mauritania Electoral, Political Parties Laws and Regulations Handbook - Strategic Information, Regulations, Procedures
Mauritius Electoral, Political Parties Laws and Regulations Handbook - Strategic Information, Regulations, Procedures
Mexico Electoral, Political Parties Laws and Regulations Handbook - Strategic Information, Regulations, Procedures
Micronesia Electoral, Political Parties Laws and Regulations Handbook - Strategic Information, Regulations, Procedures
Moldova Electoral, Political Parties Laws and Regulations Handbook - Strategic Information, Regulations, Procedures
Monaco Electoral, Political Parties Laws and Regulations Handbook - Strategic Information, Regulations, Procedures
Mongolia Electoral, Political Parties Laws and Regulations Handbook - Strategic Information, Regulations, Procedures
Morocco Electoral, Political Parties Laws and Regulations Handbook - Strategic Information, Regulations, Procedures
Mozambique Electoral, Political Parties Laws and Regulations Handbook - Strategic Information, Regulations, Procedures
Myanmar Electoral, Political Parties Laws and Regulations Handbook - Strategic Information, Regulations, Procedures
Namibia Electoral, Political Parties Laws and Regulations Handbook - Strategic Information, Regulations, Procedures
Nauru Electoral, Political Parties Laws and Regulations Handbook - Strategic Information, Regulations, Procedures
Nepal Electoral, Political Parties Laws and Regulations Handbook - Strategic Information, Regulations, Procedures
Netherlands Electoral, Political Parties Laws and Regulations Handbook - Strategic Information, Regulations, Procedures
New Zealand Electoral, Political Parties Laws and Regulations Handbook - Strategic Information, Regulations, Procedures
Nicaragua Electoral, Political Parties Laws and Regulations Handbook - Strategic Information, Regulations, Procedures
Niger Electoral, Political Parties Laws and Regulations Handbook - Strategic Information, Regulations, Procedures
Nigeria Electoral, Political Parties Laws and Regulations Handbook - Strategic Information, Regulations, Procedures
Northern Mariana Islands Electoral, Political Parties Laws and Regulations Handbook - Strategic Information, Regulations, Procedures
Norway Electoral, Political Parties Laws and Regulations Handbook - Strategic Information, Regulations, Procedures
Oman Electoral, Political Parties Laws and Regulations Handbook - Strategic Information, Regulations, Procedures
Pakistan Electoral, Political Parties Laws and Regulations Handbook - Strategic Information, Regulations, Procedures
Palestine (West Bank & Gaza) Electoral, Political Parties Laws and Regulations Handbook - Strategic Information, Regulations, Procedures
Panama Electoral, Political Parties Laws and Regulations Handbook - Strategic Information, Regulations, Procedures
Papua New Guinea Electoral, Political Parties Laws and Regulations Handbook - Strategic Information, Regulations, Procedures
Paraguay Electoral, Political Parties Laws and Regulations Handbook - Strategic Information, Regulations, Procedures
Peru Electoral, Political Parties Laws and Regulations Handbook - Strategic Information, Regulations, Procedures

TITLE
Philippines Electoral, Political Parties Laws and Regulations Handbook - Strategic Information, Regulations, Procedures
Pitcairn Islands Electoral, Political Parties Laws and Regulations Handbook - Strategic Information, Regulations, Procedures
Poland Electoral, Political Parties Laws and Regulations Handbook - Strategic Information, Regulations, Procedures
Portugal Electoral, Political Parties Laws and Regulations Handbook - Strategic Information, Regulations, Procedures
Qatar Electoral, Political Parties Laws and Regulations Handbook - Strategic Information, Regulations, Procedures
Romania Electoral, Political Parties Laws and Regulations Handbook - Strategic Information, Regulations, Procedures
Russia Electoral, Political Parties Laws and Regulations Handbook - Strategic Information, Regulations, Procedures
Rwanda Electoral, Political Parties Laws and Regulations Handbook - Strategic Information, Regulations, Procedures
Samoa (Western) Electoral, Political Parties Laws and Regulations Handbook - Strategic Information, Regulations, Procedures
Sao Tome and Principe Electoral, Political Parties Laws and Regulations Handbook - Strategic Information, Regulations, Procedures
Saudi Arabia Electoral, Political Parties Laws and Regulations Handbook - Strategic Information, Regulations, Procedures
Senegal Electoral, Political Parties Laws and Regulations Handbook - Strategic Information, Regulations, Procedures
Serbia Electoral, Political Parties Laws and Regulations Handbook - Strategic Information, Regulations, Procedures
Seychelles Electoral, Political Parties Laws and Regulations Handbook - Strategic Information, Regulations, Procedures
Sierra Leone Electoral, Political Parties Laws and Regulations Handbook - Strategic Information, Regulations, Procedures
Singapore Electoral, Political Parties Laws and Regulations Handbook - Strategic Information, Regulations, Procedures
Slovakia Electoral, Political Parties Laws and Regulations Handbook - Strategic Information, Regulations, Procedures
Slovenia Electoral, Political Parties Laws and Regulations Handbook - Strategic Information, Regulations, Procedures
Solomon Islands Electoral, Political Parties Laws and Regulations Handbook - Strategic Information, Regulations, Procedures
Somalia Electoral, Political Parties Laws and Regulations Handbook - Strategic Information, Regulations, Procedures
South Africa Electoral, Political Parties Laws and Regulations Handbook - Strategic Information, Regulations, Procedures
Spain Electoral, Political Parties Laws and Regulations Handbook - Strategic Information, Regulations, Procedures
Sri Lanka Electoral, Political Parties Laws and Regulations Handbook - Strategic Information, Regulations, Procedures
Sudan Electoral, Political Parties Laws and Regulations Handbook - Strategic Information, Regulations, Procedures
Suriname Electoral, Political Parties Laws and Regulations Handbook - Strategic Information, Regulations, Procedures
Swaziland Electoral, Political Parties Laws and Regulations Handbook - Strategic Information, Regulations, Procedures
Sweden Electoral, Political Parties Laws and Regulations Handbook - Strategic Information, Regulations, Procedures
Switzerland Electoral, Political Parties Laws and Regulations Handbook - Strategic Information, Regulations, Procedures
Syria Electoral, Political Parties Laws and Regulations Handbook - Strategic Information, Regulations, Procedures
Taiwan Electoral, Political Parties Laws and Regulations Handbook - Strategic Information, Regulations, Procedures
Tajikistan Electoral, Political Parties Laws and Regulations Handbook - Strategic Information, Regulations, Procedures
Tanzania Electoral, Political Parties Laws and Regulations Handbook - Strategic Information, Regulations, Procedures
Thailand Electoral, Political Parties Laws and Regulations Handbook - Strategic Information, Regulations, Procedures
Togo Electoral, Political Parties Laws and Regulations Handbook - Strategic Information, Regulations, Procedures
Trinidad and Tobago Electoral, Political Parties Laws and Regulations Handbook - Strategic Information, Regulations, Procedures
Tunisia Electoral, Political Parties Laws and Regulations Handbook - Strategic Information, Regulations, Procedures
Turkey Electoral, Political Parties Laws and Regulations Handbook - Strategic Information, Regulations, Procedures
Turkmenistan Electoral, Political Parties Laws and Regulations Handbook - Strategic Information, Regulations, Procedures
Uganda Electoral, Political Parties Laws and Regulations Handbook - Strategic Information, Regulations, Procedures
Ukraine Electoral, Political Parties Laws and Regulations Handbook - Strategic Information, Regulations, Procedures
United Arab Emirates Electoral, Political Parties Laws and Regulations Handbook - Strategic Information, Regulations, Procedures
United Kingdom Electoral, Political Parties Laws and Regulations Handbook - Strategic Information, Regulations, Procedures
United States Electoral, Political Parties Laws and Regulations Handbook - Strategic Information, Regulations, Procedures
Uruguay Electoral, Political Parties Laws and Regulations Handbook - Strategic Information, Regulations, Procedures
Uzbekistan Electoral, Political Parties Laws and Regulations Handbook - Strategic Information, Regulations, Procedures
Venezuela Electoral, Political Parties Laws and Regulations Handbook - Strategic Information, Regulations, Procedures
Vietnam Electoral, Political Parties Laws and Regulations Handbook - Strategic Information, Regulations, Procedures

TITLE
Yemen Electoral, Political Parties Laws and Regulations Handbook - Strategic Information, Regulations, Procedures
Zambia Electoral, Political Parties Laws and Regulations Handbook - Strategic Information, Regulations, Procedures
Zimbabwe Electoral, Political Parties Laws and Regulations Handbook - Strategic Information, Regulations, Procedures
Sudan South Electoral, Political Parties Laws and Regulations Handbook - Strategic Information, Regulations, Procedures